Emily Lawless, Arthur Mrs Bronson

The Story of Ireland

With some Additions by Mrs. Arthur Bronson

Emily Lawless, Arthur Mrs Bronson

The Story of Ireland
With some Additions by Mrs. Arthur Bronson

ISBN/EAN: 9783337139872

Printed in Europe, USA, Canada, Australia, Japan

Cover: Foto ©ninafisch / pixelio.de

More available books at **www.hansebooks.com**

HOLY ISLAND LOUGH DERG. (*From a painting by Watkins.*)

The Story of the Nations

THE
STORY OF IRELAND

BY

THE HON. EMILY LAWLESS
AUTHOR OF "HURRISH: A STUDY," ETC

WITH SOME ADDITIONS BY

MRS. ARTHUR BRONSON

NEW YORK
G. P. PUTNAM'S SONS
LONDON: T. FISHER UNWIN
1888

Press of
G. P. PUTNAM'S SONS
NEW YORK

To
THE EARL OF DUFFERIN, K.P., G.C.B., F.R.S., &c.,
VICEROY OF INDIA.

SGEUL NA H-ÉIREANN
DON ÉIREANNACH AS FIÚ.

PREFACE.

IRISH history is a long, dark road, with many blind alleys, many sudden turnings, many unaccountably crooked portions; a road which, if it has a few signposts to guide us, bristles with threatening notices, now upon the one side and now upon the other, the very ground underfoot being often full of unsuspected perils threatening to hurt the unwary.

To the genuine explorer, flushed with justified self-confidence, well equipped for the journey, and indifferent to scratches or bruises, one may suppose this to be rather an allurement than otherwise, as he spurs along, lance at rest, and sword on side. To the less well-equipped traveller, who has no pretensions to the name of explorer at all, no particular courage to boast of, and whose only ambition is to make the way a little plainer for some one travelling along it for the first time, it is decidedly a serious impediment, so much so as almost to scare such a one from attempting the *rôle* of guide even in the slightest and least responsible capacity.

Another and perhaps even more formidable objection occurs. A history beset with such distracting problems, bristling with such thorny controversies, a history, above all, which has so much bearing upon that portion of history which has still to be born, ought, it may be said, to be approached in the gravest and most authoritative fashion possible, or else not approached at all. This is too true, and that so slight a summary as this can put forward no claim to authority of any sort is evident enough. National "stories," however, no less than histories, gain a gravity, it must be remembered, and even at times a solemnity from their subject apart altogether from their treatment. A good reader will read a great deal more into them than the mere bald words convey. The lights and shadows of a great or a tragic past play over their easy surface, giving it a depth and solidity to which it could otherwise lay no claim. If the present attempt disposes any one to study at first hand one of the strangest and most perplexing chapters of human history and national destiny, its author for one will be more than content.

CONTENTS.

I.

PRIMEVAL IRELAND 1–12

Early migrations, 1—The great ice age, 3—Northern character of the fauna and flora of Ireland, 5—First inhabitants, 6—Formorian, Firbolgs, Tuatha-da-Danaans, 6—Battle of Moytura Cong, 7–9—The Scoto-Celtic invasion, 9—Annals and annalists, how far credible? 9–12.

II.

THE LEGENDS AND LEGEND-MAKERS . . 13–21

The legends, 13—Their archaic character, 14—The pursuit of Gilla Dacker and his horse, 14–18—The ollamhs, 19—Positions of the bards or ollamhs in Primitive Ireland, 19–21.

III.

PRE-CHRISTIAN IRELAND 22–31

Early Celtic law, 24—The Senchus Mor and Book of Aicill, 25—Laws of inheritance, 26–28—Narrow conception of patriotism, 30–31.

CONTENTS.

IV.

ST. PATRICK THE MISSIONARY 32-37

St. Patrick's birth, 33—Capture, slavery, and escape, 33—His return to Ireland, 33—Arrives at Tara, 34—Visits Connaught and Ulster, 34, 35—Early Irish missionaries and their enthusiasm for the work, 35-37.

V.

THE FIRST IRISH MONASTERIES . . . 38-41

"The Tribes of the Saints," 38—Small oratories in the West, 39, 40—Plan of monastic life, 40—Ready acceptance of Christianity, 41.

VI.

COLUMBA AND THE WESTERN CHURCH . . 42-49

Birth of Columba, 42—His journey to Iona, 42—His character and humanity, 43—Conversion of Saxon England, 44—Schism between Western Church and Papacy, 45—Synod of Whitby, 46—The Irish Church at home, 47-49.

VII.

THE NORTHERN SCOURGE 50-59

Ireland divided into five kingdoms, 50—The Ard-Reagh, 52—Arrival of Vikings, 53—Thorgist or Turgesius? 55—Later Viking invaders, 56—The round towers, 56-58—Dublin founded, 58—Hatred between the two races, 59.

VIII.

BRIAN OF THE TRIBUTE 60-70

Two deliverers, 60—Defeat of the Vikings at Sulcost, 61—Brian becomes king of Munster, 63—Seizes Cashel, 63—Overcomes Malachy, 63—Becomes king of Ireland, 64—Celtic theory of loyalty, 64—Fresh Viking invasion, 66—Battle of Clontarf, 67-69—Death of Brian Boru, 69.

IX.

FROM BRIAN TO STRONGBOW 71–75

Result of Brian Boru's death, 71—Chaos returns, 71—Struggle for the succession, 73—Roderick O'Connor, last native king of Ireland, 75.

X.

THE ANGLO-NORMAN INVASION 76–89

First group of knightly invaders, 76—Their relationship, 76—Giraldus Cambrensis, 78—Motives for invasion, 79—Papal sanction, 81—Dermot McMurrough, 81—He enlists recruits, 82—Arrival of Robert FitzStephen, 83—Wexford, Ossory, and Kilkenny captured, 84–86—Arrival of Strongbow, 86—Struggle with Hasculph the Dane and John the Mad, 87—Danes defeated, 87—Dublin besieged, 88—Strongbow defeats Roderick O'Connor, goes to Wexford, and embarks at Waterford, 88—Meets the king, 88—Arrival of Henry II., 89.

XI.

HENRY II. IN IRELAND 90–92

Large military forces of Henry, 90—The chiefs submit and do homage, 90, 91—Irish theory of Ard-Reagh or Over-Lord, 91—Henry in Dublin, 92—Synod at Cashel, 92—Henry recalled to England, 92.

XII.

EFFECTS OF THE ANGLO-NORMAN INVASION . 93–97

Effect of Henry's stay in Ireland, 93—His large schemes, 94—Their practical failure, 95—Rapacity of adventurers, 96—Contrast between Irish and their conquerors, 96—Civil war from the outset, 96–97.

XIII.

JOHN IN IRELAND 98–100

John's first visit, 98—His insolence and misconduct, 98—Recalled in disgrace, 98—Second visit as king, 99—His energy, 99—Overruns Meath and Ulster, 99—Returns to England, 99—Effect of his visit, 100.

XIV.

THE LORDS PALATINE 101–106

The Geraldines, 101—Their possessions in Ireland, 102—The five palatinates, 103—The heirs of Strongbow, 103—The De Burghs, 104—The Butlers, 105—Importance of the great territorial owners in Ireland, 105, 106.

XV.

EDWARD BRUCE IN IRELAND 107–112

Want of landmarks in Irish history, 107—Edward the I.'s reign, 107—Battle of Bannockburn, 108—Its effect on Ireland, 108—Scotch invasion under Edward Bruce, 108—Ravages and famine caused by him, 109—The colonists regain courage: Battle of Dundalk, 110—Edward Bruce killed, 110—Result of the Scotch invasion, 111, 112.

XVI.

THE STATUTE OF KILKENNY 113–118

Reign of Edward III., 113—A lost opportunity, 114—Duke of Clarence sent to Ireland, 114—Parliament at Kilkenny, 115—Statute of Kilkenny, 115—Its objects, 116—Two Irelands, 116—Weakness resorts to cruelty, 117—Effects of the statute, 118.

XVII.

RICHARD II. IN IRELAND 119–124

Richard the II.'s two visits to Ireland, 119—Utter disorganization of the country, 119-120—The chieftains submit and come in, 120—"Sir Art" McMurrough, 120—Richard leaves, and Art McMurrough breaks out again, 121—Earl of March killed, 121— Richard returns, 122 — Attacks Art McMurrough, 122—Failure of attack, 122—Recalled to England, 123—His defeat and death, 123—Confusion redoubles, 124.

XVIII.

THE DEEPEST DEPTHS 125–131

Monotony of Irish history, 125—State of Ireland during the Wars of the Roses, 126—Pillage, carnage, and rapine, 126, 127—The seaport towns, 128—Richard Duke of York in Ireland, 128—His conciliatory policy, 129—Battle of Towton, 129—The Kildares grow in power, 130—Geroit Mor, 130—His character, 131.

XIX.

THE KILDARES IN THE ASCENDANT . . 132–143

Effect of the battle of Bosworth, 132—Kildare still in power, 132—Lambert Simnel in Ireland, 132—Crowned in Dublin, 134—Battle of Stoke, 135—Henry VII. pardons the rebels, 135—Irish peers summoned to Court, 136—Perkin Warbeck in Ireland, 137—Quarrels between the Kildares and Ormonds, 138—Sir Edward Poynings, 138—Kildare's trial and acquital, 140—Restored to power, 141—Battle of Knocktow, 142, 143.

XX.

FALL OF THE HOUSE OF KILDARE . . . 144–150

Rise of Wolsey to power, 144—Resolves to destroy the Geraldines, 144—Geroit Mor succeeded by his son, 145—Earl of Surrey sent as viceroy, 145—Kildare restored to power, 146—Summoned to London and imprisoned, 146—Again restored and again imprisoned, 147—Situation changed, 147—Revolt of Silken Thomas, 147—Seizes Dublin, 148—Archbishop Allen murdered, 148—Sir William Skeffington to Ireland, 148—Kildare dies in prison, 149—"The Pardon of Maynooth," 149—Silken Thomas surrenders, and is executed, 150.

XXI.

THE ACT OF SUPREMACY 151–155

Lord Leonard Grey deputy, 151—Accused of treason, recalled and executed, 152—Act of Supremacy proposed, 152—Opposition of clergy, 152—Suppression of the abbeys, 153—

xviii CONTENTS.

XXIX.

THE ESSEX FAILURE 206–210

Essex appointed Lord-Lieutenant, 206—Arrival in Ireland, 208—Mistakes and disasters, 208—Death of Sir Conyers Clifford in the Curlews, 209—Essex advances north, 209—Holds a conference with Tyrone, 209—Agrees to an armistice, 209—Anger of the Queen, 210—Essex suddenly leaves Ireland, 210.

XXX.

END OF THE TYRONE WAR 211–219

Mountjoy appointed deputy, 211—Contrast between him and Essex, 213—Reasons for Mountjoy's greater success, 213—Conquest by starvation, 214—Success of method, 214—Arrival of Spanish forces at Kinsale: Mountjoy and Carew marched south and invests Kinsale, 215—Attack of Mountjoy by Tyrone, 218—Failure of attack, 218—Surrender of Spaniards, 218—Surrender of Tyrone, 219.

XXXI.

THE FLIGHT OF THE EARLS 220–225

The last chieftain rising against England, 220—Condition of affairs at close of war, 221—Tyrone's position impossible, 221—Reported plot, 222—Tyrone and Tyrconnel take flight, 222—Confiscation of their territory, 223—Sir John Davis, 224—The Ulster Settlement, 224, 225.

XXXII.

THE FIRST CONTESTED ELECTION . . . 226–228

Parliament summoned, 226—Anxiety of government to secure a Protestant majority, 226—Contested election, 227—Narrow Protestant majority, 227—Furious quarrel over election of Speaker, 228—Parliament dissolved, 228—The king appealed to, 228—Attainder of Tyrone and Tyrconnel, 228—Reversal of statute of Kilkenny, 228.

XXXIII.

OLD AND NEW OWNERS 229–231

Further plantations, 229—The Connaught landowners, 230—Their positions, 231—Charles I.'s accession and how it affected Ireland, 231—Lord Falkland appointed viceroy, 231—Succeeded by Wentworth, 231.

XXXIV.

STRAFFORD 232–239

Arrival of Wentworth in Ireland, 232—His methods and theory, 232—Dissolves parliament, 234—Goes to Connaught, 234—Galway jury fined and imprisoned, 230—His ecclesiastical policy, 237—His Irish army, 238—Return to England, 238—Attainder, trial, and death, 239.

XXXV.

'FORTY-ONE 240–245

Confusion and disorder, 240—Strafford's army disbanded, but still in the country, 241—Plot to seize Dublin Castle, 241—Plot transpires, 242—Sir Phelim O'Neill seizes Charlemont, 243—Attack upon the Protestant settlers, 243—Barbarities and counter barbarities, 244.

XXXVI.

THE WATERS SPREAD 246–250

The rising at first local, 246—Attitude of the Pale gentry, 249—They resolve to join the rising, 247—Disorganization of the northern insurgents, 248—Incapacity of Sir Phelim O'Neill, 248—Arrival of Owen Roe O'Neill and Preston, 249—Meeting of delegates at Kilkenny, 249—Charles decides upon a *coup de main*, 250.

XXXVII.

CIVIL WAR 251–256

Effect of the Ulster massacres on England, 251—An agrarian rather than religious rising, 252—The Confederates' terms,

253—Glamorgan sent to Ireland, 254—The secret treaty transpires, 254—Arrival of Rinucini, 255—Battle of Benturb, 255—Ormond surrenders Dublin to the Parliament, 256.

XXXVIII.

THE CONFUSION DEEPENS. 257–260

Total confusion of aims and parties, 258—The "poor Panther" Inchiquin, 258—Alliance between Jones and Owen Roe O'Neill, 259—Ormond advances upon Dublin, 259—Battle of Baggotrath and defeat of the Royalists, 260—Arrival of Cromwell, 260.

XXXIX.

CROMWELL IN IRELAND 261–265

Cromwell's mission, 261—Assault of Drogheda, and slaughter of its garrison, 261—Wexford garrison slaughtered, 262—Cromwell's discipline, 263—The "country sickness," 263—Confusion in the Royalist camp, 264—Signature of the Scotch covenant by the king, 284—Final surrender of O'Neill and the Irish army, 265.

XL.

CROMWELL'S METHODS 266–272

Loss of life during the eight years of war, 266—Punishment of the vanquished, 267—Executions, 267—Wholesale scheme of eviction, 268—The New Owners, 269—"The Burren," 270—Sale of women to the West Indian plantations, 270—Dissatisfaction amongst the soldiers and debenture holders, 271—Irish Cromwellians, 272.

XLI.

THE ACT OF SETTLEMENT. 273–276

The Restoration, 273—Henry Cromwell, 273—Coote and Broghill, 273—Court of claims established in Dublin, 275—Prolonged dispute, 276—Final settlement, 276—Condition of Irish Roman Catholics at close of the struggle, 276.

CONTENTS. xxi

PAGE

XLII.

OPPRESSION AND COUNTER OPPRESSION . . 277–283

Effects of the Restoration upon the Ulster Presbyterians, 277—
A new Act of Uniformity, 277—Exodus of Presbyterians from
Ireland, 278—The Popish plot, 279—Insane panic, 279—
Execution of Archbishop Plunkett, 279—Sudden reversal of
the tide, 280—Tyrconnel sent as viceroy, 280—Terror of
Protestant settlers, 281—William of Orange in England, 282
—James II. arrives in Ireland, 283.

XLIII.

WILLIAM AND JAMES IN IRELAND . . . 284–294

Popular enthusiasm for James, 284—Struggle between his
English and Irish adherents, 285—James advances to London-
derry, 285—Siege of Londonderry, 286—Its garrison relieved,
286—Debasing the coinage, 286—Reversal of the Act of
Settlement, 287—Bill of Attainder, 287—Arrival of William
III., 288—Battle of the Boyne, 289—Flight of James, 289—
First siege of Limerick, 291—Athlone captured by Ginkel,
292—Battle of Aughrim, 293, 294.

XLIV.

THE TREATY OF LIMERICK 295–298

Sarsfield refuses to surrender, 295—Second siege of Limerick,
295—The Limerick treaty, 296—Its exact purport, 296—The
military treaty, 297—Departure of the exiles, 298.

XLV.

THE PENAL CODE 299–306

A new century and new fortunes, 299—Mr. Lecky's "Eighteenth Century," 300—Reversal of all the recent Acts, 300—
The Penal Code, 301—Burke's description of it, 302—How
evaded, 303—Its effects upon Protestants and Catholics,
304-306.

XLVI.

THE COMMERCIAL CODE 307–310

The "Protestant Ascendency," 307—England's jealousy of

her Colonists, 308—Act passed prohibiting export of Irish woollen goods, 309—Effects of the Act upon Ireland, 309—Smuggling on an immense scale, 309—Collapse of industry, 310—Strained relations, 310.

XLVII.

MOLYNEUX AND SWIFT 311–319

The "Ingenious Molyneux," 311—Irish naturalists, 312—Molyneux's "Case of Ireland," 313—Effect of its publication, 315—Death of Molyneux, 315—Dean Swift, 315—His position in Irish politics, 315—The "Drapier Letters," 317—Their line of attack, 318—Effect on popular opinion, 318—Wood's halfpence suspended, 318.

XLVIII.

HENRY FLOOD 320–327

Forty dull years, 320—Parliamentary abuses, 322—Charles Lucas, 322—Flood enters Parliament, 323—His struggle with the Government, 325—Lord Townsend recalled, 325—Flood accepts office, 326—Effect of that acceptance, 326—Rejoins the Liberal side, 326—Tries to outbid Grattan, 326—Failure and end, 327.

XLIX.

HENRY GRATTAN 328–333

Unanimity of opinion about Grattan, 328—His character, 328—Enters Parliament, 330—The "Declaration of Rights," 330—Carried by the Irish Parliament, 330—Declaratory Act of George I. repealed, 331—A spell of prosperity, 331—Rocks ahead, 332—Disaster following disaster, 332—Grattan and the Union, 332—Grattan's death, 333.

L.

THE IRISH VOLUNTEERS , . . . 334–340

Revolt of the American Colonies, 334—Its effect on Ireland, 334—Disastrous condition of the country, 335—Volunteer movement begun in Belfast, 336—Rapid popularity, 336—Its effect upon politics, 338—Free Trade, 338—Declaratory Act repealed, 338—The Volunteers disband, 340.

LI.

DANGER SIGNALS 341–346

Reform the crying necessity of the hour, 341—Corruption steadily increasing, 341—Attempt to obtain free importation of goods to England, 342—Its failure, 342—Disturbed state of the country, 344—Its causes, 344—"White boys," "Oak boys," and "Steel boys," 344, 345—Faction war in the North, 345—Orange lodges, 345—"Society of United Irishmen," 346—The one hope for the future, 346.

LII.

THE FITZWILLIAM DISAPPOINTMENT . . 347–353

General desire for Catholic Emancipation, 347—Lord Sheffield's evidence, 347—The Catholic delegates received by the king, 349—Lord Fitzwilliam sent as Lord-Lieutenant, 350—Popular enthusiasm, 350—Recalled, 351—Result of his recall, 352, 353.

LIII.

'NINETY-EIGHT 354–366

Wolfe Tone, his character and autobiography, 354—The other leaders of the rebellion, 354—England and France at war, 355—Hoche's descent, 355—Panic, 357—Habeas Corpus Act suspended, 357—Misconduct of soldiers, 359—Arrest of Lord Edward Fitzgerald, 361—Outbreak of the rebellion, 361—The rising in Wexford, 362—Bagenal Harvey, 363—Arklow, New Ross, and Vinegar Hill, 363—Suppression of the rebellion, 364—Final incidents, 365—Death of Wolfe Tone, 366.

LIV.

THE UNION 367–376

State of Ireland after the rebellion, 367, 368—Pitt resolved to pass the Union, 370—Inducements offered, 370—Discrepancy of statements upon the subject, 371—Bribery or not bribery? 372—Lord Cornwallis and Lord Castlereagh, 373—The Union carried, 375.

CONTENTS.

LV.

O'CONNELL AND CATHOLIC EMANCIPATION . 377-389

The Union not followed by union, 277—The Emmett outbreak, 377—Young Daniel O'Connell, 379—The new Catholic Association, 380—The Clare election, 381—Catholic Relief Bill carried, 381—The "Incarnation of a people," 383—Repeal, 384—The O'Connell gatherings, 386—The meeting proclaimed at Clontarf, 387—Prosecution and condemnation of O'Connell, 387—Released on appeal, 387—Never regained his power, 388—Despondency and death, 388, 389.

LVI.

"YOUNG IRELAND" 390-395

"The Nation," 390—Sir C. Gavan Duffy, 390—Thomas Davis, 390—Smith O'Brien, 391—Effect of O'Connell's death on the "Young Ireland" party, 392—James Lalor, 393—His influence on Mitchell, 393—The "United Irishmen" newspaper started, 394—Arrest and transportation of Mitchell, 394—The end of the "Young Ireland" movement, 395.

LVII.

THE FAMINE 396-402

First symptoms of the potato disease, 396—The fatal night, 396—Beginning of Famine, 397—Rapid mortality, 397—Mr. Forster's reports, 398—Relief works, 399—Soup kitchens, 399—Failure of preventive measures, 399—Famine followed by ruin, 400—Clearances and Emigration, 401—Emigrant ships, 401—Permanent effects of the Famine on Ireland, 402.

LVIII.

THE LATEST DEVELOPMENT 403-416

Encumbered Estates Act, 403—Tenant League of North and South, 403—The "Brass Band," 404—A lull, 404—The Phœnix organization, 404—The Fenian "scare," 405—Rescue of Fenian prisoners at Manchester, 405—The Clerkenwell explosion, 406—The Irish Church Act, 406, 407—The Irish

Land Act of 1870, 407—Failure of Irish Education Act, and retirement of the Liberals, 408—Mr. Butt and Mr. Parnell, 408—The Land League established, 409—Return of the Liberals to power, 409—The Irish Land Act of 1881, 410—Arrest and release of Land League Leaders, 411—Murders in the Phœnix Park, 411—James Carey, 412—His death, 412—The agrarian struggle, 413—Home Rule, 414—Its eventual destiny, 414—The untravelled Future, 416.

LIX.

CONCLUSION 417–419

Irish heroes, 417—Causes of their want of popularity, 418—Irish *versus* Scotch heroes, 418—"Prince Posterity," 419.

LIST OF ILLUSTRATIONS.

[Nearly all the archæological illustrations in this volume are from "The Early Christian Architecture of Ireland," by Miss M. Stokes, who has kindly allowed them to be reproduced. The portraits are chiefly from engravings, &c., kept in the Prints Room of the British Museum.]

	PAGE
HOLY ISLAND, LOUGH DERG	*Frontispiece*
MAP OF IRELAND IN REIGN OF HENRY VII. . . .	134
CROSS IN CEMETERY OF TEMPUL BRECCAN . . .	39
WEST CROSS, MONASTERBOICE	48
DOORWAY OF MAGHERA CHURCH	51
KILBANNON TOWER	54
KELLS ROUND TOWER	57
BASE OF TUAM CROSS	62
DOORWAY OF KILLESHIN CHURCH	65
INTERIOR OF CORMAC'S CHAPEL (CASHEL) . . .	72
WEST FRONT OF ST. CRONAN'S CHURCH	77
WEST DOORWAY OF FRESHFORD CHURCH . . .	80
SIR HENRY SIDNEY (PORTRAIT OF)	175

LIST OF ILLUSTRATIONS.

	PAGE
ASKEATON CASTLE	182
CATHERINE, THE "OLD" COUNTESS OF DESMOND	186
SIR JOHN PERROT (PORTRAIT OF)	196
CAHIR CASTLE (IN 1599)	208
CAPTURE OF THE EARL OF ORMOND BY THE O'MORES	212
IRELAND IN THE REIGN OF JAMES I.	217
THOMAS WENTWORTH, EARL OF STRAFFORD, 1641	233
ARCHBISHOP USSHER (PORTRAIT OF)	236
JAMES, DUKE OF ORMOND (PORTRAIT OF)	259
HENRY CROMWELL (PORTRAIT OF)	274
"TIGER" ROCHE	305
DEAN SWIFT (PORTRAIT OF)	316
PHILIP, EARL OF CHESTERFIELD (PORTRAIT OF)	322
RIGHT HON. HENRY FLOOD (PORTRAIT OF)	324
RIGHT HON. HENRY GRATTAN, M.P. (PORTRAIT OF)	329
JAMES CAULFIELD, EARL OF CHARLEMONT (PORTRAIT OF)	337
RIGHT HON. EDMUND BURKE (PORTRAIT OF)	343
THE EARL OF MOIRA ("A MAN OF IMPORTANCE")	348
RIGHT HON. EDMUND BURKE (SKETCH FROM LIFE)	353
THEOBALD WOLFE TONE (PORTRAIT OF)	356
LORD EDWARD FITZGERALD (PORTRAIT OF)	360
THE FOUR COURTS, DUBLIN	369
MARQUIS CORNWALLIS (PORTRAIT OF)	374
ROBERT EMMETT (PORTRAIT OF)	378
DANIEL O'CONNELL, M.P. (SKETCH OF)	383

LIST OF ILLUSTRATIONS.   xxix

LESSER ILLUSTRATIONS (AT END OF CHAPTERS).

	PAGE
CROMLEGH ON HOWTH	12
MOUTH OF SEPULCHRAL CHAMBER AT DOWTH	31
ST. KEVIN'S CHURCH	41
CORMAC'S CHAPEL AND ROUND TOWER	70
ROUND TOWER AT DEVENISH	75
SOUTH WINDOW OF ST. CAEMIN'S CHURCH	89
FIGURES ON KILCARN FONT	97
TRIM CASTLE	112
FIGURES ON KILCARN FONT	131 AND 150
INITIAL LETTER (FROM THE BOOK OF KELLS)	160
ST. PATRICK'S BELL	173
INITIAL LETTER (FROM THE BOOK OF KELLS)	202
CINERARY URN	210
TARA BROOCH	219
DOORWAY OF ST. CAEMIN'S CHURCH	225
SHRINE OF ST. PATRICK'S BELL	239
ST. COLUMBA'S ORATORY	265
INITIAL LETTER (FROM THE BOOK OF KELLS)	294
CRYPT OF CHRIST CHURCH CATHEDRAL	376

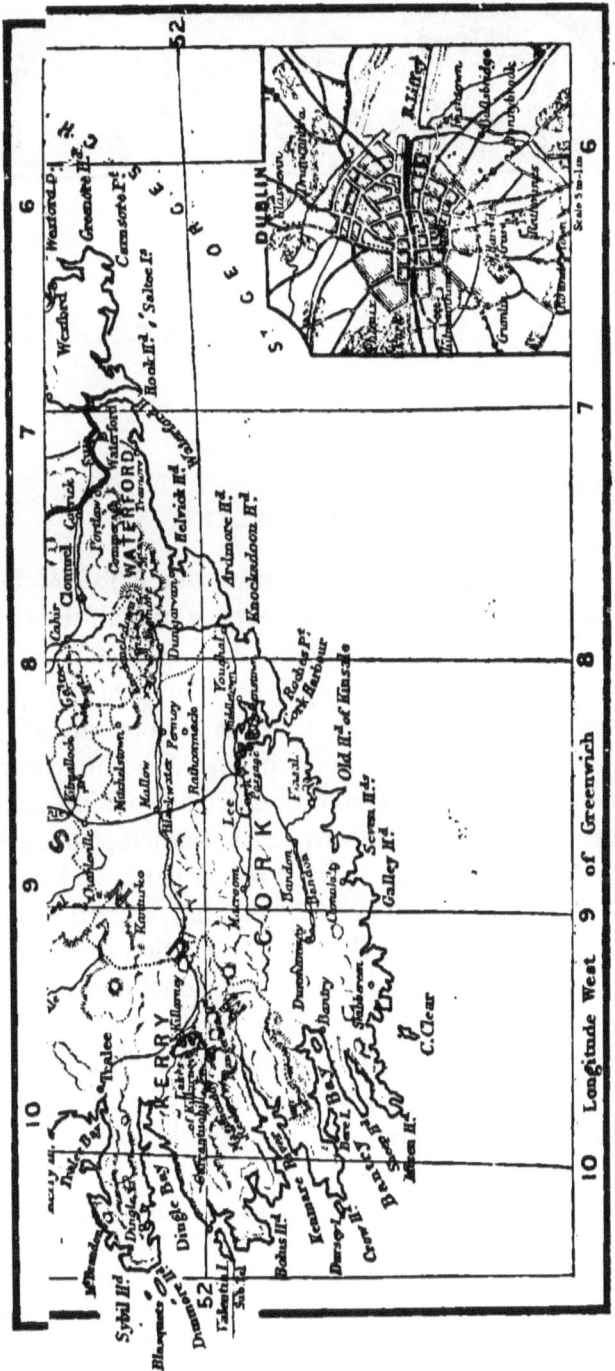

THE STORY OF IRELAND.

I.

PRIMEVAL IRELAND.

"It seems to be certain," says the Abbé McGeoghehan, "that Ireland continued uninhabited from the Creation to the Deluge." With this assurance to help us on our onward way I may venture to supplement it by saying that little is known about the first, or even about the second, third, and fourth succession of settlers in Ireland. At what precise period what is known as the Scoto-Celtic branch of the great Aryan stock broke away from its parent tree, by what route its migrants travelled, in what degree of consanguinity it stood to the equally Celtic race or races of Britain, what sort of people inhabited Ireland previous to the first Aryan invasion—all this is in the last degree uncertain, though that it was inhabited by some race or races outside the limits of that greatest of human groups seems from ethnological evidence to be perfectly clear.

When first it dawns upon us through that thick

darkness which hangs about the birth of all countries —whatever their destiny—it was a densely wooded and scantily peopled island "lying a-loose," as old Campion, the Elizabethan historian, tells us, "upon the West Ocean," though his further assertion that "in shape it resembleth an egg, plain on the sides, and not reaching forth to the sea in nooks and elbows of Land as Brittaine doeth"—cannot be said to be quite geographically accurate—the last part of the description referring evidently to the east coast, the only one with which, like most of his countrymen, he was at that time familiar.

Geographically, then, and topographically it was no doubt in much the same state as the greater part of it remained up to the middle or end of the sixteenth century, a wild, tangled, roadless land, that is to say, shaggy with forests, abounding in streams, abounding, too, in lakes—far more, doubtless, than at present, drainage and other causes having greatly reduced their number—with rivers bearing the never-failing tribute of the skies to the sea, yet not so thoroughly as to hinder enormous districts from remaining in a swamped and saturated condition, given up to the bogs, which even at the present time are said to cover nearly one-sixth of its surface.

This superfluity of bogs seems always in earlier times to have been expeditiously set down by all historians and agriculturists as part of the general depravity of the Irish native, who had allowed his good lands,—doubtless for his own mischievous pleasure—to run to waste; bogs being then supposed to differ from other lands only so far as they were made "waste and barren by superfluous moisture." About the middle of last century it began to be perceived that this view of the matter was somewhat inadequate ; the theory then prevailing being that bogs owed their origin not to water alone, but to the destruction of woods, whose remains are found imbedded in them—a view which held good for another fifty or sixty years, until it was in its turn effectually disposed of by the report of the Bogs Commission in 1810, when it was proved once for all that it was to the growth of sphagnums and other peat-producing mosses they were in the main due—a view which has never since been called in question.

A great deal, however, had happened to Ireland before the bogs began to grow on it at all. It had—to speak only of some of its later vicissitudes—been twice at least united to England, and through it with what we now know as the continent of Europe, and twice severed from it again. It had been exposed to a cold so intense as to bleach off all life from its surface, utterly depriving it of vegetation, and grinding the mountains down to that scraped bun-like outline which so many of them still retain ; had covered the whole country, highlands and lowlands alike, with a dense overtoppling cap of snow, towering often thousands of feet above the present height of the mountains, from which "central silence" the glaciers crept sleepily down the ravines and valleys, eating their way steadily seaward, and leaving behind them moraines to mark their passage, leaving also longitudinal scratches, cut, as a diamond cuts glass, upon the rocks, as may be seen by any one who takes the trouble of looking for them; finally reaching the sea in a vast sloping plateau which pushed its course steadily onward until its further advance was overborne by the buoyancy of the salt water, the ends breaking off, as the Greenland glaciers do to-day, into huge floating icebergs, which butted against one another, jammed up all the smaller bays and fiords; were carried in again and again on the rising tide; rolled hither and thither like so many colossal ninepins; played, in short, all the old rough-and-tumble Arctic games through many a cold and dismal century, finally melting away as the milder weather began slowly to return, leaving Ireland a very lamentable-looking island indeed, not unlike one of those deplorable islands scattered along the shores of Greenland and upon the edges of Baffin's Bay—treeless, grassless, brown and scalded, wearing everywhere over its surface the marks of that great ice-plough which had lacerated its sides so long.

There seems to be good geological evidence that the land connection between Ireland and Scotland continued to a considerably later period than between it and England, to which, and as far as can be seen to no other possible cause is to be attributed two very striking characteristics of its fauna, namely, its excessive meagreness and its strikingly northern character. Not only does it come far short of the already meagre English fauna, but all the distinctively southern species are the ones missing, though there is nothing in the climate to account for the fact. The Irish hare, for instance, is not the ordinary brown hare of England, but the "blue" or Arctic hare of

Scotch mountains, the same which still further to the north becomes white in winter, a habit which, owing to the milder Irish winters, it has apparently shaken off.

It would be pleasant to linger here a little over this point of distribution—so fruitful of suggestion as to the early history of the planet we occupy. To speculate as to the curious contradictions, or apparent contradictions, to be found even within so narrow an area as that of Ireland. What, for instance, has brought a group of South European plants to the shores of Kerry and Connemara, which plants are not to be found in England, even in Cornwall, which one would have thought must surely have arrested them first? Why, when neither the common toad or frog are indigenous in Ireland (for the latter, though common enough now, was only introduced at the beginning of last century) a comparatively rare little toad, the Natterjack, should be found in one corner of Kerry to all appearances indigenously? All these questions, however, belong to quite another sort of book, and to a much larger survey of the field than there is time here to embark upon, so there is nothing for it but to turn one's back resolutely upon the tempting sin of discursiveness, or we shall find ourselves belated before our real journey is even begun.

The first people, then, of whose existence in Ireland we can be said to know anything are commonly asserted to have been of Turanian origin, and are known as "Formorians." As far as we can gather, they were a dark, low-browed, stunted race, although, oddly enough, the word Formorian in early Irish legend is always used as synonymous with the word giant. They were, at any rate, a race of utterly savage hunters and fishermen, ignorant of metal, of pottery, possibly even of the use of fire; using the stone hammers or hatchets of which vast numbers remain in Ireland to this day, and specimens of which may be seen in every museum. How long they held possession no one can tell, although Irish philologists believe several local Irish names to date from this almost inconceivably remote epoch. Perhaps if we think of the Lapps of the present day, and picture them wandering about the country, catching the hares and rabbits in nooses, burrowing in the earth or amongst rocks, and being, not impossibly, looked down on with scorn by the great Irish elk which still stalked majestically over the hills; rearing ugly little altars to dim, formless gods; trembling at every sudden gust, and seeing demon faces in every bush and brake, it will give us a fairly good notion of what these very earliest inhabitants of Ireland were probably like.

Next followed a Belgic colony, known as the Firbolgs, who overran the country, and appear to have been of a somewhat higher ethnological grade, although, like the Formorians, short, dark, and swarthy. Doubtless the latter were not entirely exterminated to make way for the Firbolgs, any more than the Firbolgs to make way for the Danaans, Milesians, and other successive races; such wholesale exterminations being, in fact, very rare, especially in a country which like Ireland seems specially laid out by kindly nature for the protection of a weaker race struggling in the grip of a stronger one.

After the Firbolgs, though I should be sorry to be obliged to say how long after, fresh and more important tribes of invaders began to appear. The first of these were the Tuatha-da-Danaans, who arrived under the leadership of their king Nuad, and took possession of the east of the country. These Tuatha-da-Danaans are believed to have been large, blue-eyed people of Scandinavian origin, kinsmen and possibly ancestors of those Norsemen or " Danes " who in years to come were destined to work such woe and havoc upon the island.

Many battles took place between these Danaans and the earlier Firbolgic settlers — the native owners as no doubt they felt themselves of the country. One of the best substantiated of these, not, indeed, by history or even tradition, but by a more solid testimony, that of the stone remains left on the spot, prove, at any rate, that *some* long-sustained battle was at some remote period fought on the spot.

This is the famous pre-historic battle of Moytura, rather the Southern Moytura, for there were two ; the other, situated not far from the present town of Sligo, retaining "the largest collection of pre-historic remains," says Dr. Petrie, " in any region in the world with the exception of Carnac." This second battle of Moytura was fought upon the plain of Cong, which is washed by the waters of Lough Mask and Lough Corrib, close to where the long monotonous midland plain of Ireland becomes broken, changes into that region of high mountains and low-lying valleys, now called Connemara, but which in earlier days was always known as Iar Connaught.

It is a wild scene even now, not very much less so than it must have been when this old and half-mythical Battle of the West was fought and won. A grey plain, " stone-roughened like the graveyard of dead hosts," broken into grassy ridges, and starred at intervals with pools, repeating the larger glitter of the lake hard by. Over the whole surface of this tumbled plain rise, at intervals, great masses of rock, some natural, but others artificially up-tilted—cromlechs and dolmens, menhirs and cairns—whitened by lichen scrawls, giving them often in uncertain light the effect of so many undecipherable inscriptions, written in a long-forgotten tongue.

From the position of the battle-field it has been made out to their own satisfaction by those who have studied it on the spot, that the Firbolgs must have taken up a fortified position upon the hill called Ben-levi; a good strategic position unquestionably, having behind it the whole of the Mayo mountains into which to retreat in case of defeat. The Danaans, on the other hand, advancing from the plains of Meath, took up their station upon the hill known as Knockmaa,[1] standing by itself about five miles from the present town of Tuam, on the top of which stands a great cairn, believed to have been in existence even then—a legacy of some yet earlier and more primitive race which inhabited the country, and, therefore, possibly the oldest record of humanity to-day extant in Ireland.

Three days the battle is said to have raged with

[1] Now Castle Hacket Hill.

varying fortunes, in the course of which the Danaan king Nuad lost his arm, a loss which was repaired, we are told, by the famous artificer Credue or Cerd, who made him a silver one, and as "Nuad of the Silver Hand" he figures conspicuously in early Irish history. In spite of this, and of the death of a number of their fighting-men, the stars fought for the Tuatha-da-Danaans, who were strong men and cunning, workers in metal, and great fighters, so that at last they utterly made an end of their antagonists, occupying the whole country, and holding it, say the annalists for a hundred and ninety and six years—building earth and stone forts, many of which exist to this day, but what their end was no man can tell you, save that they, too, were, in their turn, conquered by the Milesians or "Scoti," who next overran the country, giving to it their own name of Scotia, by which name it was known down to the end of the twelfth century, and driving the earlier settlers before them, who thereupon fled to the hills, and took refuge in the forests, whence they emerged, doubtless, with unpleasant effect upon their conquerors, as another defeated race did upon *their* conquerors in later days.

As regards the early doings of these Scoti, although nearer to us in point of time, their history is, if anything, rather more vague than that of their predecessors. The source for the greater part of it is in a work known as the "Annals of the Four Masters," a compilation put together in the sixteenth century, from documents now no longer existing, and which must unfortunately, be regarded as largely fictitious. Were names, indeed, all that were wanting to give substantiality there are enough and to spare, the beginning of every Irish history positively bristling with them. Leland, for instance, who published his three sturdy tomes in the year 1773, and who is still one of our chief authorities on the subject, speaks of Ireland as having "engendered one hundred and seventy one monarchs, all of the same house and lineage; with sixty-eight kings, and two queens of Great Brittain and Ireland all sprung equally from her loins." We read in his pages of the famous brethren Heber and Heremon, sons of Milesius, who divided the island between them; of Allamh Fodla, celebrated as a healer of feuds and protector of learning, who drew the priests and bards together into a triennial assembly at Tara, in Meath; of Kimbaoth, who is praised by the annalists for having advanced learning and kept the peace. The times of peace had not absolutely arrived however, for he was not long after murdered, and wild confusion and wholesale slaughter ensued. Another Milesian prince, Thuathal, shortly afterwards returned from North Britain, and, assisted by a body of Pictish soldiers, defeated the rebels, restored order, and re-established the seat of his monarchy in Meath.

As a specimen of the sort of stories current in history of this kind, Leland relates at considerable length the account of the insult offered to this Thuathal by the provincial king of Leinster. "The king," he tells us, "had married the daughter of Thuathal, but conceiving a violent passion for her sister, pretended that his wife had died, and demanded and obtained her sister in marriage. The two ladies met in the royal house of Leinster. Astonishment and sorrow put an end to their lives!" The offender not long afterwards was invaded by his justly indignant father-in-law, and his province only preserved from desolation on condition of paying a heavy tribute, "as a perpetual memorial of the resentment of Thuathal and of the offence committed by the king of Leinster."

Another special favourite of the annalists is Cormac O'Conn, whose reign they place about the year 250, and over whose doings they wax eloquent, dwelling upon the splendour of his court, the heroism of his warlike sons, the beauty of his ten fair daughters, the doings of his famous militia, the Fenni or Fenians, and especially of his illustrious general Finn, or Fingal, the hero of the legends, and father of the poet Ossian —a warrior whom we shall meet with again in the next chapter.

And now, it will perhaps be asked, what is one in sober seriousness to say to all this? All that one can say is that these tales are not to be taken as history in any rigid sense of the word, but must for the most part be regarded as mere hints, caught from chaos, and coming down through a hundred broken mediums; scraps of adventures told around camp fires; oral traditions; rude songs handed from father to son, and altering more or less with each new teller. The early history of Ireland is in this respect much like the early history of all other countries. We have the same semi-mythical aggregations, grown up around some small kernel of reality, but so changed, swollen, distorted, that it is difficult to distinguish the true from the false; becoming vaguer and vaguer too as the mists of time and sentiment gather more and more thickly around them, until at last we seem to be swimming dimly in a "moony vapour," which allows no dull peaks of reality to pierce through it at all. "There were giants in those days," is a continually recurring assertion, characteristic of all ancient annals, and of these with the rest.

CROMLECH ON HOWTH.

II.

THE LEGENDS AND THE LEGEND MAKERS.

BETTER far than such historic shams—cardboard castles with little or no substance behind them—are the real legends. These put forward no obtrusive pretensions to accuracy, and for that very reason are far truer in that larger sense in which all the genuine and spontaneous outgrowth of a country form part and parcel of its history. Some of the best of these have been excellently translated by Mr. Joyce, whose "Celtic Romances" ought to be in the hands of every one, from the boy of twelve upwards, who aspires to know anything of the inner history of Ireland; to understand, that is to say, that curiously recurrent note of poetry and pathos which breaks continually through all the dull hard prose of the surface. A note often lost in unmitigated din and discord, yet none the less re-emerging, age after age, and century after century, and always when it does so lending its own charm to a record, which, without some such alleviations, would be almost too grim and disheartening in its unrelieved and unresulting misery to be voluntarily approached at all.

Although as they now stand none appear to be of

earlier date than the ninth or tenth century, these stories all breathe the very breath of a primitive world. An air of remote pagan antiquity hangs over them, and as we read we seem gradually to realize an Ireland as unlike the one we know now as if, like the magic island of Buz, it had sunk under the waves and been lost. Take, for instance—for space will not allow of more than a sample—the story of "The Pursuit of Gilla Dacker and his Horse," not by any means one of the best, yet characteristic enough. In it we learn that from Beltane, the 1st of May—the great Celtic festival of the sun—to Sanim, the 1st of November, the chiefs and Fenni hunted each day with their hounds through the forests and over the plains, while from Sanim to Beltane they lived in the "Betas," or houses of hospitality, or feasted high with Finn McCumal, son of Cumal, grandson of Trenmore O'Baskin, whose palace stood upon the summit of the hill of Allen, a hill now crowned with a meaningless modern obelisk, covering the site of the old historic rath, a familiar object to thousands who have looked up at it from the Curragh of Kildare, certainly with no thought in their minds of Finn McCumal or his vanished warriors.

The tale tells how one day, after hunting on the Plains of Cliach, the Fenni sat down to rest upon the hill of Colkilla, their hunting tents being pitched upon a level spot near the summit. How presently, afar off over the plain at their feet, they saw one of the conquered race of earlier inhabitants, a "Formorian" of huge size and repulsive ugliness coming towards them, leading his horse by the halter, an animal larger, it seems, than six ordinary horses, but broken down and knock-kneed, with jaws that stuck out far in advance of its head. How the heroes, idling pleasantly about in the sunshine, laughed aloud at the uncouth "foreigner" and his ugly raw-boned beast, "covered with tangled scraggy hair of a sooty black." How he came before the king and, having made obeisance, told him that his name was the Gilla Dacker, and then and there took service with him for a year, desiring at the same time that special care should be paid to his horse, and the best food given it, and care taken that it did not stray, whereat the heroes laughed again, the horse standing like a thing carved in wood and unable apparently to move a leg.

No sooner, however, was it loosed, and the halter cast off, than it rushed amongst the other horses, kicking and lashing, and seizing them with its teeth till not one escaped. Seeing which, the Fenni rose up in high wrath, and one of them seized the Gilla Dacker's horse by the halter and tried to draw it away, but again it became like a rock, and refused to stir. Then he mounted its back and flogged it, but still it remained like a stone. Then, one after the other, thirteen more of the heroes mounted, but still it stirred not. The very instant, however, that its master, the Gilla Dacker rose up angrily to depart, the old horse went too, with the fourteen heroes still upon his back, whereat the Fenni raised fresh shouts of laughter. But the Gilla Dacker, after he had walked a little way, looked back, and seeing that his horse was following, stood for a moment to tuck up his skirts. "Then, all at once changing his pace, he set out with long strides; and if you know what the speed of a swallow is, flying across a mountain-side, or the fairy wind of a March day sweeping over the plains, then you can understand Gilla Dacker, as he ran down the hillside towards the south-west. Neither was the horse behindhand in the race, for, though he carried a heavy load, he galloped like the wind after his master, plunging and bounding forward with as much freedom as if he had nothing at all on his back."

Finn and his warriors left behind on the hill stared awhile, and then resolved to go to Ben Edar, now Howth, there to seek for a ship to follow after Gilla Dacker and his horse, and the fourteen heroes. And on their way they met two bright-faced youths wearing mantles of scarlet silk, fastened by brooches of gold, who, saluting the king, told him their names were Foltlebar and Feradach, and that they were the sons of the king of Innia, and each possessed an art, and that as they walked they had disputed whose art was the greater. "And my art," said Feradach, " is this. If at any time a company of warriors need a ship, give me only my joiner's axe and my crann-tavall,[1] and I am able to provide a ship without delay. The only thing I ask them to do is this —to cover their heads close and keep them covered, while I give the crann-tavall three blows of my axe. Then I tell them to uncover their heads, and lo, there lies the ship in harbour, ready to sail!"

The Foltlebar spoke and said, " This, O king, is the art I profess: On land I can track the wild duck over

[1] A sling for projecting stones, strung rather like a cross-bow.

nine ridges and nine glens, and follow her without being once thrown out, till I drop upon her in her nest. And I can follow up a track on sea quite as well as on land, if I have a good ship and crew."

And Finn replied, "You are the very men I want; and now I take you both into my service. Though our own trackmen, the Clan Naim, are good, yet we now need some one still more skilful to follow the Gilla Dacker through unknown seas."

To these unknown seas they went, starting from Ben Edar, and sailed away west for many days over the Atlantic, seeing many strange sights and passing many unknown islands. But at last the ship stopped short in front of an island with vast rocky cliffs towering high above their heads as steep as a sheet of glass, at which the heroes gazed amazed and baffled, not knowing what to do next. But Dermot O'Dynor —called also Dermot of the Bright-face—undertook to climb it, for of all the Fenni he was the most learned in Druidical enchantments, having been early taught the secret of fairy lore by Mananan Mac Lir, who ruled over the Inis Manan or Land of Promise.

Dermot accordingly took leave of his friends and climbed the great cliff, and when he reached the top he found that it was flat and covered with tall green grass, as is often the case in these desolate wind-blown Atlantic islets. And in the very centre he found a well with a tall pillar stone beside it, and beside the pillar stone a drinking-horn chased with gold. And he took up the drinking-horn to drink, being thirsty, but the instant he touched the brim with his lips, lo! a great Wizard Champion armed to the teeth, sprang up out of the earth, whereupon he and Dermot O'Dynor fought together beside the well the livelong day until the dusk fell. But the moment the dusk fell, the wizard champion sprang with a great bound into the middle of the well, and so disappeared, leaving Dermot standing there much astonished at what had befallen him.

And the next day the same thing happened, and the next, and the next. But on the fourth day, Dermot watched his foe narrowly, and when the dusk came on, and he saw that he was about to spring into the well, he flung his arms tightly about him, and the wizard champion struggled to get free, but Dermot held him, and at length they both fell together into the well, deeper and deeper to the very bottom of the earth, and there was nothing to be seen but dim shadows, and nothing to be heard but vague confused sounds like the roaring of waves. At length there came a glimmering of light, and all at once bright day broke suddenly around them, and they came out at the other side of the earth, and found themselves in Tir-fa-ton, the land under the sea, where the flowers bloom all the year round, and no man has ever so much as heard the word Death.

What happened there; how Dermot O'Dynor met the other heroes, and how the fourteen Fenni who had been carried off were at last recaptured, would be too long to tell. Unlike most of these legends all comes right in the end; Gilla Dacker and his ugly horse disappear suddenly into space, and neither Finn himself nor any of his warriors ever see them again.

It is impossible, I think, to read this, and to an even greater degree some of the other stories, which have been translated by Mr. Joyce and others, without perceiving how thoroughly impregnated with old-world and mythological sentiment they are. An air of all but fabulous antiquity pervades them, greater perhaps than pervades the legends of any other north European people. We seem transplanted to a world of the most primitive type conceivable; a world of myth and of fable, of direct Nature interpretations, of mythology, in short, pure and simple. Even those stories which are known to be of later origin exhibit to a greater or less degree the same character; one which has come down to them doubtless from earlier half-forgotten tales, of which they are merely the final and most modern outcome.

When, too, we turn from the legends themselves to the legend-makers, everything that we know of the position of the bards (*Ollamhs* or *Sennachies*) carries out the same idea. In the earliest times they were not merely the singers and story-tellers of their race, but to a great degree they bore a religious or semi-religious character. Like the Brehons or judges they were the directors and guides of the others, but they possessed in addition a peculiarly Druidical character of sanctity, as the inheritors and interpreters of a revelation confided to them alone. A power the more formidable because no one, probably, had ever ventured to define its exact character.

The Head bard or Ollamh, in the estimation of his tribesmen, stood next in importance to the chieftain or king—higher, indeed, in some respects; for whereas to slay a king might, or might not be criminal, to slay an Ollamh entailed both outlawing in this life and a vaguer, but not the less terrible, supernatural penalty in another. Occasionally, as in the case of the Ollamh Fodhla, by whom the halls of Tara are reputed to have been built, the king was himself the bard, and so combined both offices, but this appears to have been rare. Even as late as the sixteenth century, refusal of praise from a bard was held to confer a far deeper and more abiding stigma upon a man than blame from any other lips. If they, "the bards," says an Elizabethan writer, "say ought in dispraise, the gentleman, especially the meere Irish, stand in great awe."

It is easy, I think, to see this is merely the survival of some far more potent power wielded in earlier times. In pre-Christian days especially, the penalty attaching to the curse of a Bard was understood to carry with it a sort of natural anathema, not unlike the priestly anathema of later times. Indeed there was one singular, and, as far as I am aware, unique power possessed by the Irish Bards, which goes beyond any priestly or papal anathema, and which was known as the *Clann Dichin*, a truly awful malediction, by means of which the Ollamh, if offended or injured, could pronounce a spell against the very land of his injurer; which spell once pronounced that land would produce no crop of any kind, neither could living creature graze upon it, neither was it possible even to walk over it without peril, and so it continued until the wrong, whatever it was, had been repented, and the curse of the Ollamh was lifted off from the land again.

Is it to be wondered at that men, endowed with such powers of blessing or banning, possessed of such mystic communion with the then utterly unknown powers of nature, should have exercised an all but unlimited influence over the minds of their countrymen, especially at a time when the powers of evil were still supposed to stalk the earth in all their native malignity, and no light of any revelation had broken through the thick dim roof overhead?

Few races of which the world has ever heard are as imaginative as that of the Celt, and at this time the imagination of every Celt must have been largely exercised in the direction of the malevolent and the terrible. Even now, after fourteen hundred years of Christianity, the Connaught or Kerry peasant still hears the shriek of his early gods in the sob of the waves or the howling of the autumn storms. Fish demons gleam out of the sides of the mountains, and the black bog-holes are the haunts of slimy monsters of inconceivable horror. Even the less directly baneful spirits such as Finvarragh, king of the fairies, who haunts the stony slopes of Knockmaa, and all the endless variety of *dii minores*, the cluricans, banshees, fetches who peopled the primitive forests, and still hop and mow about their ruined homes, were far more likely to injure than to benefit unless approached in exactly the right manner, and with the properly uttered conjurations. The Unknown is always the Terrible; and the more vivid an untaught imagination is, the more certain it is to conjure up exactly the things which alarm it most, and which it least likes to have to believe in.

III

PRE-CHRISTIAN IRELAND.

GETTING out of this earliest and foggiest period, whose only memorials are the stones which still cumber the ground, or those subtler traces of occupation of which philology keeps the key, and pushing aside a long and uncounted crowd of kings, with names as uncertain as their deeds, pushing aside, too, the legends and coming to hard fact, we must picture Ireland still covered for the most part with pathless forests, but here and there cleared and settled after a rude fashion by rough cattle-owning tribes, who herded their own cattle and "lifted" their neighbour's quite in the approved fashion of the Scotch Highlanders up to a century and a half ago.

Upon the whole, we may fairly conclude that matters were ameliorating more or less; that the wolves were being killed, the woods cleared—not as yet in the ferocious wholesale fashion of later days—that a little rudimentary agriculture showed perhaps here and there in sheltered places. Sheep and goats grazed then as now over the hills, and herds of cattle began to cover the Lowlands. The men, too, were possibly beginning to grow a trifle less like two-legged beasts of prey, though still rough as the very wolves they hunted; bare-legged, wild-eyed hunter-herdsmen with—who can doubt it?—flocks of children trooping vociferously at their heels.

Of the daily life, habits, dress, religion of these people—the direct ancestors of four-fifths of the present inhabitants of Ireland—we know unfortunately exceedingly little. It is not even certain, whether human sacrifices did or did not form—as they certainly did in Celtic Britain—part of that religion, though there is some evidence that it did, in which case prisoners taken in battle, or slaves, were probably the victims.

That a considerable amount of slavery existed in early Celtic Ireland is certain, though as to the rules by which it was regulated, as of almost every other detail of the life, we know little or nothing. At the time of the Anglo-Norman conquest Ireland was said to be full of English slaves carried off in raids along the coast, and these filibustering expeditions undoubtedly began in very early times. St. Patrick himself was thus carried off, and the annalists tell us that in the third century Cormac Mac Art ravaged the whole western coast of Britain, and brought away "great stores of slaves and treasures." To how late a period, too, the earlier conquered races of Ireland, such as the Formorians, continued as a distinct race from their Milesian conquerors, and whether they existed as a slave class, or, as seems more probable, as mere outcasts and vagabonds out of the pale of humanity, liable like the "Tory" of many centuries later, to be killed whenever caught; all these are matters on which we have unfortunately only the vaguest hints to guide us.

The whole texture of society must have been loose and irregular to a degree that it is difficult for us now to conceive, without central organization or social cement of any kind. In one respect—that of the treatment of his women—the Irish Celt seems to have always stood in favourable contrast to most of the other rude races which then covered the north of Europe, but as regards the rest there was probably little difference. Fighting was the one aim of life. Not to have washed his spear in an adversary's gore, was a reproach which would have been felt by a full-grown tribesman to have carried with it the deepest and most lasting ignominy. The very women were not in early times exempt from war service, nay, probably would have scorned to be so. They fought beside their husbands, and slew or got slain with as reckless a courage as the men, and it was not until the time of St. Columba, late in the sixth century, that a law was passed ordering them to remain in their homes—a fact which alone speaks volumes both for the vigour and the undying pugnacity of the race.

While, on the one hand, we can hardly thus exaggerate the rudeness of this life, we must be careful, on the other, of concluding that these people were simple barbarians, incapable of discriminating right from wrong. Men, even the wildest, rarely indeed live entirely without some law to guide them, and certainly it was so in Ireland. A rule was growing up and becoming theoretically at any rate, established, many of the provisions of which startle us by the curious modernness of their tone, so oddly do they contrast with what we know of the condition of civilization or non-civilization then existing.

Although this ancient Irish law was not drawn up until long after the introduction of Christianity, it seems best to speak of it here, as, though modified by the stricter Christian rule, it in the main depended for such authority as it possessed upon traditions existing long before; traditions regarded indeed by Celtic scholars as tracing their origin beyond the arrival of the first Celt in Ireland, outcomes and survivals, that is to say, of yet earlier Aryan rule, showing points of resemblance with the equally Aryan laws of India, a matter of great interest, carrying our thoughts back along the history of humanity to a time when those differences which seem now the most inherent and vital were as yet undreamt of, and not one of the great nations of the modern world were as much as born.

The two chief books in which this law is contained, the "Book of Aicill" and the "Senchus-Mor," have only comparatively recently been translated and made available for English readers. The law as there laid down was drawn up and administered by the Brehons, who were the judges and the law-makers of the people, and whose decision was appealed to in all matters of dispute. The most serious flaw of the system—a very serious one it will be seen—was that, owing to the scattered and tribal existence prevailing, there was no strong central rule *behind* the Brehon, as there is behind the modern judge, ready and able to enforce his decrees. At bottom, force, it must not be forgotten, is the sanction of all law, and there was no available force of any kind then, nor for many a long day afterwards, in Ireland.

It was, no doubt, owing chiefly to this defective weakness that a system of fines rather than punishments grew up, one which in later times caused much scandal to English legal writers. In such a society crime in fact was hardly recognizable except in the form of an injury inflicted upon some person or persons. An offence against the State there could not be, simply because there was no State to be offended. Everything, from murder down to the smallest and most accidental injury, was compensated for by " erics " or fines. The amount of these fines was decided upon by the Brehon, who kept an extraordinary number of imaginary rulings, descending into the most minute particulars, such as what fine was to be paid in the case of one person's cat stealing milk from another person's house, what fine in the case of one woman's bees stinging another woman, a careful distinction being preserved in this case between the case in which the sting did or did not draw blood! Even in the matter of fines it does not seem clear how the penalty was to be enforced where the person on whom it was inflicted refused to submit and where there was no one at hand to coerce him successfully.

As regards ownership of land early Irish law is very peculiar, and requires to be carefully studied. Primogeniture, regarded by all English lawyers trained under the feudal system as the very basis of inheritance, was simply unknown. Even in the case of the chieftain his rights belonged only to himself, and before his death a re-election took place, when some other of the same blood, not necessarily his eldest son, or even his son at all, but a brother, first cousin, uncle, or whoever stood highest in the estimation of the clan, was nominated as "Tanist" or successor, and received promises of support from the rest.

Elizabethan writers mention a stone which was placed upon a hill or mound having the shape of a foot cut on it, supposed to be that of the first chief or ancestor of the race, "upon which stone the Tanist placing his foot, took oath to maintain all ancient customs inviolably, and to give up the succession peaceably to his Tanist in due time."

The object of securing a Tanist during the lifetime of the chief was to hinder its falling to a minor, or some one unfit to take up the chieftainship, and this continued to prevail for centuries after the Anglo-Norman invasion, and was even adopted by many owners of English descent who had become "meere Irish," as the phrase ran, or ".degenerate English."

"The childe being oftentimes left in nonage," says Campion, "could never defend his patrimony, but by the time he grow to a competent age and have buried an uncle or two, he also taketh his turn," a custom which, as he adds, "breedeth among them continual warres."

The entire land belonged to the clan, and was held theoretically in common, and a redistribution made on the death of each owner, though it seems doubtful whether so very inconvenient an arrangement could practically have been adhered to. All sons, illegitimate as well as legitimate, shared and shared alike, holding the property between them in undivided ownership. It was less the actual land than the amount of grazing it afforded which constituted its value. Even to this day a man, especially in the West of Ireland, will tell you that he has "the grass of three cows," or "the grass of six cows," as the case may be.

It is curious that the most distinct ancient rules concerning the excessive extortion of rent are, as has been shown by Sir Henry Maine, to be found in the "Senchus Mor." Under its regulations three rents are enumerated—namely, the *rack rent* to be extorted from one of a strange tribe; the *fair* rent from one of the same tribe; and the *stipulated* rent to be paid equally to either. The Irish clan or sept was a very loose, and in many cases irregular, structure, embracing even those who were practically undistinguishable from slaves, yet from none of these could any but a *fair* or customary rent be demanded. It was only when those who by no fiction could be supposed to belong to the clan sought for land that the best price attainable might be extorted and insisted upon.

In so primitive a state of society such persons were almost sure to be outcasts, thrown upon the world either by the breaking up of other clans or by their own misdoings. A man of this class was generally what was known as a "Fuidhar" or "broken man," and answered in some respects to the slave or the serf of the early English village community. Like him he seems to have been his lord's or chief's chattel, and if killed or injured the fine or "eric" was paid

THE FAMILY.

not to his own family, but to his master. Such men were usually settled by the chief upon the unappropriated tribal lands over which his own authority tended to increase. This Fuidhar class from the first seem to have been very numerous, and depending as they did absolutely upon the chief, there grew up by degrees that class of armed retainers—kerns and galloglasses, they were called in later times—who surrounded every important chief, whether of English or Irish descent, and were by them quartered forcibly in war time upon others, and so there grew up that system of "coyne and livery," or forced entertainment for horse and men, which is to be met with again and again throughout Irish history, and which undoubtedly was one of the greatest curses of the country, tending more perhaps than any other single cause to keep its people at the lowest possible condition of starvation and misery.

No system of representation seems ever to have prevailed in Ireland. That idea is, in fact, almost purely Teutonic, and seems never to have sprung up spontaneously amongst any Celtic people. The family was the real root. Every head of a family ruled his own household, and submitted in his turn to the rule of his chief. Blood-relationship, including fosterage, was the only real and binding union; that larger connection known as the clan or sept, having the smaller one of the family for its basis, as was the case also amongst the clans of the Scotch highlands. Theoretically, all members of a clan, high and low alike, were held to be the descendants of a common ancestor, and in this way to have a real and direct claim upon one another. If a man was not in some degree akin to another he was no better than a beast, and might be killed like one without compunction whenever occasion arose.

Everything thus began and centred around the tribe or sept. The whole theory of life was purely local. The bare right of existence extended only a few miles from your own door, to the men who bore the same name as yourself. Beyond that nothing was sacred; neither age nor sex, neither life nor goods, not even in later times the churches themselves. Like his cousin of the Scotch Highlands, the Irish tribesman's life was one perpetual carnival of fighting, burning, raiding, plundering, and he who plundered oftenest was the finest hero.

All this must be steadily borne in mind as it enables us to understand, as nothing else will, that almost insane joy in and lust for fighting, that marked inability to settle down to orderly life which runs through all Irish history from the beginning almost to the very end.

Patriotism, too, it must be remembered, is in the first instance only an idea, and the narrowest of local jealousies may be, and often are, forms merely of the same impulse. To men living in one of these small isolated communities, each under the rule of its own petty chieftain, it was natural and perhaps inevitable that the sense of connection with those outside their own community should have been remarkably slight, and of nationality, as we understand the word, quite non-existent. Their own little circle of hills and valleys, their own forests and pasturage was their world, the only one practically of which they had any cognizance. To its scattered inhabitants of that day little Ireland must have seemed a region of incalculable extent, filled with enemies to kill or to be killed by; a region in which a man might wander from sunrise to sunset yet never reach the end, nay, for days together without coming to a second sea. As Greece to a Greek of one of its smaller states it seemed vast simply because he had never in his own person explored its limits.

MOUTH OF SEPULCHRAL CHAMBER AT DOWTH, NEW GRANGE.

IV.

ST. PATRICK THE MISSIONARY.

BUT a new element was about to appear upon the troubled stage, and a new figure, one whose doings, however liberally we may discount the more purely supernatural part of them, strikes us even now as little short of miraculous. There are plenty of heathen countries still; plenty of missionaries too; but a missionary at whose word an entire island—a heathen country given up, it must be remembered, to exceedingly heathen practices—resigns its own creed, and that missionary, too, no king, no warrior, but a mere unarmed stranger, without power to enforce one of the decrees he proclaimed so authoritatively, is a phenomenon which we should find some little difficulty now, or, indeed, at any time, in paralleling.

In one respect St. Patrick was less fortunate than his equally illustrious successor, Columba, since he found no contemporary, or nearly contemporary chronicler, to write his story; the consequence being that it has become so overgrown with pious myths, so tangled and matted with portents and miracles, that it is often difficult for us to see any real substance or outline below them at all.

HIS EARLY LIFE.

What little direct knowledge we have is derived from a famous Irish manuscript known as "The Book of Armagh," which contains, amongst other things, a Confession and an Epistle, believed by some authorities to have been actually written by St. Patrick himself, which was copied as it now stands by a monkish scribe early in the eighth century. It also contains a life of the saint from which the accounts of his later historians have been chiefly drawn.

According to the account now generally accepted he was born about the year 390, though as this would make him well over a hundred at the time of his death, perhaps 400 would be the safest date; was a native, not as formerly believed of Gaul, but of Dumbarton upon the Clyde, whence he got carried off to Ireland in a filibustering raid, became the slave of one Milcho, an inferior chieftain, and herded his master's sheep upon the Slemish mountains in Antrim.

Seven or eight years later he escaped, got back to Britain, was ordained, afterwards went to Gaul, and, according to one account, to Italy. But the thought of the country of his captivity seems to have remained upon his mind and to have haunted his sleeping and waking thoughts. The unborn children of the pagan island seemed to stretch our their hands for help to him. At last the inward impulse grew too strong to be resisted, and accompanied by a few followers, he set foot first on the coast of Wicklow where another missionary, Paladius, had before attempted vainly to land, and being badly received there, took boat again, and landed finally at the entrance of Strangford Lough.

From this point he made his way on foot to Meath, where the king Laoghaire was holding a pagan festival, and stopped to keep Easter on the hill of Slane where he lit a fire. This fire being seen from the hill of Tara aroused great anger, as no lights were by law allowed to be shown before the king's beacon was lit. Laoghaire accordingly sent to know the meaning of this insolence and to have St. Patrick brought before him. St. Patrick's chronicler, Maccumacthenius (one could wish that he had been contented with a shorter name!), tells that as the saint drew nigh to Tara, many prodigies took place. The earth shook, darkness fell, and certain of the magicians who opposed him were seized and tossed into the air. One prodigy certainly took place, for he seems to have won converts from the first. A large number appear to have been gained upon the spot, and before long the greater part of Meath had accepted the new creed, although its king, Laoghaire himself remained a sturdy pagan until his death.

From Tara St. Patrick went to Connaught, a province to which he seems to have been drawn from the first, and there spent eight years, founding many churches and monasteries. There also he ascended Croagh Patrick, the tall sugar-loaf mountain which stands over the waters of Clew Bay, and up to the summit of which hundreds of pilgrims still annually climb in his honour.

From Connaught he next turned his steps to Ulster, visited Antrim and Armagh, and laid the foundations of the future cathedral and bishopric in the latter place. Wherever he went converts seem to have come in to him in crowds. Even the Bards, who had most to lose by the innovation, appear to have been in many cases drawn over. They and the chiefs gained, the rest followed unhesitatingly; whole clans were baptized at a time. Never was spiritual conquest so astonishingly complete!

The tale of St. Patrick's doings; of his many triumphs; his few failures; of the boy Benignus his first Irish disciple; of his wrestling upon Mount Cruachan; of King Eochaidh; of the Bard Ossian, and his dialogues with the apostle, all this has been excellently rendered into verse by Mr. Aubrey de Vere, whose "Legends of St. Patrick" seem to the present writer by no means so well known as they ought to be. The second poem in the series, "The Disbelief of Milcho," especially is one of great beauty, full of wild poetic gleams, and touches which breathe the very breath of an Irish landscape. Poetry is indeed the medium best suited for the Patrician history. The whole tale of the saint's achievements in Ireland is one of those in which history seems to lose its own sober colouring, to become luminous and half magical, to take on all the rosy hues of a myth.

The best proof of the effect of the new revelation is to be found in that extraordinary burst of enthusiasm which marked the next few centuries. The passion for conversion, for missionary labour of all sorts, seems to have swept like a torrent over the island, arousing to its best and highest point that Celtic enthusiasm and which has never, unhappily, found such noble exercise since. Irish missionaries flung themselves upon the dogged might of heathenism, and grappled with it in a death struggle. Amongst the Picts of the Highlands, amongst the fierce Friscians of the Northern seas, beside the Lake of Constance, where the church of St. Gall still preserves the name of another Irish saint, in the Black Forest, at Schaffhausen, at Würtzburg, throughout, in fact, all Germany and North Italy, they were ubiquitous. Wherever they went their own red-hot fervour seems to have melted every obstacle; wherever they went victory seems to have crowned their zeal.[1]

Discounting as much as you choose everything that seems to partake of pious exaggeration, there can be no doubt that the period which followed the Christianizing of Ireland was one of those shining epochs of spiritual and also to a great degree intellectual enthusiasm rare indeed in the history of the world. Men's hearts, full of newly-won fervour, burned to hand on the torch in their turn to others. They went out by thousands, and they beckoned in their converts by tens of thousands. Irish hospitality —a quality which has happily escaped the tooth of criticism—broke out then with a vengeance, and extended its hands to half a continent. From Gaul, from Britain, from Germany, from dozens of scattered places throughout the wide dominions of Charlemagne, the students came; were kept, as Bede expressly tells us, free of cost in the Irish monasteries, and drew their first inspirations in the Irish schools. Even now, after the lapse of all these

[1] For an account of Irish missionaries in Germany, see Mr. Baring-Gould's "Germany," in this series, p. 46.

centuries, many of the places whence they came still reverberate faintly with the memory of that time.

Before plunging into that weltering tangle of confusion which makes up what we call Irish history, one may be forgiven for lingering a little at this point, even at the risk of some slight over-balance of proportion. With so dark a road before us, it seems good to remember that the energies of Irishmen were not, as seems sometimes to be concluded, always and of necessity directed to injuring themselves or tormenting their rulers! Neither was this period by any means a short one. It was no mere "flash in the pan;" no "small pot soon hot" enthusiasm, but a steady flame which burned undimmed for centuries. "During the seventh and eighth centuries, and part of the ninth," says Mr. Goldwin Smith, not certainly a prejudiced writer, "Ireland played a really great part in European history." "The new religious houses," says Mr. Green in his Short History, "looked for their ecclesiastical traditions, not to Rome, but to Ireland, and quoted for their guidance the instructions not of Gregory, but of Columba." "For a time," he adds, "it seemed as if the course of the world's history was to be changed, as if that older Celtic race which the Roman and German had swept before them, had turned to the moral conquest of their conquerors, as if Celtic and not Latin Christianity was to mould the destinies of the Church of the West."

V.

THE FIRST IRISH MONASTERIES.

At home during the same period the chief events were the founding of monasteries, and the settling down of monastic communities, every such monastery becoming the protector and teacher of the little Christian community in its vicinity, educating its own sons, and sending them out as a bee sends its swarms, to settle upon new ground, and to fertilize the flowers of distant harvest fields.

At one time, " The Tribes of the Saints " seem to have increased to such an extent that they threatened to absorb all others. In West Ireland especially, little hermitages sprung up in companies of dozens and hundreds, all over the rock-strewn wastes, and along the sad shores of the Atlantic, dotting themselves like sea gulls upon barren points of rock, or upon sandy wastes which would barely have sufficed, one might think, to feed a goat. We see their remains still—so tiny, yet so enduring—in the Isles of Arran ; upon a dozen rocky points all round the bleak edges of Connemara ; in the wild mountain glens of the Burren—set often with an admirable selection of site, in some sloping dell with, perhaps,

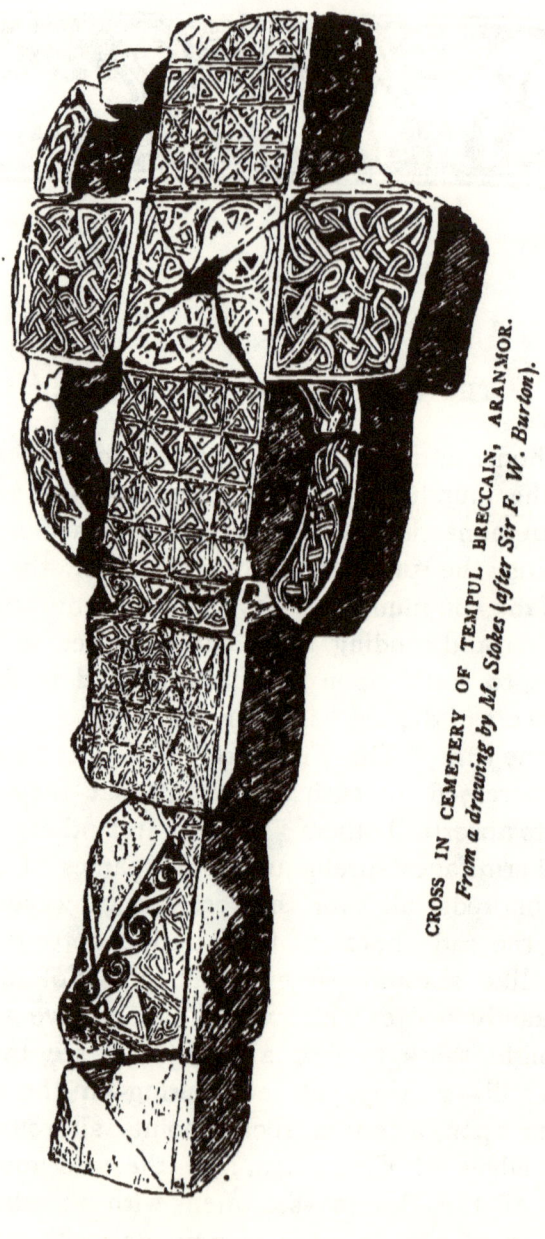

CROSS IN CEMETERY OF TEMPUL BRECCAIN, ARANMOR.
From a drawing by M. Stokes (after Sir F. W. Burton).

a stream slipping lightly by and hurrying to lose itself in the ground, always with a well or spring brimming freshly over—an object still of reverence to the neighbouring peasants. Thanks to the innate stability of their material, thanks, too, to the superabundance of stone in these regions, which makes them no temptation to the despoiler, they remain, roofless but otherwise pretty much as they were. We can look back across a dozen centuries with hardly the change of a detail.

In these little western monasteries each cell stood as a rule by itself, containing—one would say very tightly containing—a single inmate. In other places, large buildings, however, were erected, and great numbers of monks lived together. Some of these larger communities are stated to have actually contained several thousand brethren, and though this sounds like an exaggeration, there can be no doubt that they were enormously populous. The native mode of existence lent itself, in fact, very readily to the arrangement. It was merely the clan or sept re-organized upon a religious footing. "Les premières grands monastères de l'Irelande," says M. de Montalembert in his "Moines d'Occident," "ne furent donc autre chose à vrai dire qui des *clans*, reorganisés sous une forme religieuse." New clans, that is to say, cut out of the old ones, their fealty simply transferred from a chief to an abbot, who was almost invariably in the first instance of chieftain blood. "Le prince, en se faisant moine, devenait naturellement abbè, et restait ainsi dans la vie monastique, ce qu'il avait èté dans la vie sèculière le chef de sa race et de son clan."

There was thus nothing to jar with that sense of continuity, that inborn love of the past, of old ways, old habits, old modes of thought which made and still makes an Irishman—be he never so pronounced a republican—the deepest at heart of Conservatives. Whereas every later change of faith which has been endeavoured to be forced upon the country has met with a steady and undeviating resistance, Christianity, the greatest change of all, seems to have brought with it from the first no sense of dislocation. It assimilated itself quietly, and as it were naturally, with what it found. Under the prudent guidance of its first propagators, it simply gathered to itself all the earlier objects of belief, and with merely the change of a name, sanctified and turned them to its own uses.

ST. KEVIN'S CHURCH, GLENDALOUGH.

VI.

ST. COLUMBA AND THE WESTERN CHURCH.

ABOUT fifty years after the death of St. Patrick a new missionary arose, one who was destined to carry the work which he had begun yet further, to become indeed the founder of what for centuries was the real metropolis and centre of Western Christendom.

In 521 A.D., St. Columba was born in Donegal, of the royal race, say the annalists, of Hy-Nial—of the royal race, at any rate, of the great workers, doers, and thinkers all the world over. In 565, forty-four years later, he left Ireland with twelve companions (the apostolic number), and started on his memorable journey to Scotland, a date of immeasurable importance in the history of Western Christianity.

In that dense fog which hangs over these early times—thick enough to try even the most penetrating eyesight—there is a curious and indescribable pleasure in coming upon so definite, so living, so breathing a figure as that of St. Columba. In writing the early history of Ireland, one of the greatest difficulties which the historian — great or small — has to encounter is to be found in that curious unreality, that tantalizing sense of illusiveness and indefiniteness which seems to envelope every figure whose name crops up on his pages. Even four hundred years later the name of a really great prince and warrior like Brian Boru, or Boruma, awakens no particular sense of reality, nay as often as not is met by a smile of incredulity. The existence of St. Columba no one, however, has been found rash enough to dispute! His, in fact, is one of those essentially self-lit figures which seem to shed some of their own light upon every other they come in contact with, even accidentally. Across the waste of centuries we see him almost as he appeared to his contemporaries. There is something friendly— as it were, next-door-neighbourly—about the man. If we land to-day on Iona, or stand in any of the little chapels in Donegal which bear his name, his presence seems as real and tangible to us as that of Tasso at Ferrara or Petrarch at Avignon. In spite of that thick —one is inclined to say rank—growth of miracles which at times confuse Adamnan's fine portrait of his hero—cover it thick as lichens some monumental slab of marble—we can still recognize his real lineaments underneath. His great natural gifts; his abounding energy; his characteristically Irish love for his native soil; for the beloved "oaks of Derry." We see him in his goings out and his comings in; we know his faults; his fiery Celtic temper, swift to wrath, swift to forgive when the moment of anger is over. Above all, we feel the charm of his abounding humanity. Like Sterne's Uncle Toby there seems to have been something about St. Columba which "eternally beckoned to the unfortunate to come and take shelter under him," and no one apparently ever refused to respond to that appeal.

One thing it is important here to have clearly before the mind, as it is very apt to be overlooked. At the time of St. Columba's ministry, England, which during the lifetime of St. Patrick had been Roman and Christian, had now under the iron flail of its Saxon conquerors lapsed back into Paganism. Ireland, therefore, which for a while had made a part of Christendom, had been broken short off by the heathen conquest of Britain. It was now a small, isolated fragment of Christendom, with a great mass of heathenism between. We can easily imagine what a stimulus to all the eager enthusiasts of the Faith the consciousness of this neighbourhood must have been; how keen the desire to rush to the assault and to replace the Cross where it had been before.

That assault was not, however, begun by Ireland; it was begun, as every one knows, by St. Augustine, a Roman priest, sent by Pope Gregory, who landed at Ebbsfleet, in the Isle of Thanet, in the year 597—thirty-two years after St. Columba left Ireland. If the South of England owes its conversion to Rome, Northern England owes its conversion to Ireland, through the Irish colony at Iona. Oswald, the king of Northumbria, had himself taken refuge in Iona in his youth, and when summoned to reign he at once called in the Irish missionaries, acting himself, we are told, as their interpreter. His whole reign was one continuous struggle with heathenism, and although at his death it triumphed for a time, in the end the faith and energies of the missionaries carried all before them. After the final defeat of the Mercians, under their king Penda, at Winwoed, in 655, the struggle was practically over. Northern and Southern England were alike once more Christian.

One of the chief agents in this result was the Irish monk Aidan, who had fixed his seat in the little peninsula of Lindisfarne, and from whose monastery, as from another Iona, missionaries poured over the North of England. At Lichfield, Whitby, and many other places religious houses sprang up, all owing their allegiance to Lindisfarne, and through it to Iona and Ireland.

In this very fervour there lay the seeds of a new trouble. A serious schism arose between Western Christendom and the Papacy. Rome, whether spiritually or temporally, was a name which reverberated with less awe-inspiring sound in the ears of Irishmen (even Irish Churchmen) than, probably, in those of any other people at that time on the globe. They had never come under the tremendous sway of its material power, and until centuries after this period—when political and, so to speak, accidental causes drove them into its arms—its spiritual power remained to them a thing apart, a foreign element to which they gave at most a reluctant half adhesion.

From this it came about that early in the history of the Western Church serious divisions sprang up between it and the other churches, already being fast welded together into a coherent body under the yoke and discipline of Rome. The points in dispute do not strike us now of any very vital importance. They were not matters of creed at all, merely of external rule and discipline. A vehement controversy as to the proper form of the tonsure, another as to the correct day for Easter, raged for more than a century with much heat on either side; those churches which owed their allegiance to Iona clinging to the Irish methods, those who adhered to Rome vindicating its supreme and paramount authority.

At the Synod of Whitby, held in 664, these points of dispute came to a crisis, and were adjudicated upon by Oswin, king of Northumbria; Bishop Colman, Aidan's successor at Holy Island, maintaining the authority of Columba; Wilfrid, a Saxon priest who had been to Rome, that of St. Peter. Oswin's own leaning seems at first to have been towards the former, but when he heard of the great pretensions of the Roman saint he was staggered. "St. Peter, you say, holds the keys of heaven and hell?" he inquired thoughtfully, "have they also been given then to St. Columba?" It was owned with some reluctance that the Irish saint had been less favoured. "Then I give my verdict for St. Peter," said Oswin, "lest when I reach the gate of heaven I find it shut, and the porter refuse to open to me." This sounds prudent, but scarcely serious; it seems, however, to have been regarded as serious enough by the Irish monks. The Synod broke up. Colman, with his Irish brethren, and a few English ones who threw in their lot with them, forsook Lindisfarne, and sailed away for Ireland. From that moment the rift between them and their English brethren grew steadily wider, and was never afterwards thoroughly healed.

It does not, however, seem to have affected the position of the Irish Church at home, nor yet to have diminished the number of its foreign converts. Safe in its isolation, it continued to go on in its own way with little regard to the rest of Christendom, although in respect to the points chiefly in dispute it after a while submitted to the Roman decision. Armagh was the principal spiritual centre, but there were other places, now tiny villages, barely known by name to the tourist, which were then centres of learning, and recognized as such, not alone in Ireland itself, but throughout Europe. Clonard, Tallaght Clonmacnois; Slane in Meath, where Dagobert II. one of the kings of France, was educated; Kildare, where the sacred fire—not lamp—of St. Bridget was kept burning for centuries, all are places whose names fill a considerable space in the fierce dialectical controversy of that fiery theological age.[1]

This period of growth slipped all too quickly away, but it has never been forgotten. It was the golden time to which men looked wistfully back when growing trouble and discord, attack from without, and dissension from within, had torn in pieces the unhappy island which had shone like a beacon through Europe only to become its byword. The Norsemen had not yet struck prow on Irish strand, and the period between the Synod of Whitby and their appearance seems to have been really one of steady moral and intellectual growth. Heathenism no doubt still lurked in obscure places; indeed traces of it may with no

[1] For an excellent account of early Irish monastic life see "Ireland, and the Celtic Church," by Professor G. Stokes.

WEST CROSS OF MONASTERBOICE, CO. LOUTH.

great difficulty still be discovered in Ireland, but it did not hinder the light from spreading fast under the stimulus which it had received from its first founders. The love of letters, too, sprang up with the religion of a book, and the copying of manuscripts became a passion.

As in Italy and elsewhere, so too in Ireland, the monks were the painters, the illuminators, the architects, carvers, gilders, and book-binders of their time. While outside the monastery walls the fighters were making their neighbours' lives à burden to them, and beyond the Irish Sea the whole world as then known was being shaken to pieces and reconstructed, the monk sat placidly inside at his work, producing chalices, crosiers, gold and silver vessels for the churches, carving crosses, inditing manuscripts filled with the most marvellously dexterous ornament; works, which, in spite of the havoc wrought by an almost unbroken series of devastations which have poured over the doomed island, still survive to form the treasure of its people. We can have very little human sympathy, very little love for what is noble and admirable, if—whatever our creeds or our politics —we fail, as we look back across that weary waste which separates us from them, to extend our sympathy and admiration to these early workers—pioneers in a truly national undertaking which has found only too few imitators since.

VII.

THE NORTHERN SCOURGE.

WHILE from the fifth to the eighth century the work of the Irish Church was thus yearly increasing, spreading its net wider and wider, and numbering its converts by thousands, not much good can be reported of the secular history of Ireland during the same period. It is for the most part a confused chronicle of small feuds, jealousies, raids, skirmishes, retaliations, hardly amounting to the dignity of war, but certainly as distinctly the antipodes of peace.

The tribal system, which in its earlier stages has been already explained, had to some degree begun to change its character. The struggles between the different septs or clans had grown into a struggle between a number of great chieftains, under whose rule the lesser ones had come to range themselves upon all important occasions.

As early as the introduction of Christianity Ireland was already divided into four such aggregations of tribes—kingdoms they are commonly called—answering pretty nearly to the present four provinces, with the addition of Meath, which was the appanage of the house of Ulster, and included West Meath, Long-

DOORWAY OF MAGHERA CHURCH, LONDONDERRY.
(*From a drawing by George Petrie, LL.D.*)

ford, and a fragment of the King's County. Of the other four provinces, Connaught acknowledged the rule of the O'Connors, Munster that of the O'Briens, Leinster of the McMurroughs, and Ulster of the O'Neills, who were also in theory over-kings, or, as the native word was, Ard-Reaghs of the entire island.

Considering what a stout fighting race they proved in later ages—fighting often when submission would have been the wiser policy—it is curious that in early days these O'Neills or Hy-Nials seem to have been but a supine race. For centuries they were titular kings of Ireland, yet during all that time they seem never to have tried to transform their faint, shadowy sceptre into a real and active one. Malachy or Melachlin, the rival of Brian Boru, seems to have been the most energetic of the race, yet he allowed the sceptre to be plucked from his hands with an ease which, judging by the imperfect light shed by the chroniclers over the transaction, seems to be almost unaccountable.

It is difficult to say how far that light, for which the Irish monasteries were then celebrated, extended to the people of the island at large. With one exception, little that can be called cultivation is, it must be owned, discoverable, indeed long centuries after this Irish chieftains we know were innocent of the power of signing their own names. That exception was in the case of music, which seems to have been loved and studied from the first. As far back as we can see him the Irish Celt was celebrated for his love of music. In one of the earliest extant annals a *Cruit*, or stringed harp, is described as belonging to the Dashda, or Druid chieftain. It was square in form, and possessed powers wholly or partly miraculous. One of its strings, we are told, moved people to tears, another to laughter. A harp in Trinity College, known as the harp of Brian Boru, is said to be the oldest in Europe, and has thirty strings. This instrument has been the subject of many controversies. O'Curry doubts it having belonged to Brian Boru, and gives his reasons for believing that it was among the treasures of Westminster when Henry VIII. came to the throne in 1509, and that it suggested the placing of the harp in the arms of Ireland, and on the "harp grotes," a coinage of the period. However this may be we cannot doubt that music had early wrought itself into the very texture and fabric of Irish life; airs and words, wedded closely together, travelling down from mouth to mouth for countless generations. Every little valley and district may be said to have had its own traditional melodies, and the tunes with which Moore sixty years ago was delighting critical audiences had been floating unheeded and disregarded about the country for centuries.

The last ten years of the eighth century were very bad ones for Ireland. Then for the first time the black Viking ships were to be seen sweeping shorewards over the low grey waves of the Irish Channel, laden with Picts, Danes, and Norsemen, "people," says an old historian, "from their very cradles dissentious, Land Leapers, merciless, soure, and hardie." They descended upon Ireland like locusts, and wherever they came ruin, misery, and disaster followed.

KILBANNON TOWER.
(*From a drawing by George Petrie, LL.D.*)

DESTRUCTION OF THE CHURCHES.

Their first descent appears to have been upon an island, probably that of Lambay, near the mouth of what is now Dublin harbour. Returning a few years later, sixty of their ships, according to the Irish annalists, entered the Boyne, and sixty more the Liffy. These last were under the command of a leader who figures in the annals as Turgesius, whose identity has never been made very clear, but who appears to be the same person known to Norwegian historians as Thorkels or Thorgist.

Whatever his name he was undoubtedly a bad scourge to Ireland. Landing in Ulster, he burned the cathedral of Armagh, drove out St. Patrick's successors, slaughtered the monks, took possession of the whole east coast, and marching into the centre of the island, established himself in a strong position near Athlone.

Beyond all other Land Leapers, this Thorgist, or Turgesius, seems to have hated the churches. Not content with burning them, and killing all priests and monks he could find, his wife, we are told, took possession of the High Altar at Clonmacnois, and used it as a throne from which to give audience, or to utter prophecies and incantations. He also exacted a tribute of "nose money," which if not paid entailed the forfeit of the feature it was called after. At last three or four of the tribes united by despair rose against him, and he was seized and slain; an event about which several versions are given, but the most authentic seems to be that he was taken by stratagem and drowned in Lough Owel, near Mullingar, in or about the year 845.

He was not, unfortunately, the last of the Land Leapers! More and more they came, sweeping in from the north, and all seem to have made direct for the plunder of the monasteries, into which the piety of centuries had gathered most of the valuables of the country. The famous round towers, or "Clocthech" of Ireland, have been credited with a hundred fantastic origins, but are now known not to date from earlier than about the eighth or ninth century, are always found in connection with churches or monasteries, and were unquestionably used as defences against these northern invaders. At the first sight of their unholy prows, rising like water snakes above the waves, all the defenceless inmates and refugees all the church plate and valuables, and all sickly or aged brothers were hurried into these monastic keeps; the doors—set at a height of from ten to twenty feet above the ground—securely closed, the ladders drawn up, food supplies having been no doubt already laid in, and a state of siege began.

It is a pity that the annalists, who tell us so many things we neither care to hear nor much believe in, should have left us no record of any assault of the Northmen against one of these redoubtable towers. Even at the present day they would, without ammunition, be remarkably difficult nuts to crack; indeed, it is hard to see how their assault could have been successfully attempted, save by the slow process of starvation, or possibly by fires kindled immediately below the entrance, and so by degrees smoking out their inmates.

If any one ever succeeded in getting into them, we

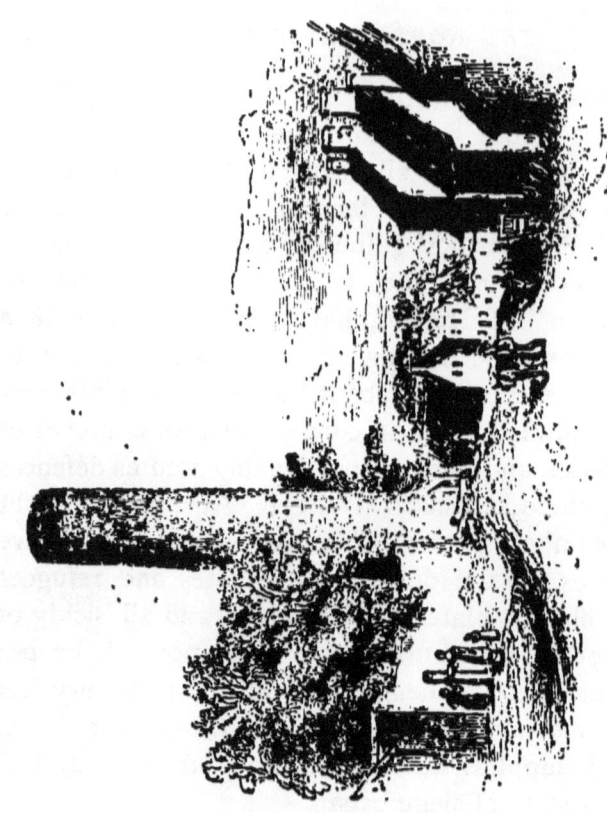

KELLS ROUND TOWER.
(From a drawing by George Petrie, LL.D.)

may be sure the Land Leapers did ! Before long they appear to have gathered nearly the whole spoil of the country into the towns, which they built and fortified for themselves at intervals along the coast. Cork, Waterford, Limerick, Wexford, and Dublin, all owe their origin in the first instance to the Northmen ; indeed it is a curious fact that Dublin can never be said, save for very short periods to have belonged to the Irish at all. It was first the capital of their northern invaders, and afterwards that, of course, of the English Government.

Three whole centuries the Danish power lasted, and internecine war raged, a war during which almost every trace of earlier civilizing influences, all those milder habits and ways of thought, which Christianity had brought in and fostered, perished well-nigh utterly. The ferocity of the invaders communicated itself to the invaded, and the whole history is one confused and continual chronicle of horrors and barbarities.

An important distinction must be made at this point between the effects of the Northern invasion in England and in Ireland. In the former the invaders and natives became after a while more or less assimilated, and, under Canute, an orderly government, composed of both nationalities, was, we know, established. In Ireland this was never the case. The reason, doubtless, is to be found in the far closer similarity of race in the former case than the latter. In Ireland the "Danes," as they are popularly called, were always strangers, heathen tyrants, hated and despised oppressors, who retorted this scorn and hatred in the fullest possible measure upon their antagonists. From the moment of their appearance down to the last we hear of them—as long, in fact, as the Danes of the seaport towns retained any traces of their northern origin—so long they continued to be the deadly foes of the rest of the island.

Even where the Northmen accepted Christianity, it does not appear to have had any strikingly ameliorating effect. Thus we read that Godfrid, son of Sitric, embraced Christianity in 948, and in the very next year we discover that he plundered and burnt all the churches in East Meath, killing over a hundred people who had taken refuge in them, and carrying off a quantity of captives. Land-leaping, too, continued in full force. "The godless hosts of pagans swarming o'er the Northern Sea," continued to arrive in fresh and fresh numbers from their inexhaustible Scandinavian breeding grounds—from Norway, from Sweden, from Denmark, even, it is said, from Iceland. The eighth, ninth, and tenth centuries are, in fact, the great period all over Europe for the incursions of the Northmen—high noon, so to speak, for those fierce and roving sons of plunder,—"People," says an old historian quaintly, "desperate in attempting the conquest of other Realmes, being very sure to finde warmer dwellings anywhere than in their own homes."

VIII.

BRIAN OF THE TRIBUTE.

AT last a time came for their oppression to be cut short in Ireland. Two valiant defenders sprang almost simultaneously into note. One of these was Malachy, or Melachlin, the Ard-Reagh and head of the O'Neills, the same Malachy celebrated by Moore as having "worn the collar of gold which he won from the proud invader." The other, Brian Boroimhe, commonly known to English writers as Brian Boru, a chieftain of the royal Dalcassian race of O'Brien, and the most important figure by far in Irish native history, but one which, like all others, has got so fogged and dimmed by prejudice and misstatement, that to many people his name seems hardly to convey any sense of reality at all.

Poor Brian Boru! If he could have guessed that he would have come to be regarded, even by some who ought to know better, as a sort of giant Cormoran or Eat-'em-alive-oh! a being out of a fairy tale, whom nobody is expected to take seriously; nay, as a symbol, as often as not, for ridiculous and inflated pretension. No one in his own day doubted his existence; no one thought of laughing at his name. Had they done so, their laughter would have come to a remarkably summary conclusion!

Brian Boroimhe, Boruma, or Boru—his name is written in all three ways—was not only a real man, but he was, what was more important, a real king, and not a mere simulacrum or walking shadow of one, like most of those who bore the name in Ireland. For once, for the only time as far as its native history is concerned, there was some one at the helm who knew how to rule, and who, moreover, did rule. His proceedings were not, it must be owned, invariably regulated upon any very strict rule of equity. He meant to be supreme, and to do so it was necessary to wrest the power from the O'Neills upon the one hand, and from the Danes on the other, and this he proceeded with the shortest possible delay to do.

He had a hard struggle at first. Munster had been overrun by the Danes of Limerick, who had defeated his brother, Mahon, king of Munster, and forced him to pay tribute. Brian himself, scorning to submit to the tyrants, had taken to the mountains with a small band of followers. Issuing from this retreat, he with some difficulty induced his brother once more to confront the aggressors. An important battle was fought at Sulcost, near Limerick, in the year 968, in which the Danes were defeated, and fled back in confusion to their walls, the Munster men, under Brian, following fast at their heels, and entering at the same time. The Danish town was seized, the fighting men were put to the sword, the remainder fled or were enslaved.

Mahon being some years afterwards slain, not by

BASE OF TUAM CROSS.

the Danes, but by certain treacherous Molloys and O'Donovans, who had joined themselves with him, Brian succeeded to the sovereignty of Munster, and shortly afterwards seized upon the throne of Cashel, which, upon the alternate system then prevailing, was at that time reigned over by one of the Euganian house of Desmond. Having avenged his brother's murder upon the O'Donovans, he next proceeded to overrun Leinster, rapidly subdued Ossory, and began to stretch out his hands towards the sovereignty of the island.

In the meantime the over-king, Malachy, had defeated the Danes at the battle of Tara, and was consequently in high honour, stronger apparently then any of his predecessors had been. In spite of this Brian by degrees prevailed. With doubtful patriotism he left the Danes for a while unpursued, attacked Meath, overran and wasted Connaught, and returning suddenly burnt the royal stronghold of Tara. After a long and wearisome struggle, Malachy yielded, and allowed Brian to become Ard-Reagh in his place, retaining only his own ancestral dominions of Meath. He seems to have been a placable, easy-going man, "loving," say the annalists, "to ride a horse that had never been handled or ridden," and caring more for this than for the cares of the State.

After this, Brian made what may be called a royal progress through the country, receiving the submission of the chiefs and inferior kings, and forcing them to acknowledge his authority. In speaking of him as king of Ireland, which in a sense he undoubtedly was, we must be careful of letting our imaginations carry us into any exaggerated idea of what is meant by that word. His name, " Brian of the Tribute," is our safest guide, and enables us to understand what was the position of even the greatest and most successful king under the Celtic system. It was the exact opposite of the feudal one, and this difference proved the source in years to come of an enormous amount of misconception, and of fierce accusations of falsehood and treachery flung profusely from both sides. The position of the over-king or Ard-Reagh was more nearly allied to that of the early French suzerain or the German emperor. He could call upon his vassal or tributary kings to aid him in war times or in any sudden emergency, but, as regards their internal arrangements—the government, misgovernment, or non-government of their several sub-kingdoms—they were free to act as they pleased, and he was not understood to have any formal jurisdiction.

For all that Brian was an unmistakable king, and proved himself to be one. He defeated the Danes again and again, reducing even those inveterate disturbers of the peace to a forced quiescence; entered Dublin, and remained there some time, taking, say the annalists, " hostages and treasure." By the year 1002 Ireland had a master, one whose influence made itself felt over its whole surface. For twelve years at least out of its distracted history the country knew the blessings of peace. Broken by defeat the Danish dwellers of the seaport towns began to turn their energies to the milder and more pacific activities of trade. The ruined monasteries were getting

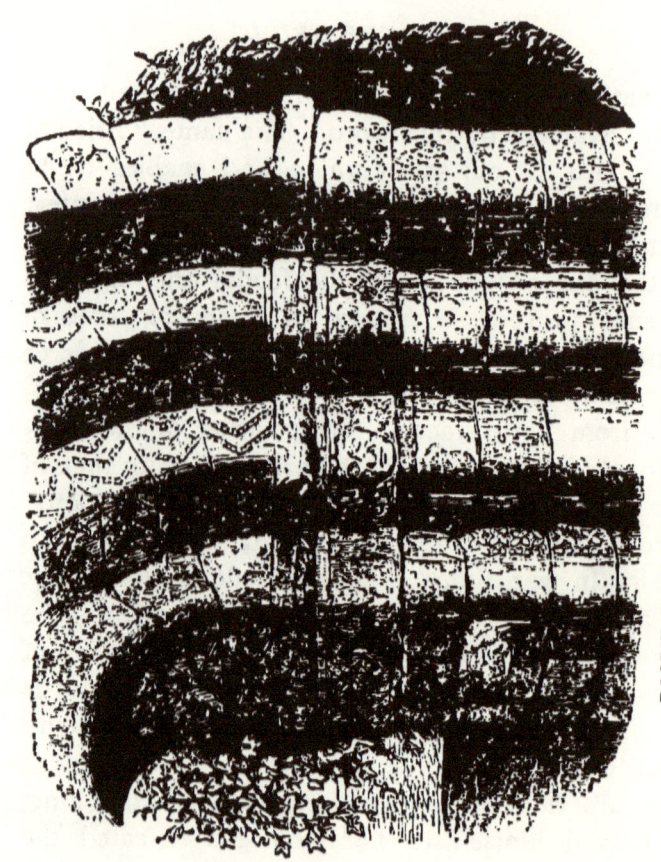

DOORWAY OF KILLESHIN CHURCH, CO. CARLOW.
(*From a Photograph.*)

rebuilt ; prosperity was beginning to glimmer faintly upon the island ; the chiefs, cowed into submission, abstained from raiding, or confined their raids to discreeter limits. Fortresses were being built, roads made, and bridges repaired in three at least of the provinces. Another twenty years of Brian's rule and the whole future history of Ireland might have been a different one.

It was not to be however. The king was now old, and the work that he had begun, and which, had he been followed by a successor like himself, might have been accomplished, was destined to crumble like a half-built house. The Danes began to stir again. A rebellion had sprung up in Leinster, the coast-line of which was strong-holded at several points with Danish towns. This rebellion they not only aided with their own strength, but further appealed for assistance to their kinsmen in Northumbria, Man, the Orkneys, and elsewhere, who responded by sending a large force under Brodar, a Viking, and Sigurd Earl of Orkney to their aid.

This force Brian gathered all his energies to oppose. With his own Munster clansmen, aided by all the fighting men of Meath and Connaught, with his five sons and with his old rival, King Malachy of Meath, fighting under his banner, he marched down to the strand of Clontarf, which stretches from the north of Dublin to the out-jutting promontory of Howth, and there, upon Good Friday, 1014, he encountered his Leinster rebels and the Viking host of invaders, ten thousand strong it is said, and a great battle was fought, a battle which, beginning before the dawn, lasted till the sun was beginning to sink.

To understand the real importance of this battle, we must first fully realize to ourselves what a very old quarrel this was. For three long weary centuries Ireland had been lying bound and broken under the heel of her pagan oppressors, and only with great difficulty and partially had escaped within the last fifteen or sixteen years. Every wrong, outrage, and ignominy that could be inflicted by one people upon another had been inflicted and would most assuredly be inflicted again were this battle, now about to be fought, lost.

Nor upon the other side were the motives much less strong. The Danes of Dublin under Sitric stood fiercely at bay. Although their town was still their own, all the rest of the island had escaped from the grasp of their race. Whatever Christianity they may occasionally have assumed was all thrown to the winds upon this great occasion. The far-famed pagan battle flag, the Raven Standard, was unfurled, and floated freely over the host. The War-arrow had been industriously sent round to all the neighbouring shores, peopled largely at that time with men of Norse blood. As the fleet swept south it had gathered in contingents from every island along the Scotch coast, upon which Viking settlements had been established. Manx men, too, and men from the Scandinavian settlements of Anglesea, Danes under Carle Canuteson, representatives, in fact, of all the old fighting pagan blood were there, and all gathered together to a battle at once of races and of creeds.

On the Irish side the command had been given by Brian to Morrogh, his eldest son, who fifteen years before had aided his father in gaining a great victory over these same Dublin Danes at a place called Glenmama, not far from Dunlaven. The old king himself abstained from taking any part in the battle. Perhaps because he wished his son—who already had been appointed his successor—to have all the glory and so to fix himself yet more deeply in the hearts of his future subjects; perhaps because he felt that his strength might not have carried him through the day; perhaps—the annalists say this is the reason—because the day being Good Friday he preferred praying for his cause rather than fighting for it. Whatever the reason it is certain that he remained in his tent, which was pitched on this occasion not far from the edge of the great woods which then covered all the rising ground to the north-west of Dublin, beginning at the bank of the river Liffy.

The onset was not long delayed. The Vikings under Sigurd and Brodar fought as only Vikings could fight. Like all battles of that period it resolved itself chiefly into a succession of single combats, which raged all over the field, extending, it is said, for over two miles along the strand. The Danish women, and the men left to guard the town, crowded the roofs, remaining all day to watch the fight. Sigurd of Orkney was killed in single combat by Thorlogh, the son of Morrogh, and grandson of Brian; Armud and several of the other Vikings fell by the hand of Morrogh, but in the end the father and son were

DEATH OF BRIAN.

both slain, although the latter survived long enough to witness the triumph of his own side.

Late in the afternoon the Northmen broke and fled ; some to their ships, some into the town, some into the open country beyond. Amongst the latter Brodar, the Viking, made for the great woods, and in so doing passed close to where the tent of the king had been fixed. The attendants left to guard Brian had by this time one by one slipped away to join the fight, and the old man was almost alone, and kneeling, it is said, at the moment on a rug in the front of his tent. The sun was low, but the slanting beams fell upon his bent head and long white beard. One of Brodar's followers perceived him and pointed him out to his leader, saying that it was the king. "King, that is no king, that is a monk, a shaveling!" retorted the Viking. "It is not, it is Brian himself," was the answer.

Then Brodar caught his axe and rushed upon Brian. Taken unawares the king nevertheless rallied his strength which in his day had been greater than that of any man of his time, and still only half risen from his knees he smote the Viking a blow across the legs with his sword. The other thereupon lifted his battle-axe, and smote the king upon his head, cleaving it down to the chin, then fled to the woods, but was caught the next day and hacked into pieces by some of the infuriated Irish.

So fell Brian in the very moment of victory, and when the combined league of all his foes had fallen before him. When the news reached Armagh, the bishop and his clergy came south as far as Swords, in Meath, where they met the corpse of the king and carried it back to Armagh, where he was buried, say the annalists, "in a new tomb" with much weeping and lamentation.

CORMAC'S CHAPEL AND ROUND TOWER, ROCK OF CASHEL.

IX.

FROM BRIAN TO STRONGBOW.

WHATEVER lamentations were uttered on this occasion were certainly not uncalled for, for a greater disaster has rarely befallen any country or people. Were proof wanted—which it hardly is—of that notorious ill-luck which has dogged the history of Ireland from the very beginning, it would be difficult to find a better one than the result of this same famous battle of Clontarf. Here was a really great victory, a victory the reverberation of which rang through the whole Scandinavian world, rejoicing Malcolm of Scotland, who without himself striking a blow, saw his enemies lying scotched at his feet, so scotched in fact, that after the defeat of Clontarf they never again became a serious peril. Yet as regards Ireland itself what was the result? The result was that all those ligaments of order which were beginning slowly to wind themselves round it, were violently snapped and scattered to the four winds. As long as Brian's grasp was over it Ireland was a real kingdom, with limitations it is true, but still with a recognized centre, and steadily growing power of combined and concerted action. At his

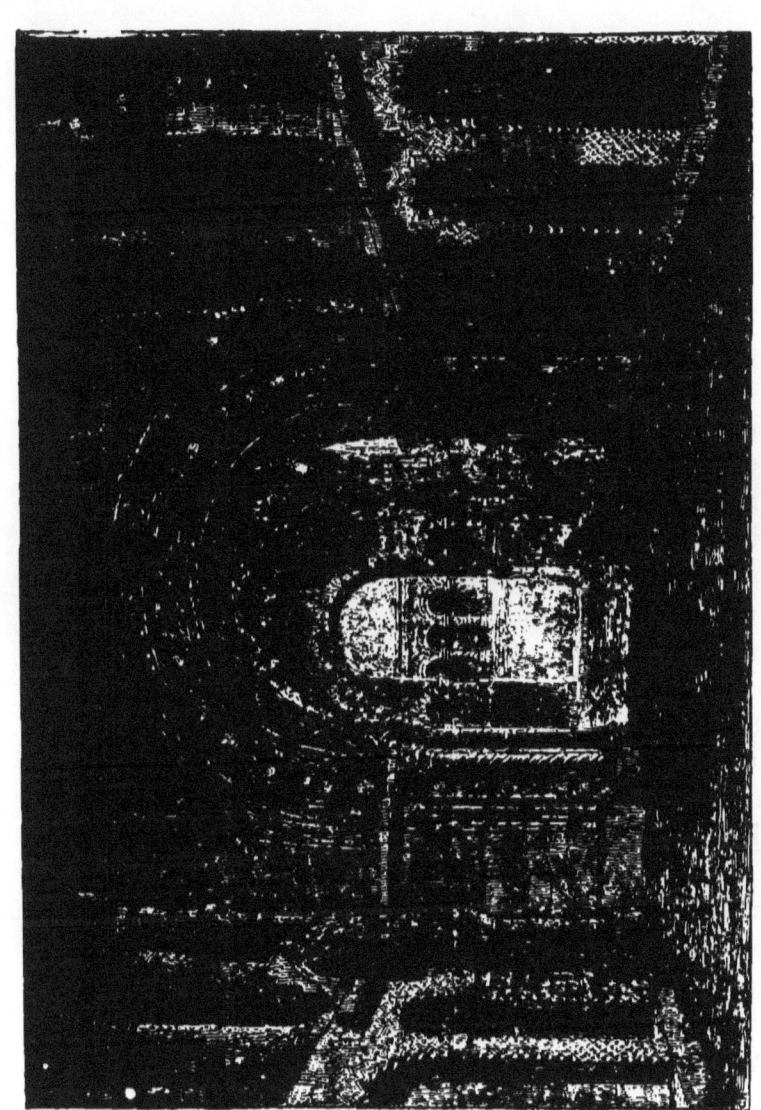

INTERIOR OF CORMAC'S CHAPEL, CASHEL. (*From a Drawing by Miss M. Stokes.*)

death the whole body politic was once more broken up, and resolved itself into its old anarchic elements again.

It would have been better far for the country had Brian been defeated, so that he, his son Morrogh, or any capable heir had survived, better for it indeed had he never ruled at all if this was to be end. By his successful usurpation the hereditary principle—always a weak one in Ireland—was broken down. The one chance of a settled central government was thus at an end. Every petty chief and princeling all over the island felt himself capable of emulating the achievements of Brian. It was one of those cases which success and only success justifies. Ireland was pining, as it had always pined, as it continued ever afterwards to pine, for a settled government; for a strong central rule of some sort. The race of Hy.-Nial had been titular kings for centuries, but they had never held the sovereignty in anything but name. Pushing their claims aside, and gathering all power into his own hands Brian had acted upon a small stage the part of Charlemagne centuries earlier upon a large one. He had succeeded, and in his success lay his justification. With his death, however, the whole edifice which he had raised crumbled away, and anarchy poured in after it like a torrent. A struggle set in at once for the sovereignty, which ended by not one of Brian's sons but the deposed King Malachy being set upon the throne. Like his greater rival he was however by this time a very old man. His spirit had been broken, and though the Danes had been too thoroughly beaten to stir, other elements of disorder abounded. Risings broke out in two of the provinces at once, and at his death the confusion became confounded. As a native rhyme runs:

> "After Malachy, son of Donald,
> Each man ruled his own tribe,
> But no man ruled Erin."

Henceforward throughout the rather more than a century and a half which intervened between the battle of Clontarf and the Norman invasion, Ireland remained a helpless waterlogged vessel, with an unruly crew, without rudder or compass, above all, without a captain. The house of O'Brien again pushed its way to the front, but none of Brian's descendants who survived the day of Clontarf seem to have shown a trace even of his capacity. A fierce feud broke out shortly after between Donchad, his son, and Turlough, one of his grandsons, and each successively caught at the helm, but neither succeeding in obtaining the sovereignty of the entire island. After the last-named followed Murhertach also of the Dalcassian house, at whose death the rule once more swung round to the house of Hy.-Nial and Donald O'Lochlin reigned nominally until his death in 1121. Next the O'Connors, of Connaught, took a turn at the sovereignty, and seized possession of Cashel which since its capture by Brian Boroimhe had been the exclusive appanage of the Dalcassians. Another O'Lochlin, of the house of O'Neill, then appears prominently in the fray, and by 1156, seems to have succeeded in seizing the over-lordship of the island, and so the tale goes on—a wearisome one, unrelieved by even a transitory gleam of order or prosperity. At last it becomes almost a relief when we reach the name of Roderick O'Connor, and know that before his death fresh actors will have entered upon the scene, and that the confused and baffling history of Ireland will, at all events, have entered upon a perfectly new stage.

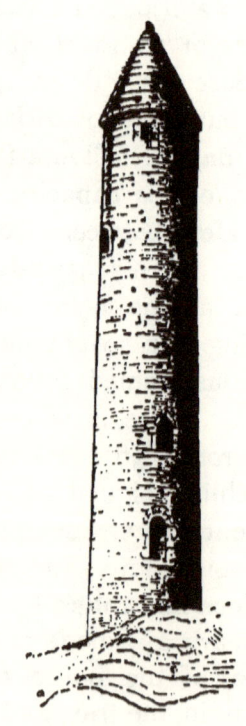

ROUND TOWER AT DEVENISH.

X.

THE ANGLO-NORMAN INVASION.

THE invasion of Ireland by the Anglo-Normans differs in several respects from other invasions and conquests, not the least singular feature about it being that nearly the whole of that famous band of knightly adventurers who took part in it, and to whose audacity it was in the first instance due, were more or less closely related to one another, either as brothers, nephews, uncles, or cousins. The connecting link between these variously-named relations was one Nesta, princess of South Wales, daughter of a Welsh king, Rice ap Tudor, a heroine whose adventures are of a sufficiently striking, not to say startling, character. By dint of a succession of alliances, some regular, others highly irregular, she became the ancestress of nearly all the great Anglo-Norman families in Ireland. Of these the Fitzgeralds, Carews, Barrys, and Cogans, are descended from her first husband, Gerald of Windsor. Robert FitzStephen, who plays, as will presently be seen, a prominent part in the conquest, was the son of her second husband, Stephen, the Castlelan of Abertivy, while Robert and Meiler Fitz-Henry, of whom we shall also hear, are said to have

WEST FRONT OF ST. CRONAN'S CHURCH, ROSCREA.
(*From a Photograph.*)

been the sons of no less a person than King Henry I. of England.

Conspicuous amongst this band of knights and adventurers was one who was himself no knight, but a priest and the self-appointed chronicler of the rest, Gerald de Barri—better known as Gerald of Wales, or Giraldus Cambrensis, who was the grandson of Nesta, through her daughter Angareta.

Giraldus is one of those writers whom, to tell the truth, we like a great deal better than they deserve. He is prejudiced to the point of perversity, and gullible almost to sublimity, uncritical even for an eminently uncritical age, accepting and retailing any and every monstrous invention, the more readily apparently in proportion to its monstrosity. For all that—despite his prejudices, despite even his often deliberate perversion of the truth, it is difficult to avoid a certain kindliness for him. To the literary student he is indeed a captivating figure. With his half-Welsh, half-Norman blood; with the nimble, excitable, distinctly Celtic vein constantly discernible in him; with a love of fighting which could hardly have been exceeded by the doughtiest of the knights, his cousins and brothers; with a pen that seems to fly like an arrow across the page; with a conceit which knows neither stint nor limit, he is the most entertaining, the most vividly alive of chroniclers; no historian certainly in any rigid sense of the word, but the first, as he was also unquestionably the chief and prince of war correspondents.

Whether we like him or not, we at any rate cannot dispense with him, seeing that nearly everything we know of the Ireland of the Conquest, we know from those marvellous pages of his, which, if often exasperating, are at any rate never dull. In them, as in a mirror, we see how, when, and where the whole plan of the campaign was laid; who took part in it; what they said, did, projected; their very motives and thoughts—the whole thing stands out fresh and alive as if it had happened yesterday.

There were no lack of motives, any of which would have been temptation enough for invasion. To the pious it took on the alluring guise of a Crusade. The Irish Church, which had obtained such glowing fame in its early days, had long since, as we have seen, grown into very bad repute with Rome. Despite that halo of early sanctity, she was held to be seriously tainted with heresy. She allowed bishops to be irregularly multiplied, and consecrated contrary to the Roman rule by one bishop only; tithes and firstfruits were not collected with any regularity; above all, the collection of Peter's pence, being the sum of one penny due from every household, was always scandalously in arrears, nay, often no attempt was made to collect it at all. She did many wrong things, but it may shrewdly be suspected that this was one of the very worst of them.

It is not a little edifying at this juncture to find the Danes of Dublin amongst those who were enlisted upon the orthodox side. Cut off by mutual hatred rather than theological differences from the Church of Ireland, they had for some time back been regularly applying to Canterbury for their supply of priests. These priests upon being sent over painted the condition of Irish heterodoxy in tints of the deepest black for their own

WEST DOORWAY OF FRESHFORD CHURCH, CO. KILKENNY.
(*From a Photograph.*)

countrymen. Even before this there had been grave complaints. Lanfranc, Anselm, St. Bernard of Clairvaux, all had had their theological ire aroused against the Irish recusants. Many of the Irish ecclesiastics themselves seem to have desired that closer union with Rome, which could only be brought about by bringing Ireland under the power of a sworn son of the Church. Henry I.—little as that most secular- /II. minded of monarchs cared probably for the more purely theological question—was fully alive to its value as supporting his own claims. He obtained from Pope Hadrian IV. (the Englishman Brakespeare), a Bull sanctioning and approving of the conquest of Ireland as prompted by "the ardour of faith and love of religion," in which Bull he is desired to enter the island and therein execute "whatever shall pertain to the honour of God, and the welfare of the land."

Fourteen years elapsed before the enterprise thus warmly commended was carried into effect. The story of Dermot McMurrough, king of Leinster, and his part in the invasion, has often been told, and does not, I think, need dwelling upon at any great length. He was a brutal, violent-tempered savage, detested in his own country, and especially by his unfortunate subjects in Leinster. How he foully wronged the honour of O'Rorke, a chieftain of Connaught; how, for this and other offences, he was upon the accession of Roderick O'Connor driven away from Ireland; how he fled to England to do homage to Henry, and seek his protection; how, finding him gone to Aquitaine, he followed him there, and in return for his vows of allegiance received letters authorizing the king's subjects to enlist if they choose for the Irish service; how armed with these he went to Wales, and there succeeded in recruiting a band of mixed Norman and Norman-Welsh adventurers—all this is recorded at large in the histories.

Of the recruits thus enlisted, the most important was Robert de Clair, Earl of Pembroke and Chepstow, nicknamed by his contemporaries, Strongbow, whom Dermot met at Bristol, and won over by a double bribe—the hand, namely, of his daughter Eva, and the succession to the sovereignty of Leinster —a succession which, upon the Irish mode of election, he had, it may be observed, no shadow of right to dispose of.

Giraldus, who seems to have been himself in Wales at the time, speaks sentimentally of the unfortunate exile, and describes him inhaling the scent of his beloved country from the Welsh coast, and feasting his eyes tenderly upon his own land : " Although the distance," he more prosaically adds, " being very great, it was difficult to distinguish mountains from clouds." As a matter of fact, Dermot McMurrough, we may be sure, was not the person to do anything of the sort. He was simply hungry—as a wild beast or a savage is hungry—for revenge, and would have plunged into any number of perjuries, or have bound himself to give away any amount of property he had no right to dispose of in order to get it. He could safely trust, too, he knew, to the ignorance of his new allies as to what was or was not a legal transfer in Ireland.

His purpose achieved, " inflamed," says Giraldus,

"with the desire to see his native land," but really the better to concoct his plans, he returned home, landing a little south of Arklow Head, and arriving at Ferns, where he was hospitably entertained during the winter by its bishop. The following spring, in the month of May, the first instalment of the invaders arrived under Robert FitzStephen, a small fleet of Welsh boats landing them in a creek of the bay of Bannow, where a chasm between the rocks was long known as " FitzStephen's stride."

Here they were met by Donald McMurrough, son of Dermot, and ten days later drew up under the walls of Wexford, having so far encountered no opposition.

In this old Danish town a stout fight was made. The townsfolk, no longer Vikings but simple traders, did what they could in their own defence. They burnt their suburbs, consisting doubtless of rude wooden huts ; shut the gates, and upon the first two assaults drove back the assailants. So violently were they repelled, "that they withdrew," Giraldus tells us, " in all great haste from the walls." His own younger brother, Robert de Barri, was amongst the wounded, a great stone falling upon his helmet and tumbling him headlong into one of the ditches, from the effects of which blow, that careful historian informs us incidentally, " Sixteen years later all his jaw teeth fell out ! "

Next morning, after mass, they renewed the assault; this time with more circumspection. Now there were at that time, as it happened, two bishops in the town, who devoted their energies to endeavouring to induce the citizens to make peace. In this attempt they were successful, more successful than might have been expected with men descended from the old Land Leapers. Wexford opened its gates, its townsmen submitting to Dermot, who thereupon presented the town to his allies, FitzStephen, true to his Norman instincts, proceeding forthwith to build a castle upon the rock of Carneg, at the narrowest point of the river Slaney, the first of that large crop of castles which subsequently sprang up upon Irish soil.

The next sharers of the struggle were the wild Ossory clans, who gathered to the defence of their territory under Donough McPatrick, an old and especially hated enemy of Dermot's. The latter had now three thousand men at his back, in addition to his Welsh and Norman allies. The Ossory men fought, as Giraldus admits, with furious valour, but upon rashly venturing out of their own forests into the open, were charged by FitzStephen, whose horsemen defeated them, killing a great number, over two hundred heads being collected and laid at the feet of Dermot, who, "turning them over, one by one, to recognize them, lifted his hands to heaven in excess of joy, and with a loud voice returned thanks to God most High." So pious was Dermot!

After this, finding that the country at large was beginning to take some note of their proceedings, the invaders fel back upon Ferns, which they fortified according to the science of the age under the superintendence of Robert FitzStephen. Roderick O'Connor, the Ard-Reagh, was by this time not unnaturally beginning to get alarmed, and had gathered his men together against the invaders. The winter, however, was now at hand, and a temporary peace was accordingly patched up; Leinster being restored to Dermot on condition of his acknowledging the over-lordship of Roderick. Giraldus recounts at much length the speeches made upon both sides on this occasion; the martial addresses to the troops, the many classical and flowery quotations, which last he is good enough to bestow upon the unlucky Roderick no less than upon his own allies. Seeing, probably, that all were alike imaginary, it is hardly necessary to delay to record them.

The next to arrive upon the scene was Maurice Fitzgerald, half brother of Robert FitzStephen and uncle of Giraldus. Strongbow meanwhile was still upon the eastern side of the channel awaiting the return of his uncle, Hervey de Montmorency, whom he had sent over to report upon the condition of affairs. Even after Hervey's return bringing with him a favourable report, he had still the king's permission to gain. Early in 1170 he again sought Henry and this time received an ambiguous reply, which, however, he chose to interpret in his own favour. He sent back Hervey to Ireland, accompanied by Raymond Fitzgerald, surnamed Le Gros, and a score of knights with some seventy archers. These, landing in Kilkenny, entrenched themselves, and being shortly afterwards attacked by the Danes of Waterford, defeated them with great slaughter, seizing a number of prisoners. Over these prisoners a dispute arose; Raymond was for sparing their lives, Hervey de Montmorency for slaying. The eloquence of the latter prevailed. "The citizens," says Giraldus, "as men condemned, had their limbs broken and were cast headlong into the sea and so drowned."

Shortly after this satisfactory beginning, Strongbow himself appeared with reinforcements. He attacked Waterford, which was taken after a short but furious resistance, and the united forces of Dermot and the Earl marched into the town, where the marriage of the latter with Eva, Dermot's daughter, was celebrated, as Maclise has represented it in his picture, amid lowering smoke and heaps of the dead and dying.

Dermot was now on the top of the wave. With his English allies and his own followers he had a considerable force around him. Guiding the latter through the Wicklow mountains, which they would probably have hardly got through unaided, he descended with them upon Dublin, and despite the efforts of St. Lawrence O'Toole, its archbishop, to effect a pacific arrangement, the town was taken by assault. The principal Danes, with Hasculph, their Danish governor, escaped to their ships and sailed hastily away for the Orkneys.

Meath was the next point to be attacked. O'Rorke, the old foe of Dermot, who held it for King Roderick, was defeated; whereupon, in defiance of his previous promises, Dermot threw off all disguise and proclaimed himself king of Ireland, upon which Roderick, as the only retaliation left in his power, slew Dermot's son who had been deposited in his hands as hostage.

It was now Strongbow's aim to hasten back and place his new lordship at the feet of his sovereign, already angry and jealous at such unlooked for and uncountenanced successes. He was not able however to do so at once. Hasculph the Dane returned suddenly with sixty ships, and a large force under a noted Berserker of the day, known as John the Mad, "warriors," says Giraldus, "armed in Danish fashion, having long breast-plates and shirts of mail, their shields round and bound about with iron. They were iron-hearted," he says, "as well as iron-armed men."

In spite of their arms and their hearts, he is able triumphantly to proclaim their defeat. Milo de Cogan, the Norman governor of Dublin, fell upon his assailants suddenly. John the Mad was slain, as were also nearly all the Berserkers. Hasculph was brought back in triumph, and promptly beheaded by the conquerors.

He was hardly dead before a new assailant, Godred, king of Man, appeared with thirty ships at the mouth of the Liffey. Roderick, in the meanwhile, had collected men from every part of Ireland, with the exception of the north which stood aloof from him, and now laid siege to Dublin by land, helped by St. Lawrence its patriotic archbishop. Strongbow was thus shut in with foes behind and before, and the like disaster had befallen Robert FitzStephen, who was at this time closely besieged in his own new castle at Wexford. Dermot their chief native ally had recently died. There seemed for a while a reasonable chance that the invaders would be driven back and pushed bodily into the sea.

Discipline and science however again prevailed. The besieged, excited both by their own danger and that of their friends in the south, made a desperate sally. The Irish army kept no watch, and was absolutely undrilled. A panic set in. The besiegers fled, leaving behind them their stores of provisions, and the conquerors thereupon marched away in triumph to the relief of FitzStephen. Here they were less successful. By force, or according to Giraldus, by a pretended tale of the destruction of all the other invaders, the Wexford men seized possession of him and the other English, and had them flung into a dungeon. Finding that Strongbow and the rest were not destroyed, but that on the contrary they were marching down on them, the Wexford men set fire to their own town and departed to an island in the harbour, carrying their prisoner with them and threatening if pursued to cut off his head.

Foiled in this attempt, Strongbow hastened to Waterford, took boat there, and flew to meet the king, whom he encountered near Gloucester with a large army. Henry's greeting was a wrathful one. His anger and jealousy had been thoroughly aroused. Not unwarrantably. But for his promptness his headstrong subjects—several of them it must be remembered of his own dominant blood—would have been perfectly capable of attempting to carve out a kingdom for themselves at his very gates. Happily Strongbow had found the task too large for his unaided energies, and, as we have seen, had barely escaped annihilation. He was ready, therefore, to accept any terms which his sovereign chose to impose. His submission appears to have disarmed the king. He allowed himself to be pacified, and after a while they returned to Ireland together. Henry II. landed at Waterford in the month of October, 1171.

SOUTH WINDOW OF ST. CAIMIN'S CHURCH, INISMAIN.

XI.

HENRY II. IN IRELAND.

THIS was practically the end of the struggle. The king had four thousand men-at-arms at his back, of whom no less than four hundred were knights. In addition his ships contained vast stores of provisions, a variety of war devices never before seen in Ireland, artizans for building bridges and making roads—a whole war train, in short. Such a display of force was felt to be irresistible. The chieftains one after the other came in and made their submission. Dermot McCarthy, lord of Desmond and Cork, was the first to do homage, followed by Donald O'Brien, Prince of Thomond; while another Donald, chieftain of Ossory, rapidly followed suit. The men of Wexford appeared, leading their prisoner with them by a chain, and presenting him as an offering to his master, who, first rating him soundly for his unauthorized proceedings, ordered him to be chained to another prisoner and shut up in Reginald's tower. Later, soothed by his own triumph, or touched, as Giraldus tells us, with compassion for a brave man, he, at the intercession of some of his courtiers, forgave and restored him to his possessions, reserving, however, the town of Wexford for himself.

From Wexford Henry marched to Dublin, having first visited Tipperary and Waterford. The Danes at once submitted and swore allegiance; so also did O'Carrol of Argial, O'Rorke of Brefny, and all the minor chieftains of Leinster; Roderick O'Connor still stood at bay behind the Shannon, and the north also remained aloof and hostile, but all the other chieftains, great and small, professed themselves willing to become tributaries of the king of England.

The idea of an Ard-Reagh, or Over-lord, was no new one, as we have seen, to any of them. Theoretically they had always acknowledged one, although, practically, he had rarely exercised any authority save over his own immediate subjects. Their feeling about Henry was doubtless the same. They were as willing to swear fealty to him as to Roderick O'Connor, more so in fact, seeing that he was stronger than Roderick, but that was all. To Henry and to his successors this recognition carried with it all the complicated dependence of feudalism, which in England meant that his land and everything else which a man possessed was his only so long as he did service for it to the king. To these new Irish subjects, who had never heard of feudalism, it entailed nothing of the sort. They regarded it as a mere vague promise of adhesion, binding them at most to a general muster or "hosting" under his arms in case of war or some common peril. This was an initial misconception, which continued, as will be seen, to be a deeper and deeper source of confusion as the years went on.

In the meanwhile Henry was established in Dublin, where he kept Christmas in high state, occupying a palace built in the native fashion of painted wicker-work, set up just outside the walls. Here he entertained the chiefs, who were naturally astonished at the splendour of his entertainments. "They learnt," Giraldus observes with satisfaction, "to eat cranes"—does this mean herons?—" a species of food which they had previously loathed ;" and, in general, were suitably impressed with the greatness and glory of the conqueror. The bishops were most of them already warmly in his favour, and at a synod shortly afterwards held at Cashel, at which all the Irish clergy were represented, the Church of Ireland was solemnly declared to be finally united to that of England, and it was laid down that, "as by Divine Providence Ireland has received her lord and king from England, so she should also submit to a reformation from the same source."

The weather that winter was so rough that hardly a ship could cross the channel, and Henry in his new kingdom found himself practically cut off from his old one. About the middle of Lent, the wind veering at last to the east, ships arrived from England and Aquitaine, bearers of very ill news to the king. Two legates were on their way, sent by the Pope, to inquire into the murder of Becket, and armed in case of an unsatisfactory reply with all the terrors of an interdict. Henry hastily made over the government of Ireland to Hugo de Lacy, whom he placed in Dublin as his representative, and sailed from Wexford upon Easter Monday. He never again revisited his new dominions, where many of the lessons inculcated by him—including possibly the delights of eating cranes—were destined before long to be forgotten.

XII.

EFFECTS OF THE ANGLO-NORMAN INVASION.

HENRY had been only six months in Ireland, but he had accomplished much—more certainly than any other English ruler ever accomplished afterwards within the same time. He had divided the ceded districts into counties; had appointed sheriffs for them; had set up three Law Courts—Bench, Pleas, and Exchequer; had arranged for the going on circuit by judges; and had established his own character for orthodoxy, and acquitted himself of his obligations to the papacy by freeing all church property from the exactions of the chiefs, and rigidly enforcing the payment of tithes.

In a still more important point—that about which he was evidently himself most tenacious—his success was even more complete. He once for all put a stop to all danger of an independent lordship by forcing those who had already received grants of land from the native chiefs to surrender them into his hands, and to receive them back direct from himself, according to the ordinary terms of feudal tenure.

That he had larger and more statesmanlike views for the new dependency than he was ever able to carry out there can be no question. As early as 1177 he appointed his youngest son John king of Ireland, and seems to have fully formed the intention of sending him over as a permanent governor or viceroy, a purpose which the misconduct of that youthful Rehoboam, as Giraldus calls him, was chiefly instrumental in foiling.

It is curious to hear this question of a royal viceroy and a permanent royal residence in Ireland coming to the front so very early in the history of English rule there. That the experiment, if fairly tried, and tried with a man of the calibre of Henry himself, might have made the whole difference in the future of Ireland, we cannot, I think, reasonably doubt. Any government, indeed, so that it was central, so that it gathered itself into a single hand and took its impress from a single mind, would have been better a thousand times than the miserable condition of half-conquest, half-rule, whole anarchy and confusion which set in and continued with hardly a break.

This is one reason more why it is so much to be regretted that Ireland, save for a few years, had never any real king or central government of her own. Had this been the case, even if she had been eventually conquered by England—as would likely enough have been the case—the result of that conquest would have been different. There would have been some one recognized point of government and organization, and the struggle would have been more violent and probably more successful at first, but less chronic and less eternally renewed in the long run. As it was, all the conditions were at their very worst. No native ruler of the calibre of a Brian Boru could ever again hope to unite all Ireland under him, since long before he arrived at that point his enemies would have called in the aid of the new colonists, who would have fallen upon and annihilated him, though after doing so they would have been as little able to govern the country for themselves as before.

This also explains what is often set down as the inexplicable want of patriotism shown by the native Irish in not combining more resolutely together against their assailants. It is true that they did not do so, but the fact is not referred to the right cause. An Englishman of the time of the Heptarchy had, if at all, little more patriotism, and hardly more sense of common country. He was a Wessex man, or a Northumbrian, or a man of the North or the East Angles, rather than an Englishman. So too in Ireland. As a people the Irish of that day can hardly be said to have had any corporate existence. They were O'Briens, or O'Neils, or O'Connors, or O'Flaherties, and that no doubt in their own eyes appeared to be quite nationality enough.

Unfortunately both for the country and for his own successors, Henry had no time to carry out his plans, and all that he had begun to organize fell away into disorder again after his departure. "That inconstant sea-nymph," says Sir John Davis, "whom the Pope had wedded to him with a ring," remained obedient only as long as her new lord was present, and once his back was turned she reverted to her own ways again. The crowd of Norman and Welsh adventurers who now filled the country were each and all intent upon ascertaining how much of that country they could seize upon and appropriate for themselves. There were many gallant men amongst them, but there was not one apparently who had the faintest trace of what is meant by public spirit. Occupied only by their own interests, and struggling solely for their own share of the spoil, they could never really hold the country, and even those parts which they did get into their hands lapsed back after a while into the old condition again.

The result was that the fighting never ended. The new colonists built castles and lived shut up in them, ruling their own immediate retainers with an odd mixture of Brehon and Norman law. When they issued forth they appeared clad from head to foot in steel, ravaging the country more like foreign mercenaries than peaceful settlers. The natives, driven to bay and dispossessed of their lands, fought too, not in armour, but, like the Berserkers of old, in their shirts, with the addition at most of a rude leather helmet, more often only with their hair matted into a sort of cap on their foreheads in the fashion known as the "gibbe," that "rascally gibbe" to which Spenser and other Elizabethan writers object so strongly. By way of defence they now and then threw up a rude stockade of earth or stone, modifications of the primitive rath, more often they made no defence, or merely twisted a jungle of boughs along the pathways to break the advance of their more heavily armed foes. The ideas of the two races were as dissimilar as their weapons. The instinct of the one was to conquer a country and subdue it to their own uses; the instinct of the other was to trust to the country itself, and depend upon its natural features, its forests, morasses, and so forth for security. The one was irresistible in attack, the other, as his conqueror soon learnt to his cost, practically invincible in defence, returning doggedly again and again, and a hundred times over to the ground from which he seemed at first to have been so easily and so effectually driven off.

All these peculiarities, which for ages continued to mark the struggle between the two races now brought face to face in a death struggle, are just as marked and just as strikingly conspicuous in the first twenty years which followed the invasion as they are during the succeeding half-dozen centuries.

FIGURES ON KILCARN FONT, MEATH.

XIII.

JOHN IN IRELAND.

Henry had gone, and the best hopes of the new dependency departed with him never to return again. Fourteen years later he despatched his son John, then a youth of nineteen, with a train of courtiers, and amongst them our friend Giraldus, who appeared to have been sent over in some sort of tutorial or secretarial capacity.

The ·expedition was a disastrous failure. The chiefs flocked to Waterford to do honour to their king's son. The courtiers, encouraged by their insolent young master, scoffed at the dress, and mockingly plucked the long beards of the tributaries. Furious and smarting under the insult they withdrew, hostile every man of them now to the death. The news spread; the more distant and important of the chieftains declined to appear. John and his courtiers gave themselves up to rioting and misconduct of various kinds. All hopes of conciliation were at an end. A successful confederation was formed amongst the Irish, and the English were for a while driven bodily out of Munster. John returned to England at the end of eight months, recalled in hot haste and high displeasure by his father.

Twenty-five years later he came back again, this time as king, with a motley army of mercenaries gathered to crush the two brothers De Lacy, who for the moment dominated all Ireland — the one, Hugo, being Earl of Ulster, and Viceroy; the other, Walter, Lord of the Palatinate of Meath.

Among his many vices John had not at least that of indolence to be laid to his charge! He marched direct from Waterford to Trim, the headquarters of the De Lacys, seized the castle, moved on next day to Kells, thence proceeded by rapid stages to Dundalk, Carlingford, Downpatrick, and Carrickfergus. Hugo de Lacy fled in dismay to Scotland. The chieftains of Connaught and Thomond joined their forces with those of the king; even the hitherto indomitable O'Neil made a proffer of submission. Leaving a garrison at Carrickfergus, John marched back by Downpatrick and Drogheda, re-entered Meath, visited Duleek, slept a night at Kells, and so back to Dublin, where he was met by nearly every Anglo-Norman baron, each and all eager to exhibit their own loyalty. His next care was to divide their territory into counties; to bind them over to supply soldiers when called upon to do so by the viceroy, and to arrange for the muster of troops in Dublin. Then away he went again to England. He had been in the country exactly sixty-six days.

Unpleasant man and detestable king as he was, John had no slight share of the governing powers of his race, and even his short stay in Ireland did some good, enough to show what might have been done had a better man, and one in a little less desperate hurry, remained to hold the reins. He had proved that, however they might ape the part, the barons were not as a matter of fact the absolute lords of Ireland ; that they had a master beyond the sea ; one who, if aroused, could make the boldest of them shake in his coat of mail. The lesson was not as well learnt as it ought to have been, but it was better at least than if it had not been learnt at all.

At that age and in its then condition a strong ruler—native if possible, if not, foreign—was by far the best hope for Ireland. Such a ruler, if only for his own sake, would have had the genuine interests of the country at heart. He might have tyrannized himself, but the little tyrants would have been kept at bay. Few countries—and certainly Ireland was not one of the exceptions—were at that time ripe for what we now mean by free institutions. Freedom meant the freedom of a strong government, one that was not at the beck of accident, and was not perpetually changing from one hand to another. The English people found this out for themselves centuries later during the terrible anarchy which resulted from the Wars of the Roses, and of their own accord put themselves under the brutal, but on the whole patriotic, yoke of the Tudors. In Ireland the petty masters unfortunately were always near ; the great one was beyond the sea and not so easily to be got at ! There was no unity ; no pretence of even-handed justice, no one to step between the oppressed and the oppressor. And the result of all this is still to be seen written as in letters of brass upon the face of the country and woven into the very texture of the character of its people.

XIV.

THE LORDS PALATINE.

THE jealousy shown by Henry and his sons towards the earliest invaders of Ireland is doubtless the reason why Giraldus—for a courtier and an ecclesiastic upon his promotion—is so remarkably explicit upon their royal failings. The Geraldines especially seem to have been the objects of this not very unnatural jealousy, and the Geraldines are, on the other hand, to Giraldus himself, objects of an almost superstitious worship. His pen never wearies of expatiating upon their valour, fame, beauty, and innumerable graces, laying stress especially — and in this he is certainly borne out by the facts—upon the great advantage which men trained in the Welsh wars, and used all their lives to skirmishing in the lightest order, had over those who had had no previous experience of the very peculiar warfare necessary in Ireland. "Who," he cries with a burst of enthusiasm, "first penetrated into the heart of the enemy's country? The Geraldines! Who have kept it in submission? The Geraldines! Who struck most terror into the enemy? The Geraldines! Against whom are the shafts of malice chiefly directed? The

Geraldines! Oh that they had found a prince who could have appreciated their distinguished worth! How tranquil, how peaceful would then have been the state of Ireland under their administration!"

Even their indignant chronicler admits however that the Geraldines did not do so very badly for themselves! Maurice Fitzgerald, the eldest of the brothers, became the ancestor both of the Earls of Kildare and Desmond; William, the younger, obtained an immense grant of land in Kerry from the McCarthys, indeed as time went on the lordship of the Desmond Fitzgeralds grew larger and larger, until it covered nearly as much ground as many a small European kingdom. Nor was this all. The White Knight, the Knight of Glyn, and the Knight of Kerry were all three Fitzgeralds, all descended from the same root, and all owned large tracts of country. The position of the Geraldines of Kildare was even more important, on account of their close proximity to Dublin. In later times their great keep at Maynooth dominated the whole Pale, while their followers swarmed everywhere, each man with a G. embroidered upon his breast in token of his allegiance. By the beginning of the sixteenth century their power had reached to, perhaps, the highest point ever attained in these islands by any subject. Whoever might be called the Viceroy in Ireland it was the Earl of Kildare who practically governed the country.

Originally there were three Palatinates—Leinster granted to Strongbow, Meath to De Lacy, and Ulster to De Courcy. To these two more were afterwards added, namely, Ormond and Desmond. The power of the Lord Palatine was all but absolute. He had his own Palatinate court, with its judges, sheriffs, and coroners. He could build fortified towns, and endow them with charters. He could create as many knights as he thought fit, a privilege of which they seem fully to have availed themselves, since we learn that Richard, Earl of Ulster, created no less than thirty-three upon a single occasion. For all practical purposes the Palatinates were thus simply petty kingdoms or principalities, independent in everything but the name.

Strongbow, the greatest of all the territorial barons, left no son to inherit his estates, only a daughter, who married William Marshall, Earl of Pembroke. Through her his estates passed to five heiresses, who married five great nobles, namely, Warrenne, Mountchesny, De Vesci, De Braosa, and Gloucester. Strongbow's Palatinate of Leinster was thus split up into five smaller Palatinates. As none of the new owners moreover chose to live in Ireland, and their revenues were merely drawn away to England, the estates were after awhile very properly declared forfeited, and went to the Crown. Thus the one who of all the adventurers had cherished the largest and most ambitious hopes in the end left no enduring mark at all in Ireland.

Connaught — despite a treaty drawn up between Henry I. and Cathal O'Connor, its native king—was granted by John to William FitzAldelm de Burgh and his son Richard, on much the same terms as Ulster had been already granted to De Courcy, on the understanding, that is to say, that if he could he might win it by the sword. De Courcy failed, but the De Burghs were wilier and more successful. Carefully fostering a strife which shortly after broke out between the two rival princes of the house of O'Connor, and watching from the fortress they had built for themselves at Athlone, upon the Shannon, they seized an opportunity when both combatants were exhausted to pounce upon the country, and wrest the greater part of it away from their grasp. They also drove away the clan of O'Flaherty—owners from time immemorial of the region known as Moy Seola, to the east of the bay of Galway—and forced them back across Lough Corrib, where they took refuge amongst the mountains of Iar Connaught, descending continually in later times in fierce hordes, and wreaking their vengeance upon the town of Galway, which had been founded by the De Burghs at the mouth of the river which carries the waters of Lough Corrib to the sea. To this day the whole of this region of Moy Seola and the eastern shores of Lough Corrib may be seen to be thickly peppered over with ruined De Burgh castles, monuments of some four or five centuries of uninterrupted fighting.

At one time the De Burghs were by far the largest landowners in Ireland. Not only did they possess an immense tract of Connaught, but by the marriage of Richard de Burgh's son to Maud, daughter of Hugh de Lacy, Earl of Ulster, they became the nominal owners of nearly all Ulster to boot. It never was more, however, than a nominal ownership, the clutch of the O'Neills and O'Donnels being found practically impossible to unloose, so that all the De Burghs could be said to hold were the southern borders of what are now the counties of Down, Monaghan, and

Antrim. When, too, William, the third Earl of Ulster, was murdered in 1333, his possessions passed to his daughter and heiress, a child of two years old. A baby girl's inheritance was not likely, as may be imagined, to be regarded at that date as particularly sacred. Ulster was at once retaken by the O'Neills and O'Connels. Two of the Burkes, or De Burghs, Ulick and Edmund, seized Connaught and divided it between them, becoming in due time the ancestors, the one of the Mayos, the other of the Clanricardes.

Another of the great houses was that of the Ormonds, descended from Theobald Walter, a nephew of Thomas à Becket, who was created hereditary cup-bearer or butler to Henry II. Theobald Walter received grants of land in Tipperary and Kilkenny, as well as at Arklow, and in 1391 Kilkenny Castle was sold to his descendant the Earl of Ormond by the heirs of Strongbow. The Ormonds' most marked characteristic is that from the beginning to the end of their career they remained, with hardly an exception, loyal adherents of the English Crown. Their most important representative was the " great duke " as he was called, James, Duke of Ormond, who bore an important part in the civil wars of Charles I., and is perhaps the most distinguished representative of all these great Norman Irish houses, unless indeed one of the greatest names in the whole range of English political history—that of Edmund Burke—is to be added to the list, as perhaps in fairness it ought.

Troublesome as it is to keep these different houses in the memory, it is hopeless to attempt without doing so to understand anything of the history of

Ireland. In England where the ruling power was vested first in the sovereign and later in the Parliament, the landowners, however large their possessions, rarely attained to more than a local importance, save of course when one of them chanced to rise to eminence as a soldier or a statesman. In Ireland the parliament, throughout nearly the whole of its separate existence, was little more than a name, irregularly summoned, and until the middle of the sixteenth century, representing only one small corner of the country. The kings never came; the viceroys came and went in a continually changing succession; practically, therefore, the great territorial barons constituted the backbone of the country—so far as it could be said to have had any backbone at all. They made war with the native chiefs, or else made alliances with them and married their daughters. They raided one another's properties, slew one another's kerns, and carried one another away prisoner. Sometimes their independent action went even further than this. The battle of Knocktow, of which we shall hear in due time, arose because the Earl of Kildare's daughter had quarrelled with her husband, the Earl of Clanricarde, and her father chose to espouse her quarrel. Two large armies were collected, nearly all the lords of the Pale and their followers being upon one side, under the banner of Kildare, a vast and undisciplined horde of natives under Clanricarde upon the other, and the slaughter is said to have exceeded 8,000. Parental affection is a very attractive quality, but when it swells to such dimensions as these it becomes formidable for the peace of a country!

XV.

EDWARD BRUCE IN IRELAND.

ONE of the greatest difficulties to be faced in the study of Irish history, no matter upon what scale, is to discover any reasonable method of dividing our space. The habit of distributing all historical affairs into reigns is often misleading enough even in England; in Ireland it becomes simply ridiculous. What difference can any one suppose it made to the great bulk of the people of that country whether a Henry, whom they had never seen, had been succeeded by an Edward they had never seen, or an Edward by a Henry? No two sovereigns could have been less alike in character or aims than Henry III. and Edward I., yet when we fix our eyes upon Ireland the difference is to all intents and purposes imperceptible.

That, though he never visited the country, Edward I., like his great-grandfather, had large schemes for the benefit of Ireland is certain. Practically, however, his schemes never came to anything, and the chief effect of his reign was that the country was so largely drawn upon for men and money for the support of his wars elsewhere as greatly to weaken the already feeble power of the Government, the result being that at the first touch of serious trouble it all but fell to pieces.

Very serious trouble indeed came in the reign of the second Edward. The battle of Bannockburn—the greatest disaster which ever befel the English during their Scotch wars—had almost as marked an effect on Ireland as on Scotland. All the elements of disaffection at once began to boil and bubble. The O'Neills—ever ready for a fray, and the nearest in point of distance to Scotland—promptly made overtures to the Bruces, and Edward Bruce, the victorious king's brother, was despatched at the head of a large army, and landing in 1315 near Carrickfergus was at once joined by the O'Neills, and war proclaimed.

The first to confront these new allies was Richard de Burgh, the "Red Earl" of Ulster, who was twice defeated by them and driven back on Dublin. The viceroy, Sir Edmund Butler, was the next encountered, and he also was defeated at a battle near Ardscul, whereupon the whole country rose like one man. Fedlim O'Connor, the young king of Connaught, the hereditary chieftain of Thomond, and a host of smaller chieftains of Connaught, Munster, and Meath, flew to arms. Even the De Lacys and several of the other Norman colonists threw in their lot with the invaders. Edward Bruce gained another victory at Kells, and having wasted the country round about, destroying the property of the colonists and slaughtering all whom he could find, he returned to Carrickfergus, where he was met by his brother, King Robert, and together they crossed Ireland, descending as far south as Cashel, and burning, pillaging, and destroying wherever they went. In 1316 the younger Bruce was crowned king at Dundalk.

Such was the panic they created, and so utterly disunited were the colonists, that for a time they carried all before them. It is plain that Edward Bruce—who on one side was descended both from Strongbow and Dermot McMurrough—fully hoped to have cut out a kingdom for himself with his sword, as others of his blood had hoped and intended before him. His own excesses, however, went far to prevent that. So frightfully did he devastate the country, and so horrible was the famine which he created, that many even of his own army perished from it or from the pestilence which followed. His Irish allies fell away in dismay. English and Irish annalists, unanimous for once, alike exclaim in horror over his deeds. Clyn, the Franciscan historian, tells us how he burned and plundered the churches. The annals of Lough Cê say that "no such period for famine or destruction of men" ever occurred, and that people "used then to eat one another throughout Erin." " They, the Scots," says the poet Spenser, writing centuries later, " utterly consumed and wasted whatsoever was before left unspoyled so that of all towns, castles, forts, bridges, and habitations they left not a stick standing, nor yet any people remayning, for those few which yet survived fledde from their fury further into the English Pale that now is. Thus was all that goodly country utterly laid waste."

Such insane destruction brought its own punishment. The colonists began to recover from their dismay. Ormonds, Kildares, and Desmonds bestirred themselves to collect troops. The O'Connors, who with all their tribe had risen in arms, had been utterly defeated at Athenry, where the young king Fedlim and no less than 10,000 of his followers are said to have been left dead. Roger Mortimer, the new viceroy, was re-organizing the government in Dublin. The clergy, stimulated by a Papal mandate, had all now turned against the invader. Robert Bruce had some time previously been recalled to Scotland, and Sir John de Bermingham, the victor of Athenry, pushing northward at the head of 15,000 chosen troops, met the younger Bruce at Dundalk. The combat was hot, short, and decisive. The Scots were defeated, Edward Bruce himself killed, and his head struck off and sent to London. The rest hastened back to Scotland with as little delay as possible. The Scotch invasion was over.

It was over, but its effects remained. From one end of Ireland to the other there was disaffection, anger, revolt. England had proved too weak or too negligent to interfere at the right time and in the right way, and although successful in the end she could not turn back the tide. There was a general feeling of disbelief in the reality of her government. A semi-national feeling had sprung up which temporarily united colonists and natives in a bond of self-defence. Norman nobles and native Irish chieftains threw in their lot together. The English yeoman class, which had begun to get established in Leinster and Munster, had been all but utterly destroyed by Edward Bruce, and the remnant now left the country in despair. The great English lords, with the exception of Ormond and Kildare, from this out took Irish names and adopted Irish dress and fashions. The two De Burghs, as already stated, seized upon the Connaught possessions of their cousin, and divided them, taking the one Galway and the other Mayo, and calling themselves McWilliam Eighter and McWilliam Oughter, or the Nether and the Further Burkes. So too with nearly all the rest. Bermingham of Athenry, in spite of his late famous victory over the Irish, did the same, calling himself McYorris; FitzMaurice of Lixnaw became McMaurice; FitzUrse of Louth, McMahon; and so on through a whole list.

Nor is it difficult to understand the motives which led to these changes. The position of an Irish chieftain—with his practically limitless powers of life and death, his wild retinue of retainers whose only law was the will of their chief — offered an irresistible temptation to men of their type, and had many more charms than the narrow and uninteresting *rôle* of liegeman to a king whom they never saw, and the obeying of whose behests brought them harm rather than good. England had shown only too plainly that she had no power to protect her Irish colonists, of what use therefore, it was asked, for them to call themselves any longer English? The great majority from that moment ceased to do so. Save within the "five obedient shires" which came to be known as the English Pale, "the king's writ no longer ran." The native Irish swarmed back from the mountains and forests, and repossessed themselves of the lands from which they had been driven. No serious attempts were made to re-establish the authority of the law over three-fourths of the island. Within a century and a half of the so-called conquest, save within one small and continually narrowing area, Ireland had ceased even nominally to belong to England.

TRIM CASTLE ON THE BOYNE.

XVI.

THE STATUTE OF KILKENNY.

It was not to be expected, however, that the larger country would for very shame let her possessions thus slip from her grasp without an effort to retain them, certainly not when a ruler of the calibre of an Edward III. came to the helm. Had his energies been able to concentrate themselves upon Ireland the stream which was setting dead against loyalty might even then have been turned back. The royal interest would have risen to the top of faction, as it did in England, and would have curbed the growing and dangerous power of the barons. That magic which surrounds the word king might—who can say that it would not?—have awakened a sentiment at once of patriotism and loyalty.

Chimerical as it may sound even to suppose such a thing, there seems no valid reason why it might not have been. No people admittedly are more intensely loyal by nature than the native Irish. By their failings no less than their virtues they are extraordinarily susceptible to a personal influence, and that devotion which they so often showed towards their own chiefs might with very little trouble have been awakened in favour of a king. It is one of the most deplorable of the many deplorable facts which stud the history of Ireland that no opening for the growth of such sentiment was ever once presented—certainly not in such a form that it would have been humanly possible for it to be embraced.

Edward III. had now his chance. Unfortunately he was too busy to avail himself of it. He had too many irons in the fire to trouble himself much about Ireland. If it furnished him with a supply of fighting men — clean-limbed, sinewy fellows who could run all day without a sign of fatigue, live on a handful of meal, and for a lodging feel luxurious with an armful of hay and the sheltered side of a stone—it was pretty much all he wanted. The light-armed Irish troop did great things at Crecy, but they were never used at home. That Half-hold, which was the ruin of Ireland, and which was to go on being its ruin for many and many a century, was never more conspicuous than during the nominal rule of the strongest and ablest of all the Angevin kings.

Something, however, for very shame he did do. In 1361 all absentee landowners, already amounting to no less than sixty-three, including the heads of several of the great abbeys, were summoned to Westminster and ordered to provide an army to accompany Lionel, Duke of Clarence, whom he had decided upon sending over to Ireland as viceroy.

Clarence was the king's third son, and had married the only daughter and heiress of William de Burgh (mentioned a little way back as a baby heiress), and through his wife had become Earl of Ulster and the nominal lord of an enormous tract of the country stretching from the Bay of Galway nearly up to the coast of Donegal. Most of this had, however, already, as we have seen, been lost. The two rebel Burkes had got possession of the Galway portion, the O'Neills, O'Connors, and other chiefs had repossessed themselves of the North. So completely indeed was the latter lost that Ulster—nominally the patrimony of the Duchess of Clarence—is not even alluded to by her husband as part of the country over which his government could attempt to lay claim.

The chief event of this visit was the summoning of a Parliament at Kilkenny, a Parliament made memorable ever after by the passing of what is still known as the Statute of Kilkenny.[1] This Statute, although it produced little effect at the time, is an extremely important one to understand, as it enables us to realize the state to which the country had then got, and explains, moreover, a good deal that would otherwise be obscure or confusing in the after history of Ireland.

Two distinct and separate set of rules are here drawn up for two distinct and separate Irelands. One is for the English Ireland, which then included about the area of ten counties, though it afterwards shrank to four and a few towns; the other is for the Ireland of the Irish and rebellious English, which included the rest of the island; the object being, not as might be supposed at first sight, to unite these two closer together, but to keep them as far apart as possible; to prevent them, in fact, if possible, from ever uniting.

[1] 40 Edward III., Irish Statutes.

A great many provisions are laid down by this Act, all bearing the same aim. Marriage and fosterage between the English and Irish are forbidden, and declared to be high treason. So, too, is the supply of all horses, weapons, or goods of any sort to the Irish; monks of Irish birth are not to be admitted into any English monastery, nor yet Irish priests into any English preferment. The Irish dress and the Irish mode of riding are both punishable. War with the natives is inculcated as a duty binding upon all good colonists. None of the Irish, except a certain number of families known as the "Five Bloods" (*Quinque sanquines*), are to be allowed to plead at any English court, and the killing of an Irishman is not to be reckoned as a crime. In addition to this, speaking the language of the country is made penal. Any one mixing with the English, and known to be guilty of this offence, is to lose his lands (if he has any), and his body to be lodged in one of the strong places of the king until he learns to repent and amend.

The original words of this part of the Act are worth quoting. They run as follows: "Si nul Engleys ou Irroies entre eux memes encontre c'est ordinance et de cei soit atteint soint sez terrez e tenez s'il eit seizez en les maines son Seignours immediate, tanque q'il vèigne a un des places nostre Seignour le Roy, et trove sufficient seurtee de prendre et user le lang Englais."

One would like—merely as a matter of curiosity—to know what appliances for the study of that not easiest of languages were provided, and before what tribunal the student had to prove his proficiency in it. When, too, we remember that English was still, to a great degree, tabooed in England itself; that the official and familiar language of the Normans was French, that French of which the Statutes of Kilkenny are themselves a specimen, the difficulty of keeping within the law at this point must, it will be owned, have been considerable.

"In all this it is manifest," says Sir John Davis, "that such as had the government of Ireland did indeed intend to make a perpetual enmity between the English and the Irish, pretending that the English should in the end root out the Irish; which, the English not being able to do, caused a perpetual war between the two nations, which continued four hundred and odd years, and would have lasted unto the world's end, if in Queen Elizabeth's reign the Irish had not been broken and conquered by the sword."

It is easy to see that the very ferocity—as it seems to us the utter and inconceivable ferocity—of these enactments is in the main a proof of the pitiable and deplorable weakness of those who passed them, and to this weakness we must look for their excuse, so far as they admitted of excuse at all. Weakness, especially weakness in high places, is apt to fall back upon cruelty to supply false strength, and a government that found itself face to face with an entire country in arms, absolutely antagonistic to and defiant of its authority, may easily have felt itself driven by sheer despair into some such false and futile exhibitions of power. The chief sufferers by these statutes were not the inhabitants of the wilder districts, who, for the most part, escaped out of reach of its provisions, beyond that narrow area where the Dublin judges travelled their little rounds, and who were governed still—when governed at all—by the Brehon laws and Brehon judges, much as in the days of Brian Boru. The real victims were the unhappy settlers of the Pale and such natives as had thrown in their lot with them, and who were robbed and harassed alike by those without and those within. The feudal system was one that always bore hardly upon the poor, and in Ireland the feudal system was at its very worst. There was no central authority; no one to interpose between the baronage and the tillers of the soil; and that state of things which in England only existed during comparatively short periods, and under exceptionally weak rulers, in Ireland was continuous and chronic. The consequence was that men escaped more and more out of this intolerable tyranny into the comparative freedom which lay beyond; forgot that they had ever been English; allowed their beards, in defiance of regulations, to grow; pulled their hair down into a "gibbes" upon their foreheads; adopted fosterage, gossipage, and all the other pleasant contraband Irish customs; married Irish wives, and became, to all intents and purposes, Irishmen. The English power had no more dangerous enemies in the days that were to come than these men of English descent, whose fathers had come over to found a new kingdom for her upon the western side of St. George's Channel.

XVII.

RICHARD II. IN IRELAND.

RICHARD THE SECOND'S reign is a more definite epoch for the Irish historian than many more striking ones, for the simple reason of two visits having been paid by him to Ireland. The first of these was in 1394, when he landed at Waterford with 30,000 archers and 40,000 men at arms, an immense army for that age, and for Ireland it was held an irresistible one.

It was certainly high time for some steps to be taken. In all directions the interests of the colonists were going to the wall. Not only in Ulster, Munster, and Connaught, but even in the East of Ireland, the natives were fast repossessing themselves of all the lands from which they had been driven. A great chieftain, Art McMurrough, had made himself master of the greater part of Leinster, and only by a humiliating use of "Black Rent," could he be kept at bay. The towns were in a miserable state; Limerick, Cork, Waterford had all again and again been attacked, and could with difficulty defend themselves. The Wicklow tribes swarmed down to the very walls of Dublin, and carried the cattle off from under the noses of the citizens.

The judges' rounds were getting yearly shorter and shorter. The very deputy could hardly ride half-a-dozen miles from the castle gates without danger of being set upon, captured, and carried off for ransom.

Richard flattered himself that he had only to appear to conquer. He was keen to achieve some military glory, and Ireland seemed an easy field to win it upon. Like many another before and after him, he found the task harder than it seemed. The great chiefs came in readily enough; O'Connors, O'Briens, O'Neills, even the turbulent McMurrough himself, some seventy-five of them in all. The king entertained them sumptuously, as Henry II. had entertained their ancestors two centuries before. They engaged to be loyal, and to answer for the loyalty of their dependants —with some mental reservations we must conclude. In return for this submission the king knighted the four chiefs just named, a somewhat incongruous piece of courtesy it must be owned. Shortly after his knighthood, Art McMurrough, "Sir Art," was thrown into prison on suspicion. He was released before long, but the release failed to wipe out the affront, and the angry chief retired, nursing fierce vengeance, to his forests.

Richard remained in Ireland nine months, during which he achieved nothing, and departed leaving the government in the hands of his heir-presumptive, Roger Mortimer, Earl of March, the grandson of Lionel, Duke of Clarence, and, therefore, in right of his mother, Earl of Ulster, and the nominal owner of an immense territory, covering nearly a third of the island, barely one acre of which, however, remained in his hands.

The king had not been gone long before Art McMurrough rose again. The young deputy was in Wicklow, endeavouring to carry out a projected colony. Hearing of this outbreak, he hastened into Meath. An encounter took place near Kells. Art McMurrough, at the head of his own men, aided by some wild levies of O'Tooles and O'Nolans, completely defeated the royal army, and after the battle the heir of the English Crown was found amongst the slain.

This Art McMurrough, or Art Kavangh, as he is sometimes called, was a man of very much more formidable stamp than most of the nameless freebooters, native or Norman, who filled the country. His fashion of making his onset seems to have been tremendous. Under him the wild horsemen and "naked knaves," armed only with skeans and darts, sent terror into the breast of their armour-clad antagonists. One of the few early illustrations of Irish history extant represents him as charging at breakneck pace down a hill. We are told that "he rode a horse without a saddle or housing, which was so fine and good that it cost him four hundred cows. In coming down the hill it galloped so hard that in my opinion," says a contemporary writer, "I never in all my life saw hare, deer, sheep, or other animal, I declare to you for a certainty, run with such speed. In his right hand he bore a great dart, which he cast with much skill."[1] No wonder that such a rider, upon such a horse, should

[1] "Metrical History of the Deposition of Richard II."

have struck terror into the very souls of the colonists, and induced them to comply with any demands, however rapacious and humiliating, rather than have to meet him face to face in the field.

The news of McMurrough's victory and of the death of his heir brought Richard back again to Ireland. He returned in hot wrath resolved this time to crush the delinquents. At home everything seemed safe. John of Gaunt was recently dead; Henry of Lancaster still in exile; the Percys had been driven over the border into Scotland. All his enemies seemed to be crushed or extinguished. With an army nearly as large as before, and with vast supplies of stores and arms, he landed at Waterford in 1399.

This time Art McMurrough quietly awaited his coming in a wood not far from the landing-place. He had only 3,000 men about him, so prudently declined to be drawn from that safe retreat of the assailed. The king and his army sat down on the outskirts of the wood. It was July, but the weather was desperately wet. The ground was in a swamp, the rain incessant; there was nothing but green oats for the horses. The whole army suffered from damp and exposure. Some labourers were hastily collected, and an attempt made to cut down the wood. This, too, as might be expected, proved a failure, and Richard, in disgust and vexation, broke up his camp, and with great difficulty, dragging his unwieldy army after him, fell back upon Dublin.

The Leinster chief was not slow to avail himself of the situation. He now took a high hand, and demanded to be put in possession of certain lands he claimed through his wife, as well as to retain his chieftaincy. A treaty was set on foot, varied by the despatch of a flying column to scour his country. In the middle of the negotiation startling news arrived. Henry of Lancaster had landed at Ravenspur, and all England was in arms. The king set off to return, but bad weather and misleading counsel kept him another sixteen days on Irish soil. It was a fatal sixteen days. When he reached Milford Haven it was to find the roads blocked, and to be met by the news that all was lost. The army of Welshmen, gathered by Salisbury, had dispersed, finding that the king did not arrive. His own army of 30,000 men caught the panic, and melted equally rapidly. He tried to negotiate with his cousin, but too late. At Chester he fell into the hands of the victor, and, within a few weeks after leaving Ireland, had passed to a prison, and from there to a grave. He was the last English king to set foot upon its soil until nearly exactly three centuries later, when two rivals met to try conclusions upon the same blood-stained arena.

From this out matters grew from bad to worse. Little or no attempt was made to enforce the law save within the ever-narrowing boundary of what about this time came to be known as the Pale. Outside, Ireland grew to be more and more the Ireland of the natives. Art McMurrough ruled over his own country triumphantly till his death, and levied tribute right and left with even-handed impartiality upon his neighbours. "Black Rent," indeed, began to take the form of a regularly recognized tribute; O'Neill receiving £40 a year from the county of Louth, O'Connor of Offaly, £60 from the county of Meath, and others in like proportion. In despair of any assistance from England some of the colonists formed themselves into a fraternity which they called the "Brotherhood of St. George," consisting of some thirteen gentlemen of the Pale with a hundred archers and a handful of horsemen under them.

The Irish Government continued to pass Act after Act, each more and more ferocious as it became more and more ineffective. Colonists were now empowered to take and behead any natives whom they found marauding, or whom they even suspected of any such intention. All friendly dealing with natives was to be punished as felony. All who failed to shave their upper lip at least once a fortnight were to be imprisoned and their goods seized. Englishmen who married Irish women were to be accounted guilty of high treason, and hung, drawn, and quartered at the convenience of the viceroy. Such feeble ferocity tells its own tale. Like some angry shrew the unhappy executive was getting louder and shriller the less its denunciations were attended to.

XVIII.

THE DEEPEST DEPTHS.

THE most salient fact in Irish history is perhaps its monotony. If that statement is a bull it is one that must be forgiven for the sake of the truth it conveys. Year after year, decade after decade, century after century, we seem to go swimming slowly and wearily on through a vague sea of confusion and disorder; of brutal deeds and yet more brutal retaliations; of misgovernment and anarchy; of a confusion so penetrating and all-persuasive that the mind fairly refuses to grapple with it. Even killing—exciting as an incident—becomes monotonous when it is continued *ad infinitum*, and no other occurrence ever comes to vary its tediousness. Campion the Elizabethan historian, whose few pages are a perfect magazine of verbal quaintness, apologizes in the preface to his "lovyng reader, for that from the time of Cambrensis to that of Henry VIII." he is obliged to make short work of his intermediable periods; "because that nothing is therein orderly written, and that the same is time beyond any man's memory, wherefore I scramble forward with such records as could be sought up, and am enforced to be the briefer."

"Scrambling forward" is, indeed, exactly what describes the process. We, too, must be content "to be the briefer," and to "scramble forward" across these intermediate and comparatively eventless periods in order to reach what lies beyond. The age of the Wars of the Roses is one of great gloom and confusion in England; in Ireland it is an all but complete blank. What intermittent interest in its affairs had been awakened on the other side of the channel had all but wholly died away in that protracted struggle. That its condition was miserable, almost beyond conception, is all that we know for certain. In England, although civil war was raging, and the baronage were energetically slaughtering one another, the mass of the people seem for the most part to have gone unscathed. The townsfolk were undisturbed; the law was protected; the law officers went their rounds; there seems even to have been little general rapine and pillage. The Church, still at its full strength, watched jealously over its own rights and over the rights of those whom it protected. In Ireland, although there was nothing that approached to the dignity of civil war, the condition of the country seems to have been one of uninterrupted and almost universal carnage, pillage, and rapine. The baronage of the Pale raided upon the rest of the country, and the rest of the country raided upon the Pale. Even amongst churchmen it was much the same. Although there was no religious dissension, and heresy was unknown, the jealousy between the churchmen of the two rival races, seems to have been as deep as between the laymen, and their hatred of one another probably even greater. As has been seen in a former chapter, no priest or monk of Irish blood was ever admitted into an English living or monastery, and the rule appears to have been quite equally applicable the other way.

The means, too, for keeping these discordant elements in check were ludicrously inefficient. The whole military establishment during the greater part of this century consisted of some 80 archers, and about 40 " spears ;" the whole revenue amounted to a few hundred pounds per annum. The Parliament was a small and irregular body of barons and knights of the shires, with a few burgesses, unwillingly summoned from the towns, and a certain number of bishops and abbots, the latter, owing to the disturbed state of the country, being generally represented by their proctors. It was summoned at long intervals, and met sometimes in Dublin, sometimes in Drogheda, at other times in Kilkenny, as occasion suggested. Even when it did meet legislation was rarely attempted, and its office was confined mainly to the voting of subsidies. The country simply drifted at its own pleasure down the road to ruin, and by the time the battle of Bosworth was fought, the deepest depths of anarchy had probably been sounded.

The seaport towns alone kept up some little semblance of order and self-government, and seem to have shown some slight capacity for self-defence. In 1412, Waterford distinguished itself by the spirited defence of its walls against the O'Driscolls, a piratical clan of West Cork, and the following year sent a ship into the enemy's stronghold of Baltimore, whose crew seized upon the chief himself, his three brothers, his son, his uncle, and his wife, and carried them off in triumph to Waterford, a feat which the annals of the town commemorate with laudable pride. Dublin, too, showed a similar spirit, and fitted out some small vessels which it sent on a marauding expedition to Scotland, in reward for which its chief magistrate, who had up to that time been a Provost, was invested with the title of Mayor. "The king granted them license," says Camden, "to choose every year a Mayor and two baliffs." Also that its Mayor "should have a gilt sword carried before him for ever."

Several eminent figures appear amongst the "ruck of empty names" which fill up the list of fifteenth-century Irish viceroys. Most of these were mere birds of passage, who made a few experiments at government — conciliatory or the reverse, as the case might be—and so departed again. Sir John Talbot, the scourge of France, and antagonist of the Maid of Orleans, was one of these. From all accounts he seems to have quite kept up his character in Ireland. The native writers speak of him as a second Herod. The colonist detested him for his exactions, while his soldiery were a scourge to every district they were quartered upon. He rebuilt the bridge of Athy, however, and fortified it so as to defend that portion of the Pale, and succeeded in keeping the O'Moores, O'Byrnes, and the rest of the native marauders to some degree at bay.

In 1449, Richard, Duke of York, was sent to Ireland upon a sort of honorary exile. He took the opposite tack of conciliation. Although Ormond was a prominent member of the Lancastrian party, he at once made gracious overtures to him. Desmond, too, he won over by his courtesy, and upon the birth of his son George—afterwards the luckless Duke of Clarence—the rival earls acted as joint sponsors, and when, in 1451, he left Ireland, he appointed Ormond his deputy and representative.

Nine years later he came back, this time as a fugitive. The popularity which he had already won stood him then in good stead. Seizing upon the government, he held it in the teeth of the king and Parliament for more than a year. The news of the battle of Northampton tempted him to England. His son, the Earl of March, had been victorious, and Henry VI. was a prisoner. He was not destined, however, to profit by the success of his own side. In a temporary Lancastrian triumph he was outnumbered, and killed by the troops of Queen Margaret at Wakefield.

His Irish popularity descended to his son. A considerable number of Irish Yorkist partisans, led by the Earl of Kildare, fought beside the latter at the decisive and sanguinary battle of Towton, at which battle the rival Earl of Ormond, leader of the Irish Lancastrians, was taken prisoner, beheaded by the victors, and all his property attained, a blow from which the Butlers were long in recovering.

No other great Irish house suffered seriously. In England the older baronage were all but utterly swept away by the Wars of the Roses, only a few here and there surviving its carnage. In Ireland it was not so. A certain number of Anglo-Norman names disappear at this point from its annals, but the greater number of those with which the reader has become familiar continue to be found in their now long-established homes. The Desmonds and De Burghs still reigned undisputed and unchallenged over their several remote lordships. Ulster, indeed, had long since become wholly Irish, but within the Pale the minor barons of Norman descent—Fingals, Gormanstons, Dunsanys, Trimbelstons and others—remained where their Norman fathers had established themselves, and where their descendants for the most part may be found still. The house of Kildare had grown in strength during the temporary collapse of its rival, and from this out for nearly a century towers high over every other Irish house. The Duke of York was the last royal viceroy who actually held the sword. Others, though nominated, never came over, and in their absence the Kildares remained omnipotent, generally as deputies, and even when that office was for a while confided to other hands, their power was hardly diminished. Only the barren title of Lord-Lieutenant was withheld, and was as a rule bestowed upon some royal personage, several times upon children, once in the case of Edward IV.'s son upon an actual infant in arms.

In 1480, Gerald, eighth Earl of Kildare, called by his own following, Geroit Mor, or Gerald the Great, became deputy, and, from that time forward under five successive kings, and during a period of 33 years, he "reigned" with hardly an interval until his death in 1513.

Geroit Mor is perhaps the most important chief

governor who ruled Ireland upon thorough-going Irish principles. "A mighty man of stature, full of honour and courage." Stanihurst describes him as being "A knight in valour;" and "princely and religious in his words and judgments" is the flattering report of the "Annals of the Four Masters." "His name awed his enemies more than his army," says Camden. "The olde earle being soone hotte and soone cold was of the Englishe well beloved," is another report. "In hys warres hee used a retchlesse (reckless) kynde of diligence, or headye carelessnesse," is a less strong commendation, but probably not less true.

He was a gallant man unquestionably, and as far as can be seen an honest and a well-intentioned one, but his policy was a purely personal, or at most a provincial, one. As for the interests of the country at large they seem hardly to have come within his ken. That fashion of looking at the matter had now so long been the established rule that it had probably ceased indeed to be regarded as a failing.

FIGURES ON KILCARN FONT, MEATH.

XIX.

THE KILDARES IN THE ASCENDANT.

WHEN the Battle of Bosworth brought the adherents of the Red Rose back to triumph, Gerald Mor was still Lord-deputy. He was not deposed, however, on that account, although the Butlers were at once reinstated in their own property, and Sir Thomas Butler was created Earl of Ormond. According to a precedent now prevailing for several reigns, the Lord-Lieutenancy was conferred upon the Duke of Bedford, the king's uncle, Kildare continuing, however, practically to exercise all the functions of government as his deputy.

A dangerous plot, started by the discomfited Yorkist faction, broke out in Ireland in 1487. An impostor, named Lambert Simnel, was sent by the Duchess of Burgundy, and trained to simulate the son of Clarence who, it will be remembered, had been born in Ireland, and whose son was therefore supposed to have a special claim on that country. Two thousand German mercenaries were sent with him to support his pretensions.

This Lambert Simnel seems to have been a youth of some talent, and to have filled his ugly im-

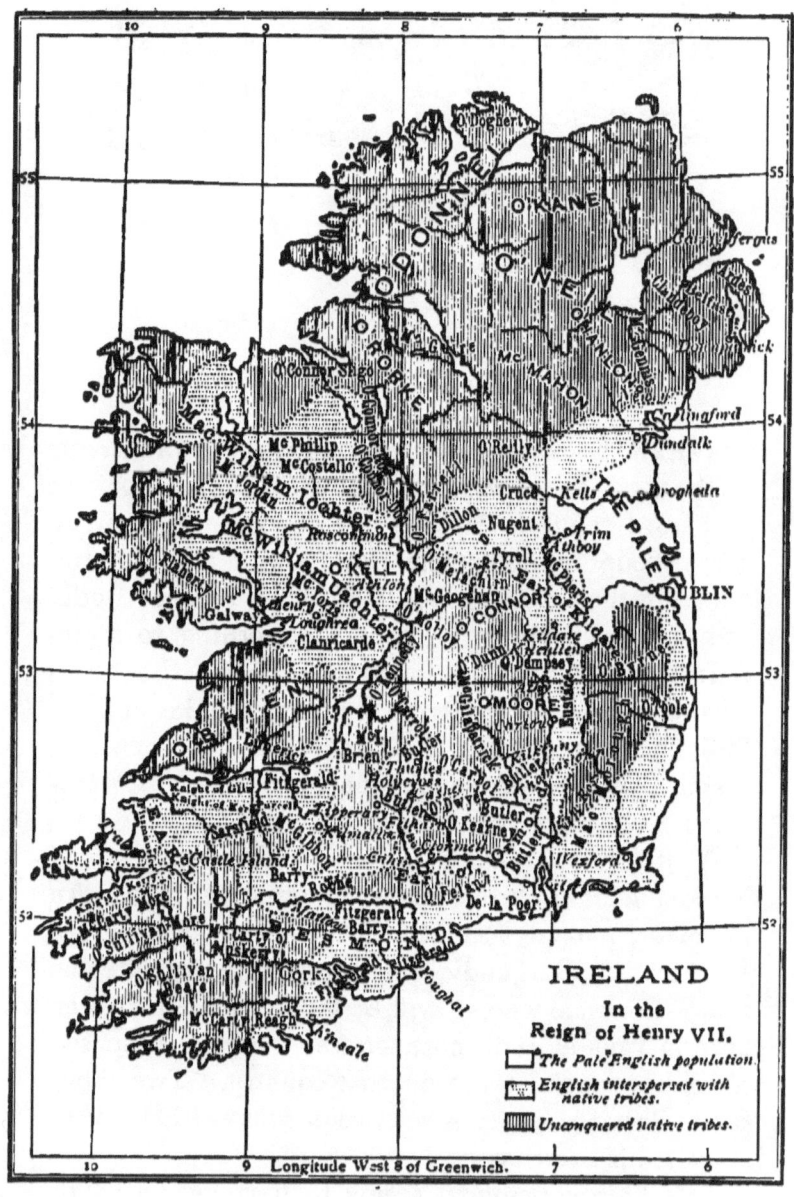

poster's *rôle* with as much grace as it admitted of Bacon, in his history of the reign, tells us that "he was a comely youth, not without some extraordinary dignity of grace and aspect." The fashion in which he retailed his sufferings, pleaded his youth, and appealed to the proverbial generosity of the Irish people, to protect a hapless prince, robbed of his throne and his birthright, seems to have produced an immense effect. Kildare, there is reason to suspect, was privy to the plot, but of others there is no reason to think this, and with a single exception—that of the Earl of Howth—all the lords of the Pale and many of the bishops, including the Archbishop of Dublin, seem to have welcomed the lad—he was only fifteen—with the utmost enthusiasm, an enthusiasm which Henry's production of the real son of Clarence had no effect at all in diminishing.

Lambert Simnel was conducted in high state to Dublin, and there crowned in the presence of the Earl of Kildare, the chancellor, and other State officers. The crown used for the purpose was taken off the head of a statue of The Virgin in St. Mary's Abbey, and—a quainter piece of ceremonial still—the youthful monarch was, after the ceremony, hoisted upon the shoulders of the tallest man in Ireland, "Great Darcy of Platten," and, in this position, promenaded through the streets of Dublin so as to be seen by the people, after which he was taken back in triumph to the castle.

His triumph was not, however, long-lived. Emboldened by this preliminary success, his partizans took him across the sea and landed with a considerable force at Fondray, in Lancashire, the principal leaders on this occasion being the Earl of Lincoln, Thomas Fitzgerald, brother to the Earl of Kildare, Lord Lovell, and Martin Schwartz, the commander of the German forces.

The enthusiasm that was expected to break out on their arrival failed however to come off. "Their snowballs," as Bacon puts it, "did not gather as they went." A battle was fought at Stoke, at which 4,000 of the rebels fell, including Thomas Fitzgerald, the Earl of Lincoln, and the German general Martin Schwartz, while Lambert Simnel with his tutor, Simon the priest, fell into the king's hands, who spared their lives, and appointed the former to the office of turnspit, an office which he held for a number of years, being eventually promoted to that of falconer, and as guardian of the king's hawks he lived and died.

He was not the only culprit whom Henry was willing to pardon. Clemency indeed was his strong point, and he extended it without stint again and again to his Irish rebels. He despatched Sir Richard Edgecombe, a member of the royal household, shortly afterwards upon a mission of conciliation to Ireland. The royal pardon was to be extended to Kildare and the rest of the insurgents on condition of their submission. Kildare's pride stood out for a while against submission on any conditions, but the Royal Commissioner was firm, and the terms, easy ones it must be owned, were at last accepted, and an oath of allegiance sworn to. Kildare, thereupon, was confirmed in his deputyship, and Sir Richard Edgecombe having first partaken of "much excellent good cheere" at the earl's castle at Maynooth, returned peaceably to England.

The Irish primate, one of the few ecclesiastics who had refused to support the impostor, was then, as it happened, in London, and placed strongly before the king the impolicy of continuing Kildare in office. Apparently his remonstrance had its effect, for Henry issued a summons to the deputy and all the Irish nobility to attend at Court, one which was obeyed with hardly an exception. A dramatic turn is given to this visit by the fact that Lambert Simnel, the recently crowned king, was promoted for the occasion to serve wine at dinner to his late Irish subjects. The poor scullion did his office with what grace he might, but no one, it is said, would touch the wine until it came to the turn of the Earl of Howth, the one Irish peer, as we have seen, who had declined to accept the impostor in his heyday of success. "Nay, but bring me the cup if the wine be good," quoth he, being a merry gentleman, "and I shall drink it both for its sake and mine own, and for thee also as thou art, so I leave thee, a poor innocent!"

Howth, whose speech is recorded by his own family chronicler, received three hundred pounds as a reward for his loyalty, the rest returned as they came, lucky, they must have felt under the circumstances, in returning at all.

Simnel was not the last Yorkist impostor who found credit and an asylum in Ireland. Peterkin, or Perkin Warbeck was the next whom the indefatigable Duchess of Burgundy started on the same stage and upon the same errand. This time the prince supposed to be personated was the youngest son of Edward IV., one of the two princes murdered in the tower. He is also occasionally spoken of as a son of Clarence, and sometimes as an illegitimate son of Richard III.—any royal personage, in fact, whose age happened to suit. In spite of the slight ambiguity which overhung his princely origin, he was received with high honour in Cork, and having appealed to the Earls of Desmond and Kildare, was accepted by the former with open arms. "You Irish would crown apes!" Henry afterwards said, not indeed unwarrantably. This time Kildare was more cautious, though his brother, Sir James Fitzgerald, warmly espoused the cause of the impostor. Perkin Warbeck remained in Ireland about a year, when he was invited to France and, for a while, became the centre of the disaffected Yorkists there. He was a very poor specimen of the genus impostor, and seems even to have been destitute of the commonplace quality of courage.

In spite of the unusual prudence displayed by him on this occasion, Kildare was, in 1497, removed from the deputyship, which was for a time vested in Walter Fitzsimons, Archbishop of Dublin, a declared enemy of the Geraldines. Sir James Ormond who represented his brother, the earl, was appointed Lord Treasurer in place of the Baron of Portlester, Kildare's uncle, who had held the office for thirty-eight years. Fresh quarrels thereupon broke out between the Butlers and the rival house, and each harassed the lands of the other in the usual approved style. A meeting was at last arranged to take place in St. Patrick's Cathedral between the two leaders, but a riot breaking out Sir James barred himself up in alarm in the Chapter House. Kildare arriving at the door with offers of peace, a hole had to be cut to enable the two to communicate. Sir James fearing treachery declined to put out his hand, whereupon Kildare boldly thrust in his, and the rivals shook hands. The door was then opened; they embraced, and for a while peace was patched up. The door, with the hole still in it, was extant up to the other day.

The quarrels between these two great houses were interminable, and kept the whole Pale and the greater part of Ireland in eternal hot water. Their war-cries of "Crom-a-Boo" and "Butler-a-Boo" filled the very air, and had to be solemnly prohibited a few years later by special Act of Parliament. By 1494 the complaints against Kildare had grown so loud and so long that the king resolved upon a new experiment, that of sending over an Englishman to fill the post, and Sir Edward Poynings was pitched upon as the most suitable for the purpose.

He arrived accompanied by a force of a thousand men-at-arms, and five or six English lawyers, who were appointed to fill the places of chancellor, treasurer, and other offices from which the present occupiers, most of whom had been concerned either in the Warbeck or Simnel rising, were to be ejected.

It was at a parliament summoned at Drogheda, whither this new deputy had gone to quell a northern rising, that the famous statute known as Poynings' Act was passed, long a rock of offence, and even still a prominent feature in Irish political controversy.

Many of the statutes passed by this Parliament—such as the one just mentioned forbidding war cries, others forbidding the levying of private forces, forbidding the " country's curse " Coyne and livery, and other habitual exactions were undoubtedly necessary and called for by the circumstances of the case. The only ones now remembered however are the following. First, that no parliament should be summoned by the deputy's authority without the king's special license for that purpose. Secondly, that all English statutes should henceforward be regarded as binding upon Ireland; and thirdly, that all Acts referring to Ireland must be submitted first to the king and Privy Council, and that, when returned by them, the Irish Parliament should have no power to modify them further. This, as will be seen, practically reduced the latter to a mere court for registering laws already passed elsewhere, passed too often without the smallest regard to the special requirements of the country. A condition of subserviency from which it only escaped again for a short time during the palmy days of the eighteenth century.

By this same parliament Kildare was attained—rather late in the day—on the ground of conspiracy, and sent prisoner to London. He lay a year in prison, and was then brought to trial, and allowed to plead his own cause in the king's presence. The audacity, frank humour, and ready repartee of his great Irish subject seems to have made a favourable impression upon Henry, who must himself have had more sense of humour than English historians give us any impression of. One of the principal charges against the earl was that he had burned the church at Cashel. According to the account given in the Book of Howth he readily admitted the charge, but declared positively that he would never have thought of doing so had he not been solemnly assured that the archbishop was at the time inside it. The audacity of this defence is not a little heightened by the fact that the archbishop in question was at the moment sitting in court and listening to it.

Advised by the king to provide himself with a good counsel, "By St. Bride"—his favourite oath—said he, "I know well the fellow I would have, yea, and the best in England, too!" Asked who that might be. "Marry, the king himself." The note of comedy struck at the beginning of the trial lasted to the end. The earl's ready wit seems to have dumbfounded his accusers, who were not unnaturally indignant at so unlooked for a result. "All Ireland," they swore, solemnly, "could not govern the Earl of Kildare." "So it appears," said Henry. "Then let the Earl of Kildare govern all Ireland."

Whether the account given by Irish historians of this famous trial is to be accepted literally or not, the result, at any rate, was conclusive. The king seems to have felt, that Kildare was less dangerous as sheep-dog —even though a head-strong one—than as wolf, even a wolf in a cage. He released him and restored him to his command. Prince Henry, according to custom, becoming nominally Lord-Lieutenant, with Kildare as deputy under him. The earl's wife had lately died, and before leaving England he strengthened himself against troubles to come by marrying Elizabeth St. John, the king's cousin, and having left his son Gerald behind as hostage for his good behaviour, sailed merrily home to Ireland.

Perkin Warbeck meanwhile had made another foray upon Munster, where he was supported by Desmond, and repulsed with no little ignominy by the townsfolk of Waterford; after which he again departed and was seen no more upon that stage. Kildare—whose own attainder was not reversed until after his arrival in Ireland—presided over a parliament, one of whose first acts was to attaint Lord Barrymore and the other Munster gentlemen for their share in this rising. He also visited Cork and Kinsale, leaving a garrison behind him; rebuilt several towns in Leinster which had been ruined in a succession of raids; garrisoned the borders of the Pale with new castles, and for the first time in its history brought ordnance into Ireland, which he employed in the siege of Belrath Castle. A factor destined to work a revolution upon Irish traditional modes of warfare, and upon none with more fatal effect than upon the house of Fitzgerald itself.

That Kildare's authority, even during this latter period of his government was wholly exercised in the cause of tranquility it would be certainly rash to assert. At the same time it may be doubted whether any better choice was open to the king—short of some very drastic policy indeed. That he used his great authority to overthrow his own enemies and to aggrandize his own house goes almost without saying

The titular sovereignty of the king could hope to count for little beside the real sovereignty of the earl, and the house of Kildare naturally loomed far larger and more imposingly in Ireland than the house of Tudor. Despotism in some form was the only practical and possible government, and Earl Gerald was all but despotic within the Pale, and even outside it was at any rate stronger than any other single individual. The Desmond Geraldines lived remote, the Butlers, who came next to the Geraldines in importance, held Kilkenny, Carlow, and Tipperary, but were cut off from Dublin by the wild mountains of Wicklow, and the wilder tribes of O'Tooles, and O'Brynes who held them. They were only able to approach it through Kildare, and Kildare was the head-quarters of the Geraldines.

One of Earl Gerald's last, and, upon the whole, his most remarkable achievement was that famous expedition which ended in the battle of Knocktow already alluded to in an earlier chapter, in which a large number of the lords of the Pale, aided by the native allies of the deputy, took part. In this case there was hardly a pretence that the expedition was undertaken in the king's service. It was a family quarrel pure and simple, between the deputy and his son-in-law McWilliam, of Clanricarde. The native account tells us that the latter's wife " was not so used as the earl (her father) could be pleased with," whereupon "he swore to be revenged upon this Irishman and all his partakers." The notion of a Fitzgerald stigmatizing a De Burgh as an Irishman is delightful, and eminently characteristic of the sort of wild confusion prevailing on the subject. The whole story indeed is so excellent, and is told by the narrator with so much spirit, that it were pity to curtail it, and as it stands it would be too long for these pages. The result was that Clanricarde and his Irish allies were defeated with frightful slaughter, between seven and eight thousand men, according to the victors, having been left dead upon the field! Galway, previously held by Clanricarde, was re-occupied, and the deputy and his allies returned in triumph to Dublin, whence the archbishop was despatched in hot haste to explain matters to the king.

A slight incident which took place at the end of this battle is too characteristic to omit. "We have done one good work," observed Lord Gormanston, one of the Lords of the Pale, confidentially to the Lord-deputy. "And if we now do the other we shall do well." Asked by the latter what he meant, he replied, "We have for the most part killed our enemies, if we do the like with all the Irishmen that we have with us it were a good deed."[1] Happily for his good fame Kildare seems to have been able to resist the tempting suggestion, and the allies parted on this occasion to all appearances on friendly terms.

[1] Book of Howth.

XX.

FALL OF THE HOUSE OF KILDARE.

THE battle of Knocktow was fought five years before the death of Henry VII. Of those five years and of the earlier ones of the new reign little of any vital importance remains to be recorded in Ireland. With the rise of Wolsey to power however a new era set in. The great cardinal was the sworn enemy of the Geraldines. He saw in them the most formidable obstacle to the royal power in that country. The theory that the Kildares were the only people who could carry on the government had by this time become firmly established. No one in Ireland could stand against the earl, and when the earl was out of Ireland the whole island was in an uproar. The confusion too between Kildare in his proper person, and Kildare as the king's Viceroy was, it must be owned, a perennial one, and upon more than one occasion had all but brought the government to an absolute standstill.

Geroit Mor had died in 1513 of a wound received in a campaign with the O'Carrolls close to his own castle of Kilkea, but almost as a matter of course his son Gerald had succeeded him as Viceroy and carried on the government in much the same fashion; had made raids on the O'Moores and O'Reillys and others of the "king's Irish enemies," and been rewarded with grants upon the lands which he had captured from the rebels. The state of the Pale was terrible. "Coyne and livery," it was declared, had eaten up the people. The sea, too, swarmed with pirates, who descended all but unchecked upon the coast and carried off men and women to slavery. Many complaints were made of the deputy, and by 1520 these had grown so loud and long that Henry resolved upon a change, and like his predecessor determined to send an English governor, one upon whom he could himself rely.

The choice fell upon the Earl of Surrey, son of the conqueror of Flodden. Surrey's survey of the field soon convinced him to his own satisfaction that no half measures was likely to be of any avail. The plan proposed by him had certainly the merit of being sufficiently sweeping. Ireland was to be entirely reconquered. District was to be taken after district, and fortresses to be built to hold them according as they were conquered. The occupation was thus to be pushed steadily on until the whole country submitted, after which it was to be largely repopulated by English colonists. The idea was a large one, and would have taken a large permanent army to carry out. The loss too of life would have been appalling, though not, it was represented to the king, greater than was annually squandered in an interminable succession of petty wars. Probably the expense was the real hindrance. At any rate Surrey's plan was put aside for the time being, and not long afterwards at his own urgent prayer he was allowed to lay down his uneasy honours and return to England.

Meanwhile Earl Gerald the younger had been rapidly gaining favour at Court, had accompanied Henry to France, and like his father before him, had wooed and won an English bride. Like his father, too, he possessed that winning charm which had for generations characterized his house. Quick-witted and genial, with the bright manner and courteous ease of high-bred gentlemen, such—even on the showing of those who had no love for them—was the habitual bearing of these Leinster Geraldines. The end was that Kildare after a while was allowed to return to Ireland, and upon Surrey's departure, and after a brief and very unsuccessful tenure of office by Sir Pierce Butler, the deputyship was restored to him.

Three years later he was again summoned, and this time, on Wolsey's urgent advice, thrown into the Tower. Heavy accusations had been made against him, the most formidable of which was that he had used the king's ordnance to strengthen his own castle of Maynooth. The Ormonds and the cardinal were bent upon his ruin. The earl, however, faced his accusers boldly; met even the great cardinal himself in a war of words, and proved to be more than his equal. Once again he was acquitted and restored to Ireland, and after a while the deputyship was restored to him, John Allen, a former chaplain of Wolsey's, being however appointed Archbishop of Dublin, and Chancellor, with private orders to keep a watch upon Kildare, and to report his proceedings to the English Council.

Yet a third time in 1534 he was summoned, and now the case was more serious. The whole situation had in fact in the meanwhile utterly changed, Henry was now in the thick of his great struggle with Rome. With excommunication hanging over his head, Ireland had suddenly become a formidable peril. Fears were entertained of a Spanish descent upon its coast. One of the emperor's chaplains was known to be intriguing with the Earl of Desmond. Cromwell's iron hand too was over the realm and speedily made itself felt in Ireland. Kildare was once more thrown into the Tower, from which this time he was never destined to emerge. He was ill already of a wound received the previous year, and the confinement and trouble of mind—which before long became acute—brought his life to a close.

His son Thomas — generally known as Silken Thomas from the splendour of his clothes—had been rashly appointed vice-deputy by his father before his departure. In the month of August, a report reached Ireland that the earl had been executed, and the whole house of Geraldine was forthwith thrown into the wildest convulsions of fury at the intelligence. Young Lord Thomas — he was only at the time twenty-one—hot-tempered, undisciplined, and brimful of the pride of his race—at once flew to arms. His first act was to renounce his allegiance to England. Galloping up to the Council with a hundred and fifty Geraldines at his heels, he seized the Sword of State, marched into the council-room, and addressing the Council in his capacity of Vice-deputy, poured forth a speech full of boyish fanfaronade and bravado. "Henceforth," said he, "I am none of Henry's deputy! I am his foe! I have more mind to meet him in the field, than to serve him in office." With other words to the like effect he rendered up the Sword, and once more springing upon his horse, galloped out of Dublin.

He was back again before long, this time with intent to seize the town. There was little or no defence. Ormond was away; the walls were decayed; ordnance was short—a good deal of it, the Geraldine enemies said, had been already removed to Maynooth. White, the commander, threw himself into the castle; the gates were opened; Lord Thomas cantered in and took possession of the town, the garrison remaining placidly looking on.

Worse was to come. Allen, the archbishop, and the great enemy of the Fitzgeralds made an attempt to escape to England, but was caught and savagely murdered by some of the Geraldine adherents upon the sea coast near Clontarf. When the news of these proceedings—especially of the last named—reached England, the sensation naturally was immense. Henry hastily despatched Sir William Skeffington with a considerable force to restore order, but his coming was long delayed, and when he did arrive his operations were feeble in the extreme. Ormond had marched rapidly up from the south, and almost singlehanded defended the interests of government. Even after his arrival Skeffington, who was old, cautious, and enfeebled by bad health, remained for months shut up in Dublin doing nothing, the followers of Lord Thomas wasting the country at pleasure, and burning the towns of Trim and Dunboyne, not many miles from its walls.

The Earl of Kildare had meanwhile died in prison, broken-hearted at the news of this ill-starred rising, in which he doubtless foresaw the ruin of his house. It was not until the month of March, eight months after his arrival in Ireland, that Sir William ventured to leave Dublin, and advance to the attack of Maynooth Castle, the great Leinster stronghold and Paladium of the Geraldines. Young Kildare, as he now was, was away in the south, but managed to throw some additional men into the castle, which was already strongly fortified, and believed in Ireland to be impregnable. The siege train imported by the deputy shortly dispelled that illusion. Whether, as is asserted, treachery from within aided the result or not, the end was not long delayed. After a few days Skeffington's cannons made a formidable breach in the walls. The English soldiery rushed in. The defenders threw down their arms and begged mercy, and a long row of them, including the Dean of Kildare and another priest who happened to be in the castle at the time were speedily hanging in front of its walls. "The Pardon of Maynooth" was from that day forth a well-known Irish equivalent for the gallows!

This was the end of the rebellion. The destruction of Maynooth Castle seems to have struck a cold chill to the very hearts of the Geraldines. For a while, Earl Thomas and his brother-in-law, the chief of the

O'Connors, tried vainly to sustain the spirits of their followers. The rising seems to have melted away almost of its own accord, and within a few months the young leader himself surrendered to Lord Leonard Grey, the English commander, upon the understanding that his life was to be spared. Lord Leonard was his near relative, and therefore no doubt willing, as far as was compatible with safety to himself, to do the best he could for his kinsman. Whether a promise was formally given, or whether as was afterwards asserted "comfortable words were spoken to Thomas to allure him to yield" the situation was considered too grave for any mere fanciful consideration of honour to stand in the way. Lord Thomas was not executed upon the spot, but he was thrown into prison, and a year later with five of his uncles, two of whom at least had had no share whatever in the raising, he was hanged at Tyburn. Of all the great house of the Leinster Geraldines only a boy of twelve years old survived this hecatomb.

FIGURES ON KILCARN FONT, MEATH.

XXI.

THE ACT OF SUPREMACY.

IN spite of his feeble health and feebler energies, Sir William Skeffington was continued Lord-deputy until his death, which took place not many months after the fall of Maynooth—" A good man of war, but not quick enough for Ireland "—seems to have been the verdict of his contemporaries upon him. He was succeeded by Lord Leonard Grey, against whom no such charge could be made. His energy seems to have been immense. He loved, we are told, to be "ever in the saddle." Such was the rapidity of his movements, and such the terror they inspired that for a while a sort of awe-struck tranquillity prevailed. He overran Cork; broke down the castles of the Barrys and Munster Geraldines; destroyed the famous bridge over the Shannon across which the O'Briens of Clare had been in the habit of descending from time immemorial upon the Pale, and after these various achievements returned triumphantly to Dublin.

His Geraldine connection proved however his ruin. He was accused of favouring the adherents of their fallen house, and even of conniving at the escape of its last legitimate heir; of playing " Bo Peep " with him, as Stanihurst, the historian puts it. Ormond and the deputy were never friends, and Ormond had won—not undeservedly—great weight in the councils of Henry. "My Lord-deputy," Lord Butler, Ormond's son had declared, "is the Earl of Kildare born over again." Luttrell, on the other hand, declared that "Ormond hated Grey worse than he had hated Kildare." All agreed that Lord Leonard was difficult to work with. He seems to have been a well-intentioned man, a hard worker, and a keen soldier, but neither subtle enough nor conciliatory enough for his place. He was accused of treasonable practices, and a list of formidable charges made against him. At his own request he was summoned to court to answer these. To a good many he pleaded guilty—half in contempt as it would seem—and threw himself upon the mercy of the king. No mercy however followed. Like many another "well-meaning English official" of the period, his life ended upon the scaffold.

A more astute and cautious man, Sir Anthony St. Leger, next took the helm in Ireland. His task was chiefly one of diplomacy, and he carried it out with much address. In 1537 a parliament had been summoned in Dublin for the purpose of carrying out the Act of Supremacy. To this proposal the lay members seem to have been perfectly indifferent, but, as was to be expected, the clergy stood firmer. So resolute were they in their opposition that the parliament had to be prorogued, and upon its re-assembling, a Bill was hastily forced through by the Privy Council, declaring that the proctors, who had long represented the clergy in the Lower House, had henceforward no place in the Legislature. The Act of Supremacy was then passed: thirteen abbeys were immediately suppressed, and the firstfruits made over to the king in place of the Pope. The foundation of the new edifice was felt to have been securely laid.

This was followed five years later by another Act, by which the property of over four hundred religious houses was confiscated. That the arguments which applied forcibly enough in many cases for the confiscations of religious houses in England had no application in Ireland, was a circumstance which was not allowed to count. In England, the monasteries were rich; in Ireland, they were, for the most part, very poor: in England, they absorbed the revenues of the parishes; in Ireland, the monks as a rule served the parishes themselves: in England, popular condemnation had to a great degree already forestalled the legal enactment; in Ireland, nothing of the sort had ever been thought of: in England, the monks were as a rule distinctly behind the higher orders of laity in education; in Ireland, they were practically the only educators. These however were details. Uniformity was desirable. The monasteries were doomed, and before long means were found to enlist most of the Irish landowners, Celts no less than Normans, in favour of the despoliation.

At a great parliament summoned in Dublin in 1540, all the Irish lords of English descent, and a large muster of native chieftains were for the first time in history assembled together under one roof. O'Tooles and O'Byrnes from their wild Wicklow mountains; the McMurroughs from Carlow, the O'Connor, the O'Dunn, the O'Moore; the terrible McGillapatrick from his forests of Upper Ossory—all the great O's and Macs in fact of Ireland were called together to meet the Butlers, the Desmonds, the Barrys, the Fitzmaurices—their hereditary enemies now for four long centuries. One house alone was not represented, and that the greatest of them all. The sun of the Kildares had set for a while, and the only surviving member of it was a boy, hiding in holes and corners, and trusting for the bare life to the fealty of his clansmen.

Nothing that could reconcile the chiefs to the new religious departure was omitted upon this occasion. Their new-found loyalty was to be handsomely rewarded with a share of the Church spoil. Nor did they show the smallest reluctance, it must be said, to meet the king's good dispositions half way. The principal Church lands in Galway were made over to McWilliam, the head of the Burkes; O'Brien received the abbey lands in Thomond; other chiefs received similar benefices according to their degree, while a plentiful shower of less substantial, but still appreciated favours followed. The turbulent McGillapatrick of Ossory was to be converted into the decorous-sounding Lord Upper Ossory. For Con O'Neill as soon as he chose to come in, the Earldom of Tyrone was waiting. McWilliam Burke of Galway was to become Earl of Clanricarde; O'Brien of Clare, Earl of Thomond and Baron of Inchiquin. Parliamentary robes, and golden chains; a house in Dublin for each chief during the sitting of Parliament—these

DISTRIBUTION OF CHURCH LANDS. 155

were only a portion of the good things offered by the deputy on the part of his master. Could man or monarch do more? In a general interchange of civilities the "King's Irish enemies" combined with their hereditary foes to proclaim him no longer Lord, but King of Ireland—" Defender of the Faith, and of the Church of England and Ireland on earth the Supreme Head."

FONT IN KILCARN CHURCH, CO. MEATH.

XXII.

THE NEW DEPARTURE.

So far so good. Despite a few trifling clouds which overhung the horizon, the latter years of Henry VIII.'s life and the short reign of his successor may claim to count among the comparatively halcyon periods of Irish history. The agreement with the landowners worked well, and no serious fears of any purpose to expel them from their lands had as yet been awakened. Henry's policy was upon the whole steadily conciliatory. Tyrant as he was, he could be just when his temper was not roused, and he kept his word loyally in this case. To be just and firm, and to give time for those hitherto untried varieties of government to work, was at once the most merciful and most politic course that could be pursued. Unfortunately for the destinies of Ireland, unfortunately for the future comfort of her rulers, there was too little patience to persevere in that direction. The Government desired to eat their loaf before there was fairly time for the corn to sprout. The seed of conciliation had hardly begun to grow before it was plucked hastily up by the roots again. The plantations of Mary's reign, and the still larger operations carried on in that of her sister, awakened a deep-seated feeling of distrust, a rooted belief in the law as a mysterious and incomprehensible instrument invented solely for the perpetration of injustice, a belief which is certainly not wholly extinguished even in our own day.

For the present, however, "sober ways, politic shifts, and amicable persuasions" were the rule. Chief after chief accepted the indenture which made him owner in fee simple under the king of his tribal lands. These indentures, it is true, were in themselves unjust, but then it was not as it happened a form of injustice that affected them unpleasantly. Con O'Neill, Murrough O'Brien, McWilliam of Clanricarde, all visited Greenwich in the summer of 1543, and all received their peerages direct from the king's own hands. The first named, as became his importance, was received with special honour, and received the title of Earl of Tyrone, with the second title of Baron of Dungannon for any son whom he liked to name. The son whom he did name—apparently in a fit of inadvertence—was one Matthew, who is confidently asserted to have not been his son at all, but the son of a blacksmith, and who in any case was not legitimate. An odd choice, destined, as will be seen, to lead to a good deal of bloodshed later on.

One or two of the new peers were even persuaded to send over their heirs to be brought up at the English Court, according to a gracious hint from the king. Young Barnabie FitzPatrick, heir to the new barony of Upper Ossory, was one of these, and the descendent of a long line of turbulent Mc Gillapatricks, grew up there into a douce-mannered

English-seeming youth, the especial friend and chosen companion of the mild young prince.

While civil strife was thus settling down, religious strife unfortunately was only beginning to awaken. The question of supremacy had passed over as we have seen in perfect tranquillity; it was a very different matter when it came to a question of doctrine. Unlike England, Ireland had never been touched by religious controversy. The native Church and the Church of the Pale were sharply separated from one another it is true, but it was by blood, language, and mutual jealousies, not by creed, doctrine, or discipline. As regards these points they were all but absolutely identical. The attempt to change their common faith was instantly and vehemently resisted by both alike. Could a Luther or a John Knox have arrived, with all the fervour of their popular eloquence, the case might possibly have been different. No Knox or Luther however, showed the slightest symptom of appearing, indeed hardly an attempt was made to supply doctrines to the new converts. The few English divines that did come knew no Irish, those who listened to them knew no English. The native priests were silent and suspicious. A general pause of astonishment and consternation prevailed.

The order for the destruction of relics broke this silence, and sent a passionate thrill of opposition through all breasts, lay as well as clerical. When the venerated remains of the golden days of the Irish Church were collected together and publicly destroyed, especially when the staff of St. Patrick, the famous Baculum Cristatum, part of which was believed to have actually touched the hands of the Saviour, was burnt in Dublin in the market-place, a spasm of shocked dismay ran through the whole island. Men who would have been scandalized by no other form of violence were horror-stricken at this. Differences of creed were so little understood that a widespread belief that a new era of paganism was about to be inaugurated sprang up all over Ireland. To this belief the friars, who, though driven from their cloisters, were still numerous, lent their support, as did the Jesuits, who now for the first time began to arrive in some numbers. Even the acceptance of the supremacy began to be rebelled against now that it was clearly seen what it was leading to. An order to read the new English liturgy was met with sullen resistance—"Now shall every illiterate fellow read mass!" cried Archbishop Dowdal of Armagh, in hot wrath and indignation. Brown, the Archbishop of Dublin, was an ardent reformer, so also was the Bishop of Meath, but to the mass of their brethren they simply appeared to be heretics. A proposal was made to translate the Prayer-book into Irish, but it was never carried into effect, indeed, even in the next century when Bishop Bedell proposed to undertake the task he received little encouragement.

The attempt to force Protestantism upon the country produced one, and only one, important result. It broke down those long-standing barriers which had hitherto separated Irishmen of different blood and lineage, and united them like one man against the Crown. When the common faith was touched the common sense of brotherhood was kindled. "The English and Irish," Archbishop Brown wrote in despair to Cromwell, "both oppose your lordship's orders, and begin to lay aside their own quarrels." Such a result might be desirable in itself, but it certainly came in the form least likely to prove propitious for the futuos tranquillity of the country. Even those towns where loyalty had hitherto stood above suspicion received the order to dismantle their churches and destroy all "pictures and Popish fancies" with sullen dislike and hostility. Galway, Kilkenny, Waterford, each and all protested openly. The Irish problem— not so very easy of solution before—had suddenly received a new element of confusion. One that was destined to prove a greater difficulty than all the rest put together.

INITIAL LETTER FROM THE BOOK OF KELLS.

XXIII.

THE FIRST PLANTATIONS.

WITH Mary's accession the religious struggle was for a while postponed. Some feeble attempts were even made to recover the Church property, but too many people's interests were concerned for much to be done in that direction. Dowdal, Archbishop of Armagh, who had been deprived, was restored to his primacy. Archbishop Brown and the other conforming bishops were deprived. So also were all married clergy, of whom there seem to have been but few; otherwise there was no great difference. As far as the right of exercising her supremacy was concerned, Mary relished Papal interference nearly as little as did her father.

Although the religious struggle was thus for a time postponed, the other vital Irish point—the possession of the land—now began to be pressed with new vigour. Fercal, Leix, and Offaly, belonging to the fierce tribes of the O'Moores, O'Dempseys, O'Connors, and O'Carrols, lay upon the Kildare frontier of the Pale, and had long been a standing menace to their more peaceful neighbours. It was now determined that this tract should be added to the still limited area of shire land. The chiefs, it is true, had been indentured by Henry, but since then there had been outbreaks of the usual sort, and it was considered by the Government that nowhere could the longed-for experiment of a plantation be tried with greater advantage.

There was little or no resistance. The chiefs, taken by surprise, submitted. The English force sent against them, under the command of Sir Edward Bellingham, was irresistible. O'Moore and O'Connor were seized and sent prisoners to England. Dangen, which had so often resisted the soldiers of the Pale was taken. The tribesmen whose fathers had fed their cattle from time immemorial upon the unfenced pastures of the plains were driven off, and took refuge in the forests, which still covered most of the centre of Ireland. The more profitable land was then leased by the Crown to English colonists —Cosbies, Barringtons, Pigotts, Bowens, and others. Leix and a portion of Offaly were called Queen's County, in compliment to the queen, the remainder King's County, in compliment to Philip. Dangen at the same time becoming Phillipstown, and Campa Maryborough. The experiment was regarded as eminently successful, and congratulations passed between the deputy and the English Council, but it awakened a deep-seated sense of insecurity and ill-usage, which argued poorly for the tranquillity of the future.

Of the rest of Mary's reign little needs to be here recorded. That indelible brand of blood which it has left on English history was all but unfelt in Ireland.

There had been few Protestant converts, and those few were not apparently emulous of martyrdom. No Smithfield fires were lighted in Dublin, indeed it is a curious fact that in the whole course of Irish history—so prodigal of other horrors—no single execution for heresy is, it is said, recorded. A story is found in the Ware Papers, and supported by the authority of Archbishop Ussher, which, if true, shows that this reproach to Irish Protestantism—if indeed it is a reproach—was once nearly avoided. The story runs that one Cole, Dean of St. Paul's, was despatched by Mary with a special commission to "lash the heretics of Ireland." That Cole slept on his way at an inn in Chester, the landlady of which happened to have a brother, a Protestant then living in Dublin. This woman, hearing him boast of his commission, watched her opportunity, and stole the commission out of his cloak-bag, substituting for it a pack of cards. Cole unsuspiciously pursued his way, and presenting himself authoritatively before the deputy, declared his business and opened his bag. There, in place of the commission against the heretics, lay the pack of cards with the knave of clubs uppermost!

The story goes on to say that the dean raged in discomfited fury, but that the deputy, though himself a Roman Catholic, took the matter easily. "Let us have another commission," he said, "and meanwhile we will shuffle the cards." The cards were effectually shuffled, for before any further steps could be taken Mary had died.

XXIV.

WARS AGAINST SHANE O'NEILL.

UPON the 17th of November, 1558, Mary died, and upon the afternoon of the same day Elizabeth was proclaimed queen. A new reign is always accounted a new starting-point, and in this case the traditional method of dividing history is certainly no misleader. The old queen had been narrow, dull-witted, bigoted; an unhappy woman, a miserable wife, plagued with sickness, plagued, above all, with a conscience whose mission seems to have been to distort everything that came under its cognizance. A woman even whose good qualities—and she had several—only seemed to push her further and further down the path of disaster.

The new queen was twenty-six years old. Old enough, therefore, to have realized what life meant, young enough to have almost illimitable possibilities still unrevealed to her. No pampered royal heiress, either, for whom the world of hard facts had no reality, and the silken shams of a Court constituted the only standpoint, but one who had already with steady eyes looked danger and disaster in the face and knew them for what they were. With a realm under her hand strong already, and destined before her death to grow stronger still; with a spirit too, strong enough and large enough for her realm; stronger perhaps in spite of her many littlenesses than that of any of the men she ruled over.

And Ireland? How was it affected by this change of rulers? At first fairly well. The early months of the new reign were marked by a policy of conciliation. Protestantism was of course, re-established, but there was no eagerness to press the Act of Conformity with any severity, and Mass was still said nearly everywhere except in the Pale.

As usual, troubles began in the North. Henry VIII., it will be remembered, had granted the hereditary lands of Tyrone to Con O'Neill, with remainder to Matthew, the new Baron of Dungannon, whereas lands in Ulster, as elsewhere in Ireland, had always hitherto, by the law of Tanistry, been vested in the tribe, who claimed the right to select whichever of their late chiefs' sons they themselves thought fit. This right they now proceeded to exercise. Matthew, if he was Con's son at all, which was doubtful, was unquestionably illegitimate, and, therefore, by English as well as Irish law, wrongfully put in the place. On the other hand, a younger son Shane—called affectionately "Shane the Proud" by his clansmen—was unquestionably legitimate, and what was of much more importance, was already the idol of every fighting O'Neill from Lough Foyle to the banks of the Blackwater.

Shane is one of those Irish heroes—rather perhaps Ulster heroes, for his aspirations were hardly national

—whom it is extremely difficult to mete out justice to with a perfectly even hand. He was unquestionably three-fourths of a savage—that fact we must begin in honesty by admitting—at the same time, he was a very brilliant, and, even in many respects attractive, savage. His letters, though suffering like those of some other distinguished authors from being translated, are full of touches of fiery eloquence, mixed with bombast and the wildest and most monstrously inflated self-pretension. His habits certainly were not commendable. He habitually drank, and it is also said ate a great deal more than was good for him. He ill-used his unlucky prisoners. He divorced one wife to marry another, and was eager to have a third in the lifetime of the second, making proposals at the same time to the deputy for the hand of his sister, and again and again petitioning the queen to provide him with some " English gentlewoman of noble blood, meet for my vocation, so that by her good civility and bringing up the country would become civil." In spite however of these and a few other lapses from the received modern code of morals and decorum, Shane the Proud is an attractive figure in his way, and we follow his fortunes with an interest which more estimable heroes fail sometimes to awaken.

The Baron of Dungannon was in the meantime dead, having been slain in a scuffle with his half-brother's followers—some said by his half-brother's own hand—previous to his father's death. His son, however, who was still a boy, was safe in England, and now appealed through his relations to the Government, and Sir Henry Sidney, who in Lord

Sussex's absence was in command, marched from Dublin to support the English candidate. At a meeting which took place at Dundalk Shane seems however to have convinced Sidney to some degree of the justice of his claim, and hostilities were delayed until the matter could be reported to the queen.

Upon Sussex's return from England they broke out again. Shane, however, had by this time considerably strengthened his position. Not only had he firmly established himself in the allegiance of his own tribe, but had found allies and assistants outside it. There had of late been a steady migration of Scotch islanders into the North of Ireland, "Redshanks" as they were familarly called, and a body of these, got together by Shane and kept as a body-guard, enabled him to act with unusual rapidity and decision. Upon Sussex attempting to detach two chieftains, O'Reilly of Brefny and O'Donnell of Tyrconnel, who owed him allegiance, Shane flew into Brefny and Tyrconnel, completely overawed the two waverers, and carried off Calvagh O'Donnell with his wife, who was a sister-in-law of the Earl of Argyle. The following summer he encountered Sussex himself and defeated him, sending his army flying terror-stricken back upon Armagh. This feat established him as the hero of the North. No army which Sussex could again gather together could be induced to risk the fate of its predecessor. The deputy was a poor soldier, feeble and vacillating in the field. He was no match for his fiery assailant; and after an attempt to get over the difficulty by suborning one Neil Grey to make away with the too successful

Shane, he was reduced to the necessity of coming to terms. An agreement was entered into with the assistance of the Earl of Kildare, by which Shane agreed to present himself at the English Court, and there, if he could, to make good his claims in person before the queen.

Few scenes are more picturesque, or stand out more vividly before our imagination than this visit of the turbulent Ulster chieftain to the capital of his unknown sovereign. As he came striding down the London streets on his way to the Palace, the citizens ran to their doors to stare at the redoubtable Irish rebel with his train of galloglasses at his heels—huge bareheaded fellows clad in saffron shirts, their huge naked axes swung over their shoulders, their long hair streaming behind them, their great hairy mantles dangling nearly to their heels. So attended, and in such order, Shane presented himself before the queen, amid a buzz, as may be imagined, of courtly astonishment. Elizabeth seems to have been equal to the situation. She motioned Shane, who had prostrated himself, clansman fashion upon the floor, to rise, "check'd with a glance the circle's smile," eyeing as she did so, not without characteristic appreciation, the redoubtable thews and sinews of this the most formidable of her vassals.

Her appreciation, equally characteristically, did not hinder her from taking advantage of a flaw in his safe-conduct to keep Shane fuming at her Court until he had agreed to her own terms. When at last he was allowed to return home it was with a sort of compromise of his claim. He was not to call himself

Earl of Tyrone—a distinction to which, in truth, he seems to have attached little importance—but he was allowed to be still the O'Neill, with the additional title of "Captain of Tyrone." To which the wits of the Court added—

> "Shane O'Neill, Lord of the North of Ireland;
> Cousin of St. Patrick. Friend of the Queen of England;
> Enemy of all the world besides."

Shane and his galloglasses went home, and for some two years he and the Irish Government left one another comparatively alone. He was supreme now in the North, and ruled his own subjects at his own pleasure and according to his own rude fashion. Sussex made another attempt not long after to poison him in a gift of wine, which all but killed him and his entire household, which still included the unhappy "Countess" and her yet more unhappy husband Calvagh O'Donnell, whom Shane kept securely ironed in a cell at the bottom of his castle. The incident did not add to his confidence in the Queen's Government, or incline him to trust himself again in their hands, which, all things considered, was hardly surprising.

That in his own wild way Shane kept the North in order even his enemies admitted. While the East and West of Ireland were distracted with feuds, and in the South Ormond and Desmond were wasting one another's country with unprecedented ferocity. Ulster was comparatively peaceable and prosperous. Chiefs who made themselves objectionable to Shane felt the weight of his arm, but that perhaps had not a little to say to this tranquillity. Mr. Froude—no exaggerated admirer of Irish heroes—tells us *apropos* of this time, " In O'Neill's county alone in Ireland were peasants prosperous, or life and property safe," though he certainly adds that their prosperity flourished largely upon the spoils collected by them from the rest of the country.

That Shane himself believed that he had so far kept his word with Elizabeth is pretty evident, for in a letter to her written in his usual inflated style about the notorious Sir Thomas Stukeley, he entreats that she will pardon the latter "for his sake and in the name of the services which he had himself rendered to England." Whether Elizabeth, or still more Sidney, were equally convinced of those services is an open question.

Shane's career however was rapidly running to a close. In 1565 he made a sudden and unexpected descent upon the Scots in Antrim, where, after a fierce combat, an immense number of the latter were slaughtered, a feat for which he again had the audacity to write to Elizabeth and assure her that it was all done in her service. Afterwards he made a descent on Connaught, driving back with him into his own country over 4000 head of cattle which he had captured. His game, however, was nearly at an end. Sir Henry Sidney was now back to Ireland, this time with the express purpose of crushing the rebel, and had marched into Ulster with a considerable force for that purpose. Shane, nevertheless, still showed a determined front. Struck up an alliance with Argyle, and wrote to France for instant aid to hold Ulster against Elizabeth, nay, in spite of his recent achievement, he seems to have even hoped to win the Scotch settlers over to his side. Sidney however was this time in earnest, and was a man of very different calibre from Sussex, in whom Shane had previously found so easy an antagonist. He marched right across Ulster, and entered Tyrconnel; reinstated the O'Donnells who had been driven thence by Shane; continued his march to Sligo, and from there to Connaught, leaving Colonel Randolph and the O'Donnells to hold the North and finish the work which he had begun.

Randolph's camp was pitched at Derry—not then the *protégée* of London, nor yet famed in story, but a mere insignificant hamlet, consisting of an old castle and a disused graveyard. It was this latter site that the unlucky English commander selected for his camp, with, as might be expected, the most disastrous results. Fever broke out, the water proved to be poisonous, and in a short time half the force were dead or dying, Randolph himself being amongst the former. An explosion which occurred in a magazine finished the disaster, and the scared survivors escaped in dismay to Carrickfergus. Local superstition long told tales of the fiery portents and miracles by which the heretic soldiery were driven from the sacred precincts which their presence had poluted.

With that odd strain of greatness which ran through her, Elizabeth seems to have accepted this disaster well, and wrote " comfortable words " to Sidney upon the subject. For the time being, however, the attack upon Shane devolved of necessity wholly upon his native foes.

Aided by good fortune they proved for once more than a match for him. Encouraged by the disaster of the Derry garrison, Shane made a hasty advance into Tyrconnel, and crossed with a considerable force over the ford of Lough Swilly, near Letterkenny. He found the O'Donnells, though fewer in number than his own forces, established in a strong position upon the other side. From this position he tried to drive them by force, but the O'Donnells were prepared, and Shane's troops coming on in disorder were beaten back upon the river. The tide had in the meantime risen, and there was therefore no escape. Penned between the flood and the O'Donnells, over 3000 of his men perished, many by drowning, but the greater number being hacked to death upon the strand. Shane himself narrowly escaped with his life by another ford.

The Hero of the North was now a broken man. Such a disaster was not to be retrieved. The English troops were again coming rapidly up. The victorious O'Donnells held all the country behind him. A French descent, even if it had come, would hardly have saved him now. In this extremity a desperate plan occurred to him. Followed by a few horsemen, and accompanied by the unhappy "Countess" who had so long shared his curious fortunes, he rode off to the camp of the Scotch settlers in Antrim, there to throw himself on their mercy and implore their support. It was an insane move. He was received with seeming courtesy, and a banquet spread in his honour. Lowering looks however were bent upon him from every side of the table. Captain Pierce, an English officer, had been busy the day before stirring up the smouldering embers of anger. Suddenly a taunt was flung out by one of the guests at the discomfited hero. Shane—forgetting perhaps where he was—sprang up to revenge it. A dozen swords and skeans blazed out upon him, and he fell, pierced by three or four of his entertainers at once. His body was then tossed into an old ruined chapel hard by, where the next day his head was hacked off by Captain Pierce, and carried to Sidney, who sent it to be spiked upon Dublin Castle. It was but too characteristic an end of an eminently characteristic career.

ST. PATRICK'S BELL.

XXV.

BETWEEN TWO STORMS.

BY 1566 Sir Henry Sidney became Lord-deputy, not now in the room of another, but fully appointed. With the possible exception of Sir John Perrot, he was certainly the ablest of all the viceroys to whom Elizabeth committed power in Ireland. Unlike others he had the advantage, too, of having served first in the country in subordinate capacities, and so earning his experience. He even seems to have been fairly popular, which, considering the nature of some of his proceedings, throws a somewhat sinister light, it must be owned, upon those of his successors and predecessors.

After the death and defeat of Shane the Proud a lull took place, and the new deputy took the opportunity of making a progress through the south and west of the island, which he reports to be all terribly wasted by war. Many districts, he says, "had but one-twentieth part of their former population." Galway, worn out by incessant attacks, could scarcely defend her walls. Athenry had but four respectable householders left, who "sadly presenting the rusty keys of their once famous town, confessed themselves unable to defend it."

SIR HENRY SIDNEY, LORD-DEPUTY FROM 1565 TO 1587.
(*From an engraving by Harding.*)

Sidney was one of the first to relinquish what had hitherto been the favourite and traditional policy of all English governors, that, namely, of playing one great lord or chieftain against another, and to attempt the larger task of putting down and punishing all signs of insubordination especially in the great. In this respect he was the political parent of Strafford, who acted the same part sixty years later. He had not—any more than his great successor—to reproach himself either with feebleness in the execution of his policy. The number of military executions that mark his progress seem to have startled his own coadjutors, and even to have evoked some slight remonstrance from Elizabeth herself. "Down they go at every corner!" the Lord-deputy writes at this time triumphantly in an account of his own proceedings, "and down, God willing, they shall go."

A plan for appointing presidents of provinces had been a favourite with the late deputy, Sussex, and was now revived. Sir Edward Fitton, one of the judges of the Queen's Bench, was appointed to the province of Connaught—a miserably poor appointment as it turned out; Sir John Perrot a little later to Munster; Leinster for the present the deputy reserved for himself. This done he returned, first pausing to arrest the Earl of Desmond and carrying him and his brother captive to Dublin and eventually to London, where according to the queen's orders he was to be brought in order that she might adjudicate herself in the quarrel between him and Ormond.

The two earls—they were stepson and stepfather by the way—had for years been at fierce feud, a feud which had desolated the greater part of the South of Ireland. It was a question of titles and ownership, and therefore exclusively one for the lawyers. The queen, however, was resolved that it should be decided in Ormond's favour. Ormond was "sib to the Boleyns;" Ormond had been the playmate of "that sainted young Solomon, King Edward," and Ormond therefore, it was quite clear, must know whether the lands were his own or not.

Against the present Desmond nothing worse was charged than that he had enforced what he considered his palatinate rights in the old, high-handed, time-immemorial fashion. His father, however, had been in league with Spain, and he himself was held to be contumacious, and had never been on good terms with any of the deputies.

On this occasion he had, however, surrendered himself voluntarily to Sidney. Nevertheless, upon his arrival he was kept a close prisoner, and upon attempting, some time afterwards, to escape, was seized, and only received his life on condition of surrendering the whole of his ancestral estates to the Crown, a surrender which happened to fit in very conveniently with a plan upon which the attention of the English Council was at that time turned.

The expenses of Ireland were desperately heavy, and Elizabeth's frugal soul was bent upon some plan for their reduction. A scheme for reducing the cost of police duty by means of a system of military colonies had long been a favourite one, and an opportunity now occurred for turning it into practice. A number of men of family, chiefly from Devonshire and Somersetshire, undertook to migrate in a body to Ireland, taking with them their own farm servants, their farm implements, and everything necessary for the work of colonization. The leader of these men was Sir Peter Carew, who held a shadowy claim over a vast tract of territory, dating from the reign of Henry II., a claim which, however, had been effectually disposed of by the lawyers. The scheme as it was first proposed was a truly gigantic one. A line was to be drawn from Limerick to Cork, and everything south of that line was to be given over to the adventurers. As for the natives, they said, they would undertake to settle with them. All they required was the queen's permission. Everything else they could do for themselves.

So heroic a measure was not to be put in force at once. As far as Carew's claims went, he took the matter, however, into his own hands by forcibly expelling the occupiers of the lands in question, and putting his own retainers into them. As fortune would have it, amongst the first lands thus laid hold of were some belonging to the Butlers, brothers of Lord Ormond, and therefore probably the only Irish landowners whose cry for justice was pretty certain just then to be heard in high quarters. Horrible tales of the atrocities committed by Carew and his band was reported by Sir Edward Butler, who upon his side was not slow to commit retaliations of the same sort. A spasm of anger, and a wild dread of coming contingencies flew through the whole South of Ireland. Sir James Fitzmaurice, cousin of the Earl of Desmond, broke into open rebellion; so did also both the younger Butlers. Ormond himself, who was in England, was as angry as the fiercest, and informed Cecil in plain terms that "if the lands of good subjects were not to be safe, he for one would be a good subject no longer."

It was no part of the policy of the Government to alienate the one man in Ireland upon whose loyalty they could depend at a pinch. By the personal efforts of the queen his wrath was at last pacified, and he agreed to accept her earnest assurance that towards him at least no injury was intended. This done, he induced his brothers to withdraw from the alliance, while Sir Henry Sidney, sword in hand, went into Munster and carried out the work of pacification in the usual fashion, burning villages, destroying the harvest, driving off cattle, blowing up castles, and hanging their garrisons in strings over the battlements. After which he marched to Connaught, leaving Sir Humphrey Gilbert behind him to keep order in the south.

For more than two years Sir James Fitzmaurice continued to hold out in his rocky fastness amongst the Galtese mountains. A sort of grim humour pervades the relations between him and Sir John Perrot, the new President of Munster. Perrot had boasted upon his arrival that he would soon "hunt that fox out of his hole." The fox, however, showed a disposition to take the part of the lion, sallying out unexpectedly, ravaging the entire district, burning Kilmallock, and returning again to his mountains before he could be interfered with. The following year he marched into Ulster, and on his way home burnt Athlone, the English garrison there looking helplessly on; joined the two Mac-an-Earlas as they were called, the sons of Lord Clanricarde, and assisted them to lay waste Galway, and so returned triumphantly across the Shannon to Tipperary. Once Perrot all but made an end of him, but his soldiers took that convenient opportunity of mutinying, and so baulked their leader of his prey. Another time, in despair of bringing the matter to any conclusion, the president proposed that it should be decided by single combat between them, a proposal which Fitzmaurice prudently resisted on the ground that though Perrot's place could no doubt readily be supplied, his own was less easily to fill, and that therefore for his followers' sake he must decline.

At last the long game of hide-and-seek was brought to an end by Sir James offering to submit, to which Perrot agreeing, he took the required oaths in the church of Kilmallock, the scene of his former ravages, and kissed the president's sword in token of his regret for "the said most mischievous part." This farce gravely gone through, he sailed for France, and Munster for a while was at peace. It was only a temporary lull though. The Desmond power was still too towering to be left alone, and both its defenders and the Government knew that they were merely indulging in a little breathing time before the final struggle.

XXVI.

THE DESMOND REBELLION.

THE tale of the great Desmond rebellion which ended only with the ruin of that house, and with the slaughter or starvation of thousands of its unhappy adherents, is one of those abortive tragedies of which the whole history of Ireland is full. Our pity for the victims' doom, and our indignation for the cold-blooded cruelty with which that doom was carried out, is mingled with a reluctant realization of the fact that the state of things which preceded it was practically impossible, that it had become an anomaly, and that as such it was bound either to change or to perish.

From the twelfth century onwards, the Desmond Geraldines had been lords, as has been seen, of a vast tract of Ireland, covering the greater part of Munster. Earlier and perhaps more completely than any of the other great Norman houses, they had become Irish chieftains rather than English subjects, and the opening of Elizabeth's reign found them still what for centuries past they had been, and with their power, within their own limits, little if at all curtailed. The Desmond

CAHIR CASTLE, TIPPERARY, TAKEN BY THE EARL OF ESSEX IN 1599.
(*From the "Pacata Hibernia."*)

of the day had still his own judges or Brehons, by whose judgment he professed to rule. He had still his own palatinate courts; he still collected his dues by force, driving away his clansmen's cattle, and distraining those who resisted him. Only a few years before this time, during an expedition of the kind, he and Ormond had encountered one another in the open field at Affane, upon the Southern Blackwater, each side flying their banners, and shouting their war cries as if no queen's representative had ever been seen or heard of.

Such a state of things, it was plain, could not go on indefinitely, would not indeed have gone on as long but for the confusion and disorder in which the country had always been plunged, and especially the want of all settled communication. The palatinate of Ormond, it is true, was theoretically in much the same state, but then Ormond was a keener sighted and a wiser man than Desmond, and knew when the times demanded redress. He had of late even made some effort to abolish the abominable system of "coyne and livery," although, as he himself frankly admits, he was forced to impose it again in another form not long afterwards.

Sir James meanwhile had left Ireland, and at every Catholic Court in Europe was busily pleading for aid towards a crusade against England. Failing in France, he appealed to Philip of Spain. Philip, however, at the moment was not prepared to break with Elizabeth, whereupon Fitzmaurice, undeterred by failure, presented himself next before the Pope. Here he was more successful, and preparations for the collection of a considerable force was at once set on foot, a prominent English refugee, Dr. Nicolas Saunders, being appointed to accompany it as legate.

Saunders, who had distinguished himself not long before by a violent personal attack against Elizabeth, threw himself heart and soul into the enterprise, and in a letter to Philip pointed out all the advantages that were to be won by it to the Catholic cause. "Men," he assured him, "were not needed." Guns, powder, a little money, and a ship or two with stores from Spain, and the whole country would soon be at his feet.

Although absurdly ignorant, as his own letters prove, of a country of which he had once been nominally king, Philip knew rather more probably about the circumstance of the case than Saunders, and he met these insinuating suggestions coldly. A fleet in the end was fitted out and sent from Civita Vecchia, under the command of an English adventurer Stukeley, the same Stukeley in whose favour we saw Shane O'Neill appealing to Elizabeth. Though it started for Ireland it never arrived there. Touching at Lisbon, Stukeley was easily persuaded to give up his first scheme, and to join Sebastian, king of Portugal, in a buccaneering expedition to Morocco, and at the battle of Alcansar both he and Sebastian with the greater part of their men were killed.

Fitzmaurice meanwhile had gone to Spain by land, and had there embarked for Ireland, accompanied by his wife, two children, Saunders, the legate, Allen, an Irish priest, a small party of Italians and Spaniards, and a few English refugees, and bringing with them a banner especially consecrated by the Pope for this service.

Their landing-place was Dingle, and from there they crossed to Smerwick, where they fortified the small island peninsula of Oilen-an-Oir, or "Gold Island," where they were joined by John and James Fitzgerald, brothers of the Earl of Desmond, and by a party of two hundred O'Flaherties from Iar Connaught, who, however, speedily left again.

But Desmond still vacillated helplessly. Now that the time had come he could not make up his mind what to do, or with whom to side. He was evidently cowed. His three imprisonments lay heavily upon his soul. He knew the power of England better too than most of his adherents, and shrank from measuring his own strength against it. What he did not realize was that it was too late now to go back. He had stood out for what he considered his own rights when it would have been more politic to have submitted, and now he wanted to submit when it was only too plain to all who could read the signs of the times that the storm was already upon him, and that no humility or late-found loyalty could avail to avert that doom which hung over his house.

If Desmond himself was slow to rise, the whole South of Ireland was in a state of wild tumult and excitement when the news of the actual arrival of Fitzmaurice and the legate became known. Nor in the south alone. In Connaught and the Pale the excitement was very little less. Kildare, like Desmond, held back fearing the personal consequences of rebellion, but all the younger lords of the Pale were eager to throw in their lot with

CATHERINE, THE "OLD" COUNTESS OF DESMOND.
(Reputed to have been killed at the age of 120 by a fall from a cherry tree.)
(*From the Burne Collection.*)

Fitzmaurice. Alone amongst the Irishmen of his day, he possessed all the necessary qualifications of a leader. He had already for years successfully resisted the English. He was known to be a man of great courage and tenacity, and his reputation as a general stood deservedly high in the opinion of all his countrymen.

That extraordinary good fortune, however, which has so often befallen England at awkward moments, and never more conspicuously than during the closing years of the sixteenth century, did not fail now. Fitzmaurice started for Connaught to encourage the insurrection which had been fast ripening there under the brutal rule of Sir Nicolas Malby, its governor. A trumpery quarrel had recently broken out between the Desmonds and the Mayo Bourkes, and this insignificant affair sealed the fate of what at one moment promised to be the most formidable rebellion which had ever assailed the English power in Ireland. At a place called Barrington's Bridge, not far from Limerick, where the little river Muckern or Mulkearn was then crossed by a ford, Fitzmaurice was set upon by the Bourkes. Only a few followers were with him at the time, and in turning to expostulate with one of his assailants, he was killed by a pistol shot, and fell from his horse. This was upon the 18th of August, 1579. From that moment the Desmond rising was doomed.

Desmond meanwhile still sat vacillating in his own castle of Askeaton, neither joining the rising, nor yet exerting himself vigorously to put it down. Malby, who had newly arrived from Connaught, took steps to hasten his decision. Ordering the earl to come to him, and the latter still hesitating, he marched against Askeaton, utterly destroyed the town up to the walls of the castle, burning everything in the neighbourhood, including the abbey and the tombs of the Desmonds, the castle itself only escaping through the lack of ammunition.

This hint seems to have sufficed. Desmond was at last convinced that the time for temporizing was over. He rose, and all Munster rose with him. Ormond was still in London, and hurried over to find all in disorder. Drury had lately died, and the only other English commander, Malby, was crippled for want of men, and had been obliged to retreat into Connaught. The new deputy, Sir William Pelham, had just arrived, and he and Ormond now proceeded to make a concerted attack. Advancing in two separate columns they destroyed everything which came in their way; men, women, children, infants, the old, the blind, the sick all alike were mercilessly slaughtered; not a roof, however humble, was spared; not a living creature that crossed their path survived to tell the tale. Lady Fitzmaurice and her two little children seem to have been amongst the number of these nameless and uncounted victims, for they were never heard of again. From Adare and Askeaton to the extreme limits of Kerry, everything perishable was destroyed. The two commanders met one another at Tralee, and from this point carried on their raid in unison, and returned, to Askeaton and Cork, leaving the whole country a desert behind them. There was little or no resistance. The Desmond clansmen were not soldiers; they were unarmed, or armed only with spears and skeans. They had just lost their only leader. They could do nothing but sullenly watch the progress of the English forces. Desmond, his two brothers, and the legate were already fugitives. The rising seemed to be all but crushed, when a new incident occurred to spur it into a momentary vitality.

Four Spanish vessels, containing 800 men, chiefly Italians, had managed to pass unperceived by the English admiral, Winter's, fleet, and to land at Smerwick, where they established themselves in Fitzmaurice's dismantled fort. They found everything in confusion. They had brought large supplies of arms for their Irish allies, but there were apparently no Irish allies to give them to. The legate and Desmond had first to be found, and now that arms had come, the Munster tribesmen had for the most part been killed or dispersed. Ormond and Pelham's terrible raid had done its work, and the heart of the rising was broken. The Pale, however, had now caught the fire, and though Kildare, its natural leader, still hung back, Lord Baltinglass and some of the bolder spirits flew to arms, and threw themselves into the Wicklow highlands where they joined their forces with those of the O'Byrnes, and were presently joined by Sir John of Desmond and a handful of Fitzgeralds.

Lord Grey de Wilton had by this time arrived in Ireland as deputy. Utterly inexperienced in Irish wars, he despised and underrated the capabilities of those opposed to him, and refused peremptorily to listen to the advice of more experienced men. Hastening south, his advanced guard was caught by Baltinglass and the other insurgents in the valley of Glenmalure. A well-directed fire was poured into the defile; the English troops broke, and tried to flee, and were shot down in numbers amongst the rocks.

Lord Grey had no time to retrieve this disaster. Leaving the Pale to the mercy of the successful rebels, he hastened south, and arrived in Kerry before Smerwick fort. Amongst the small band of officers who accompanied him on this occasion were Walter Raleigh and Edmund Spenser, both then young men, and both of them all but unknown to fame.

The English admiral, Winter, with his fleet had long been delayed by bad weather. When at length it arrived, cannon were landed and laid in position upon the sand hills. Next day the siege commenced. There was heavy firing on both sides, but the fort was soon found to be untenable. The garrison thereupon offered to capitulate, and an unconditional surrender was demanded. There being no alternative, these terms were accepted. Lord Grey thereupon "put in certain bands," under the command of Captain Raleigh. "The Spaniard," says Spenser, who was an eye-witness of the whole scene, "did absolutely yield himself, and the fort, and all therein, and only asked mercy." This, "it was not thought good," he adds, "to show them." They were accordingly all slaughtered in cold blood, a few women and priests who were with them hanged, the officers being reserved for ransom. "There was no other way," Spenser observes in conclusion, "but to make that end of them as thus was done." [1]

[1] "View of the State of Ireland," pp. 5, 11.

This piece of work satisfactorily finished, Grey returned rapidly to Dublin to crush the Leinster insurgents. Kildare and Delvin, though they had kept themselves clear of the rebellion, were arrested and thrown into prison. Small bands of troopers were sent into the Wicklow mountains to hunt out the insurgents. Baltinglass escaped to the Continent, but the two Eustaces his brothers, with Garrot O'Toole and Feagh McHugh were caught, killed, and their heads sent to Dublin. Clanricarde's two sons, the Mac-an-Earlas, were out in the Connemara mountains and could not be got at; but Malby again overran their country, burning houses and slaughtering without mercy. In Dublin, the Anglo-Irishmen of the Pale were being brought to trial for treason, and hung or beheaded in batches. Kildare was sent to England to die in the Tower. With the exception of the North, which on this occasion had kept quiet, the whole country had become one great reeking shambles; what sword and rope and torch had spared, famine came in to complete.

The Earl of Desmond was now a houseless fugitive, hunted like a wolf or mad dog through the valleys and over the mountains of his own ancestral " kingdom." His brothers had already fallen. Sir John Fitzgerald had been killed near Cork, and his body hung head downwards, by Raleigh's order, upon the bridge of the river Lee. The other brother, Sir James, had met with a similar fate. Saunders, the legate, had died of cold and exposure. Desmond alone escaped, time after time, and month after month. Hunted, desperate, in want of the bare necessities of life, he was still in his own eyes the Desmond, ancestral owner of nearly a hundred miles of territory. Never in his most successful period a man of any particular strength of character, sheer pride seems to have upheld him now. He scorned to make terms with his hated enemy, Ormond. If he yielded to any one, he sent word, it would be only to the queen herself in person. He was not given the chance. Hunted over the Slievemish mountains, with the price of £1,000 on his head, one by one the trusty companions who had clung to him so faithfully were taken and killed. His own course could inevitably be but a short one. News reached the English captain at Castlemain one night that the prey was not far off. A dozen English soldiers stole up the stream in the grey of the morning. The cabin where the Desmond lay was surrounded, the door broken in, and the earl stabbed before there was time for him to spring from his bed. The tragedy had now been played out to the bitterest end. As formerly with the Leinster Geraldines, so now with the Munster ones, of the direct heirs of the house only a single child was left, a feeble boy, afterwards known by the significant title of the " Tower Earl," with the extinguishing of whose sickly tenure of life the very name of Desmond ceases to appear upon the page of Irish history.

XXVII.

BETWEEN TWO MORE STORMS.

Two great risings against Elizabeth's power in Ireland had thus been met and suppressed. A third and a still more formidable one was yet to come. The interval was filled with renewed efforts at colonization upon a yet larger scale than before. Munster, which at the beginning of the Desmond rising had been accounted the most fertile province in Ireland, was now little better than a desert. Not once or twice' but many times the harvest had been burnt and destroyed, and great as had been the slaughter, numerous as were the executions, they had been far eclipsed by the multitude of those who had died of sheer famine.

Spenser's evidence upon this point has been often quoted, but no other words will bring the picture before us in the same simple, awful vividness; nor must it be forgotten that the man who tells it was under no temptation to exaggerate having himself been a sharer in the deeds which had produced so sickening a calamity.

"They were brought to such wretchedness," he says, "that any stony heart would rue the same. Out of every corner of the woods and glens, they came, creeping forth upon their hands, for their legs could not bear them. They looked like anatomies of death; they spoke like ghosts crying out of their graves. They did eat the dead carrions, where they did find them, yea and one another soon after, in as much as the very carcases they spared not to scrape out of their graves; and if they found a plot of watercresses or shamrocks, there they thronged as to a feast."

To replace this older population, thus starved, slaughtered, made away with by sword and pestilence with new colonists was the scheme of the hour. Desmond's vast estate, covering nearly six hundred thousand Irish acres, not counting waste land, had all been declared forfeit to the Crown. This and a considerable portion of territory also forfeit in Leinster was now offered to English colonists upon the most advantageous terms. No rent was to be paid at first, and for ten years the undertakers were to be allowed to send their exports duty free.

Many eminent names figure in the long list of these "undertakers"; amongst them Sir Walter Raleigh, Sir Christopher Hatton, Sir Wareham St. Leger, Edmund Spenser himself, Sir Thomas Norris, and others, all of whom received grants of different portions. But "the greater," says Leland, "their rank and consequence, the more were they emboldened to neglect the terms of their grant." Instead of completing their stipulated number of tenantry, the same persons often were admitted as tenants to different undertakers, and in the same seniory sometimes served at once as freeholder, leaseholder, and copyholder, so as to fill up the necessary number of each denomination.

The whole scheme of colonization proved, in short, a miserable failure. English farmers and labourers declined to come over in sufficient numbers. Those that did come left again in despair after a time. The dispossessed owners hung about, and raided the goods of the settlers whenever opportunity offered. The exasperation on both sides increased as years went on; the intruders becoming fewer and more tyrannical, the natives rapidly growing more numerous and more desperate. It was plain that the struggle would break out again at the first chance which offered itself.

That occasion arose not in Munster itself, but at the opposite end of the island. In Ulster the great southern rising had produced singularly little excitement. The chiefs for the most part had remained aloof, and to a great degree, loyal. The O'Donnells, who had been reinstated it will be remembered in their own territory by Sidney, kept the peace. Sir John Perrot, who after the departure of Grey became Lord-deputy, seems in spite of his severity to have won confidence. Old Tyrlough Luinagh who had been elected O'Neill at the death of Shane, seems even to have felt a personal attachment for him, which is humorously shown by his consenting on several occasions to appear at his court in English attire, habiliments which the Irish, like the the Scotch chiefs, objected to strongly as tending to make them ridiculous. "Prythee at least, my lord," he is reported to have said on one of these occasions, "let my chaplain attend me in his Irish

Sʳ John Perrot.
LORD-DEPUTY FROM 1584 TO 1588.

mantle, that so your English rabble may be directed from my uncouth figure and laugh at him."

Perrot, however, had now fallen under the royal displeasure; had been recalled and sent to the Tower, a common enough climax in those days to years spent in the arduous Irish service. His place was taken in 1588 by Sir William Fitzwilliam, who had held it nearly thirty years earlier. Fitzwilliam was a man of very inferior calibre to Perrot. Avaricious by nature he had been highly dissatisfied with the poor rewards which his former services had obtained. Upon making some remonstrance to that effect he had been told that the "position of an Irish Lord-deputy was an honourable one and should challenge no reward." Upon this hint he seems now to have acted. Since the Lord-deputy was not to be better rewarded, the Lord-deputy, he apparently concluded, had better help himself. The Spanish Armada had been destroyed a few years back, and ships belonging to it had been strewed in dismal wreck all along the North, South, and West coasts of Ireland. It was believed that much gold had been hidden away by the wretched survivors, and fired with the hope of laying his own hands upon this treasure, Sir William first issued a permission for searching, and then started himself upon the search. He marched into Ulster in the dead of winter, at considerable cost to the State, and with absolutely no result. Either, as was most likely, there was no treasure, or the treasure had been well hidden. Furious at this disappointment he arrested two upon his own showing of the most loyal and law-abiding landowners in Ulster, Sir Owen

McToole and Sir John O'Dogherty; dragged them back to Dublin with him, flung them into the castle, and demanded a large sum for their liberation.

This was a high-handed proceeding in all conscience, but there was worse to come ; it seemed as if the new deputy had laid himself out for the task of inflaming Ulster to the highest possible pitch of exasperation, and so of once more awakening the scarce extinguished flames of civil war. McMahon, the chief of Monaghan, had surrendered his lands, held previously by tanistry, and had received a new grant of them under the broad seal of England, to himself and his heirs male, and failing such heirs to his brother Hugh. At his death Hugh went to Dublin and requested to be put into possession of his inheritance. This Fitzwilliam agreed to, and returned with him to Monaghan, apparently for the purpose. Hardly had he arrived there, however, before he trumped up an accusation to the effect that Hugh McMahon had collected rents two years previously by force—the only method, it may be said in passing, by which in those unsettled parts of the country rents ever were collected at all. It was not an offence by law being committed outside the shire, and he was therefore tried for it by court-martial. He was brought before a jury of private soldiers, condemned, and executed in two days. His estate was thereupon broken up, the greater part of it being divided between Sir Henry Bagnall, three or four English officers, and some Dublin lawyers, the Crown reserving for itself a quit rent. Little wonder if the other Ulster landowners felt that their turn would come next, and that no loyalty could assure a man's safety so long as he had anything to lose that was worth the taking.

At this time the natural leader of the province was not Tyrlough Luinagh, who though called the O'Neill was an old man and failing fast. The real leader was Hugh O'Neill, son of Matthew the first Baron of Dungannon, who had been killed, it will be remembered, by Shane O'Neill, by whose connivance Hugh's elder brother had also, it was believed, been made away with. Hugh had been educated in England, had been much at Court, and had found favour with Elizabeth, who had confirmed him in the title of Earl of Tyrone which had been originally granted to his grandfather.

Tyrone was the very antipodes of Shane, the last great O'Neill leader. He was much more, in fact, of an English politician and courtier than an Irish chieftain. He had served in the English army; had fought with credit under Grey in Munster, and was intimately acquainted with all the leading Englishmen of the day. Even his religion, unlike that of most Irish Catholics of the day, seems to have sat but lightly upon him. Captain Lee, an English officer, quartered in Ulster, in a very interesting letter to the queen written about this time, assures her confidentially that, although a Roman Catholic, he "is less dangerously or hurtfully so than some of the greatest in the English Pale," for that when he accompanied the Lord-deputy to church " he will stay and hear a sermon ;" whereas they "when they have reached the church door depart as if they were wild cats." He adds, as a further recommendation, that by way of domestic chaplain he has at present but "one little cub of an English priest." Lord Essex in still plainer terms told Tyrone himself when he was posing as the champion of Catholicism : " Dost *thou* talk of a free exercise of religion! Why thou carest as little for religion as my horse."

Such a man was little likely to rush blindly into a rebellion in which he had much to lose and little to gain. He knew, as few Irishmen knew, the strength of England. He knew something also of Spain, and of what had come of trusting for help in that direction. Hitherto, therefore, his influence had been steadily thrown upon the side of order. He had more than once assisted the deputy to put down risings in the north, and, on the whole, had borne his part loyally as a dutiful subject of the queen.

Now, however, he had come to a point where the ways branched. He had to choose his future course, and there were many causes pushing him all but irresistibly into an attitude of rebellion. One of these was the arbitrary arrest of his brother-in-law Hugh O'Donnell, called Red Hugh, who had been induced to come on board a Government vessel by means of a friendly invitation, and had been then and there seized, flung under hatches, and carried off as a hostage to Dublin Castle, from which, after years of imprisonment, he had managed to escape by stealth in the dead of winter, and arrived half dead of cold and exposure in his own country, where his treatment had aroused the bitterest and most implacable hostility in the breast of all the clan. A more directly personal affair, and the one that probably more than any other single cause pushed Tyrone over the frontiers of rebellion, was the following. Upon the death of his wife he had fallen in love with Bagnall, the Lord-Marshall's, sister, and had asked for her hand. This Bagnall, for some reason, refused, whereupon Tyrone, having already won the lady's heart, carried her off, and they were married, an act which the marshall never forgave.

From that moment he became his implacable enemy, made use of his position to ply the queen and Council with accusations against his brother-in-law, and when Tyrone replied to those charges the answers were intercepted. It took some time to undermine Elizabeth's confidence in the earl, having previously had many proofs of his loyalty. It took some time, too, to induce Tyrone himself to go in the direction in which every event seemed now to be pushing him. Once, however, his mind was made up and his retreat cut off, he set to work at his preparations upon a scale which soon showed the Government that they had this time no fiery half-savage Shane, no incapable vacillating Desmond to deal with.

An alliance with the O'Donnells and the other chiefs of the north was his first step. He was by no means to be contented however with a merely provincial rising. He despatched messages to Connaught, and enlisted the Burkes in the affair; also the O'Connor of Sligo, the McDermot and other western chiefs. In Wicklow the O'Byrnes, always ready for a fray, agreed to join the revolt, with all that was left of the tribes of Leix and Offaly. These, with the Kavanaghs and others, united to form a solemn union, binding themselves to stand or fall together. To Spain Tyrone sent letters urging the necessity of an immediate despatch of troops. With the Pope he also put himself into communication, and the rising was openly and avowedly declared to be a Catholic one. Just at this juncture old Tyrlough Luinagh died, and Tyrone forthwith assumed the soul-stirring name of " The O'Neill " for himself. Let the Spanish allies only arrive in time and the rule of England it was confidently declared would shortly in Ireland be a thing of the past.

INITIAL LETTER FROM THE BOOK OF KELLS.

XXVIII.

BATTLE OF THE YELLOW FORD.

THE northern river Blackwater—there are at least three Blackwaters in Ireland—forms the southern boundary of the county Tyrone, which takes a succession of deep loops or elbows in order to follow its windings. At the end of the sixteenth century and for centuries previously it had marked the boundary of the territory of the chiefs or princes of Tyrone, and here, therefore, it was that the struggle between the earl and the queen's troops advancing from Dublin was necessarily fought out.

A good deal of desultory fighting took place at first, without any marked result upon either side. Tyrone got possession of the English fort which commanded the passage of the river, but it was in turn snatched from him by the lately arrived deputy, Lord Borough, who, however, was so severely wounded in the affray that he had to fall back upon Newry, where he not long afterwards died. Ireland was thus for the moment without a governor, and when after a temporary armistice, which Tyrone spun out as long as possible in hopes of his Spanish allies appearing, hostilities recommenced, the command devolved upon his brother-in-law and chief enemy, Sir Henry Bagnall.

Bagnall had between four and five thousand men under him, Tyrone having about the same number, or a little less. A few years previously a very small body of English troops had been able, as we have seen, to put to flight fully three times their own number of Irish. In the last dozen years circumstances however had in this respect very materially changed. The Desmond followers had been for the most part armed only with skeans and spears, much as their ancestors had been under Brian Boru. One English soldier armed with a gun could put to flight a dozen such assailants as easily as a sportsman a dozen wolves. Tyrone's men, on the other hand, were almost as well armed as their antagonists. Some of these arms had come from Spain, others had been purchased at high prices from the English soldiery, others again from dealers in Dublin and elsewhere. Man to man, and with equal arms, the Ulster men were fully equal to their assailants, as they were now about to prove.

In August, 1598, Bagnall advancing from the south found Tyrone engaged in a renewed attack upon the fort of Blackwater, which he had invested, and was endeavouring to reduce by famine. At the advance of Bagnall he withdrew however to a strong position a few miles from the fort, and there awaited attack.

The battle was not long delayed. The bitter personal hatred which animated the two leaders seems to have communicated itself to the men, and the struggle was unprecedently fierce and bloody. In

the thick of the engagement Bagnall, lifting his
beaver for a moment to get air, was shot through the
forehead and fell. His fall was followed by the complete
rout of his army. Fifteen hundred soldiers
and thirteen officers were killed, thirty-four flags
taken, and all the artillery, ammunition, and provisions
fell into the victor's hands. The fort immediately
surrendered, and the remains of the royal
army fled in confusion to Armagh, which shortly
abandoning, they again fled south, not attempting
to re-form until they took refuge at last in Dundalk.

Such an event as this could have but one result.
All the waverers were decided, and all determined to
throw in their lot with the victor. The talisman
of success is of more vital importance to an Irish
army than probably to any other, not because
the courage of its soldiers is less, but because their
imagination is greater, and more easily worked upon.
A soldier is probably better without too much imagination.
If the auguries are unfavourable he instinctively
augments, and exaggerates them tenfold.
Now, however, all the auguries were favourable.
Hope stood high. The Catholic cause had never
before showed so favourably. From Malin Head to
Cape Clear all Ireland was in a wild buzz of excitement,
and every fighting kern and gallowglass clutched
his pike with a sense of coming triumph.

XXIX.

THE ESSEX FAILURE.

ELIZABETH was now nearly seventy years of age, and this was her third war in Ireland. Nevertheless, she and her Council girded themselves resolutely to the struggle. There could at least be no half-hearted measure now; no petty pleas of economy; no penurious doling out of men and money. No one, not even the queen herself, could reasonably question the gravity of the crisis.

The next person to appear upon the scene is Robert Devereux, Earl of Essex, whose brilliant mercurial figure flashes for a moment across the wild and troubled stage of Ireland, only the next to vanish like some Will-o'-the-wisp into an abyss of darkness and disaster.

At that moment his fame as a soldier stood as high if not higher than that of any of his cotemporaries. If Raleigh or Sidney had more military genius, if his old rival, Sir Henry Norris, was a more capable general, the young earl had eclipsed all others in mere dash and brilliancy, and within the last few years had dazzled the eyes of the whole nation by the success of his famous feat in Spain, "The most

ASKEATON CASTLE, THE PROPERTY OF THE EARLS OF DESMOND.
(From the "Pacata Hibernia," of Sir G. Carew.)

brilliant exploit," says Lord Macaulay, "achieved by English arms upon the Continent, between Agincourt and Blenheim."

Essex was now summoned to the queen and given the supreme command in Ireland, with orders to proceed at once to the reduction of Tyrone. An army of 20,000 infantry and 1,300 horse were placed under him, and the title of Lord-Lieutenant conferred, which had not been granted to any one under royal blood for centuries. He started with a brilliant train, including a number of well-born volunteers, who gladly offered their services to the popular favourite, and landed in Dublin early in the month of April, 1599.

His disasters seem to have dated from the very moment of his setting foot on Irish soil. Contrary to orders, he had appointed his relative, the Earl of Southampton, to the command of the horse, an appointment which even after peremptory orders from the queen he declined to cancel. He went south when he was eagerly expected to go north. Spent a whole fortnight in taking the single castle of Cahir; lingered about the Limerick woods in pursuit of a nephew of the late Desmond, derisively known as the "Sugane Earl," or "Earl of Straw," who in the absence of the young heir had collected the remnants of the Desmond followers about him, and was in league with Tyrone. A few weeks later a party of English soldiers were surprised by the O'Byrnes in Wicklow, and fled shamefully; while almost at the same moment—by a misfortune which was certainly no fault of Essex's, but which went to swell the list of his disasters—Sir

Conyers Clifford, the gallant governor of Connaught, was defeated by the O'Donnells in a skirmish among the Curlew mountains, and both he and Sir Alexander Ratcliffe, the second in command, left dead upon the field.

Essex's very virtues and better qualities, in fact, were all against him in this fatal service. His natural chivalrousness, his keen perception of injustice, a certain elevation of mind which debarred him from taking the stereotyped English official view of the intricate Irish problem; an independence of vulgar motives which made him prone to see two sides of a question—even where his own interests required that he should see but one—all these were against him; all tended to make him seem vacillating and ineffective; all helped to bring about that failure which has made his six months of command in Ireland the opprobrium ever since of historians.

Even when, after more than one furiously reproachful letter from the queen, and after his army had been recruited by an additional force of two thousand men, he at last started for the north, nothing of any importance happened. He and Tyrone held an amicable and unwitnessed conference at a ford of the little river Lagan, at which the enemies of the viceroy did not scruple afterwards to assert that treason had been concocted. What, at any rate, is certain is that Essex agreed to an armistice, which, with so overwhelming a force at his own disposal, naturally awakened no little anger and astonishment. Tyrone's personal courtesy evidently produced a strong effect upon the other earl. They were old acquaintances, and Tyrone was no doubt able to place his case in strong relief. Essex, too, had that generosity of mind which made him inconveniently open to expostulation, and he knew probably well enough that the wrongs of which Tyrone complained were far from imaginary ones.

Another and a yet more furious letter from the queen startled him for his own safety. Availing himself of a permission he had brought with him to return should occasion seem to require it, he left the command in the hands of subordinates, flew to Dublin, and embarked immediately for England. What befel him upon his arrival is familiar to every school child, and the relation of it must not be allowed to divert us from following the further course of events in Ireland.

CINERARY URN.
(*From a Tumulus near Dublin.*)

XXX.

END OF THE TYRONE REBELLION.

A VERY different man from the chivalrous and quixotic Essex now took the reins. Charles Blount, Lord Mountjoy, had expected to be sent to Ireland when Essex had suddenly been appointed with ampler powers and a more extended consequence, and the disappointment had caused him to follow the course of that ill-starred favourite with ill-concealed jealousy to its tragic end.

Mountjoy was himself a man of cold, clear-sighted, self-seeking temperament. In almost all English histories dealing with this period his steadiness and solid unshowy qualities are contrasted with Essex's flightiness and failure, to the natural disadvantage of the latter. This, however, is not perhaps quite the last word upon the matter, and it is only fair to Essex that this should be realized.

No master hand has as yet made this special portion of Irish history his own. When he does so—if the keen edge of his perceptions, that is to say, has not been dimmed by too strong an earlier prepossession—we shall perhaps learn that the admitted failure of Essex, so disastrous to himself, was more honourable than the admitted and the well-rewarded success

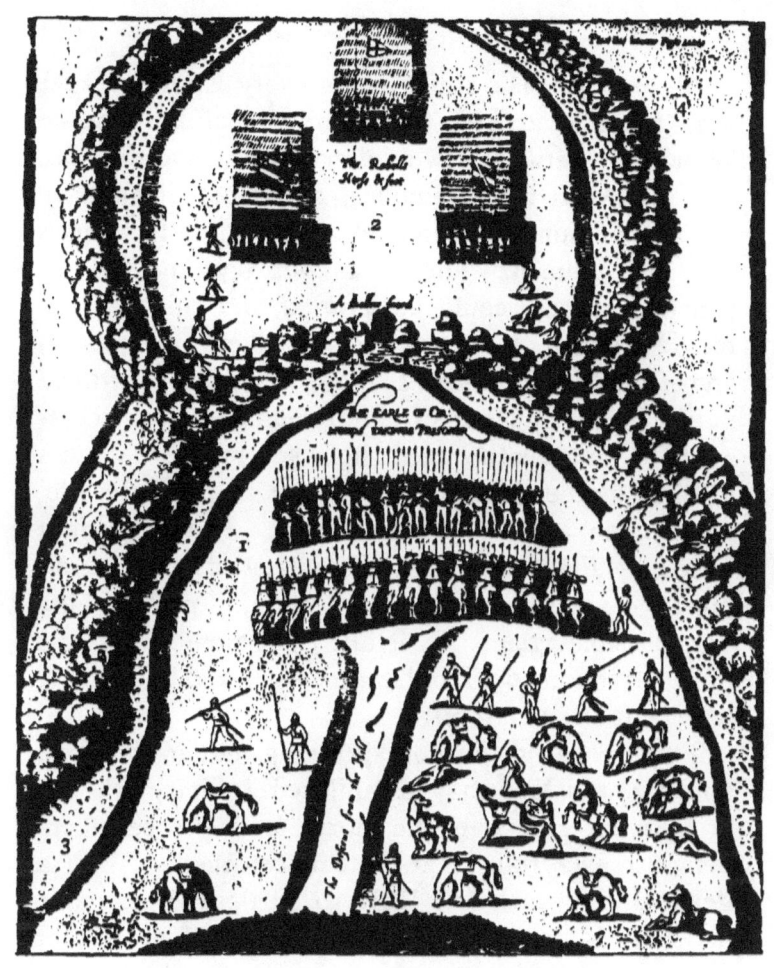

CAPTURE OF THE EARL OF ORMOND BY THE O'MORES.
(*From the " Pacata Hibernia," of Sir G. Carew.*)

1. Ormond and his followers ; 2. Rebel horse and foot ; 3. Rebels concealed in woods ; 4. Bogs.

of Mountjoy. The situation, as every English leader soon found, was one that admitted of no possible fellowship between two alternatives, success and pity; between the commonest and most elementary dictates of humanity, and the approval of the queen and her Council. There was but one method by which a success could be assured, and this was the method which Mountjoy now pushed relentlessly, and from which Essex's more sensitively attuned nature evidently shrank. The enemies it was necessary to annihilate were not so much Tyrone's soldiers, as the poor, the feeble, the helpless, the old, the women, and the little children. Famine—oddly called by Edward III. the "gentlest of war's handmaids"—was here the only certain, perhaps the only possible agent. By it, and by it alone, the germs of insurrection could be stamped out and blighted as it were at their very birth.

There was no further shrinking either from its application. Mountjoy established military stations at different points in the north, and proceeded to demolish everything that lay between them. With a deliberation which left little to be desired he made his soldiers destroy every living speck of green that was to be seen, burn every roof, and slaughter every beast which could not be conveniently driven into camp. With the aid of Sir George Carew, who enthusiastically endorsed his policy, and has left us a minute account of their proceedings, they swept the country before them. The English columns moved steadily from point to point, establishing themselves wherever they went, in strongly fortified outposts, from which points flying detachments were sent to ravage all the intermediate districts. The ground was burnt to the very sod ; all harvest utterly cleared away ; starvation in its most grisly forms again began to stalk the land ; the people perished by tens of thousands, and the tales told by eye-witnesses of what they themselves had seen at this time are too sickening to be allowed needlessly to blacken these pages.

As a policy nothing, however, could be more brilliantly successful. At the arrival of Mountjoy the English power in Ireland was at about the lowest ebb it ever reached under the Tudors. Ormond, the Lieutenant-General of the kingdom, had recently been taken captive by the O'Mores in Leinster, by whom he was held for an enormous ransom. Success, with all its glittering train, seemed to have gone bodily over to Tyrone. There was hardly a town in the whole island that remained in the hands of the Deputy. Before Mountjoy left all this was simply reversed. Not only had the royal power regained everything that had been snatched from it, but from sea to sea it stood upon a far firmer and stronger basis than it had ever done before.

Gradually, as the area over which the power of the Deputy and his able assistant grew wider and wider, that of the Tyrone fell away and faded. "The consequence of an Irish chieftain above all others," observes Leland most weightily, "depended upon opinion." A true success, that is to say, of which the gleaming plumes and trophies were not immediately visible, would have been far more disastrous than a real failure which could have been gilded over with a little delusive gleam of triumph. There was no gleams, real or imaginary, now. Tyrone was fast coming to the end of his resources. Surrender or starvation were staring him with ugly insistence in the face. The war, in fact, was on the point of dying out from sheer exhaustion, when a new element came to infuse momentary courage into the breasts of the insurgents. Fifty Spanish ships, with Don Juan d'Aguilar and three thousand soldiers on board, sailed into Kinsale harbour, where they proceeded to disembark and to occupy the town.

The instant the news of this landing reached Mountjoy, he, with characteristic vigour, hurried south with every soldier he could collect, so as to cut off the new arrivals before their allies had time to appear. Not a moment was lost. The Spaniards had landed on the 20th of September, 1601, and by the 23rd the first English soldiers appeared before the town, and before the end of the month Mountjoy and Carew had concentrated every man they had in Ireland around Kinsale.

Tyrone and O'Donnell also hurried south, but their progress was slower, and when they arrived they found their allies closely besieged on all sides. Taking advantage of a frost, which had made the bogs passable, O'Donnell stole round the English forces and joined another party of Spaniards who had just effected a landing at Castlehaven. All Kerry was now up in arms, under two local chiefs, O'Sullivan Beare and O'Driscoll. The struggle had resolved itself into the question which side could hold out longest. The English had the command of the sea, but were the

Spanish fleet to return their position would become to the last degree perilous. The game for Tyrone to play was clearly a waiting one. The Spaniards in Kinsale were weary however of their position, and urged him to try and surprise the English camp. Reluctantly, and against his own judgment, he consented. The surprise failed utterly. Information of it had already reached Carew. The English were under arms, and after a short struggle Tyrone's men gave way. Twelve hundred were killed, and the rest fled in disorder. The Spaniards thereupon surrendered Kinsale, and were allowed to re-embark for Spain; many of the Irish, including O'Donnell, accompanying them.

This was practically the end. Tyrone retreated to the north, collecting the remnants of his army as he went. Carew went south to wreak a summary vengeance upon O'Sullivan Beare, and the other Kerry insurgents, while Mountjoy, following in the wake of Tyrone, hemmed him gradually further and further north, repeating at the same time that wasting process which had already been only too brilliantly successful.

Tyrone had wit enough to see that the game was played out. On the other hand, Mountjoy was eager to bring the war to an end before the queen's death, now hourly expected. Terms were accordingly come to. The earl made his submission, and agreed to relinquish the title of O'Neill, and to abjure for ever all alliances with foreign powers or with any of the enemies of the Crown. In return he was to receive a full pardon for himself and his followers, and all his titles and lands were to be confirmed to him.

Two days after this the queen's death was announced. We are told that Tyrone, upon hearing of it, burst into a flood of tears. As he had been in arms against her up to a week before, it can scarcely have been a source of very poignant anguish. Probably he felt that had he guessed the imminence of the event he might have made better terms.

TARA BROOCH.

XXXI.

THE FLIGHT OF THE EARLS.

THIS was the last serious attempt on the part of any individual Irish chieftain to rise against the power of England. The next rebellion of which we shall hear arose from perfectly different causes, and was general rather than individual, grew indeed before its conclusion to the larger and more imposing dimensions of a civil war.

In one respect this six years' struggle was less productive of results than either of the two previous ones. At the end of it, Tyrone was still Tyrone; still the first of Irish subjects; his earldom and his ancestral possessions were still his. Nay, on crossing a few months later to England, and presenting himself to the English Court, he was graciously received by the new king, and seemed at first to stand in all respects as if no rebellion had been planned by him, or so nearly carried to a successful issue.

This state of things was a source, as may readily be conceived, of boundless rage to every English officer and official who had taken part in the late campaign. To see "that damnable rebel Tyrone" apparently in high honour caused them to rage and gnash their teeth. "How did I labour," cries one of them, "for that knave's destruction! I adventured perils by sea and land; went near to starving; eat horseflesh in Munster, and all to quell that man, who now smileth in peace at those who did hazard their lives to destroy him!"

Sheriffs, judges, commissioners, all the new officials who now began to hurry to the north, shared in this sentiment, and all had their eyes set in wrathful animosity upon Tyrone, all were bent in finding him out in some new treason. That after all that had happened he should end his days in peace and honour was not inconceivable merely, but revolting. He himself complained about this time that he could not "drink a full carouse of sack but the State in a few hours was advertised thereof." It was, in fact, an impossible situation. Tyrone was now sixty-two, and would have been willing enough therefore, in all probability, to rest and be thankful. It was impossible, he found, for him to do so. He was harassed by spies, plunged into litigation with regard to his seignorial rights, and whatever case was tried the lawyers invariably found for his antagonists. Rory O'Donnell, a brother of Red Hugh, who had been created Earl of Tyrconnel by James, was in a like case. Both were regarded with detestation by every official in Ireland; both had not long before had a price set on their heads; both, it was resolved by all in authority, would, sooner or later, therefore, begin to rebel again.

Whether they did so or not has never been satisfactorily decided. The evidence on the whole goes to prove that they did not. The air, however, was thick just then with plots, and in 1607, a mysterious and anonymous document, of which Lord Howth was reported to be the author, was found in the Dublin Council Chamber, which hinted darkly at conspiracies and perils of various kinds to the State, in which conspiracies Tyrone, it was equally darkly hinted, was in some manner or other involved.

It was rather a poor plot, still it served its turn. Tyrone received warning from his friends abroad that he was about to be arrested, and so serious was the peril deemed that a vessel was specially sent by them to bring him away in safety. He at once communicated with Tyrconnel, and after a short consultation the two Earls with their families resolved to take advantage of the opportunity and depart at once. This at the time, and indeed generally, has been construed into a proof of their guilt. It may have been so, but, on the other hand, it may just as well not have been. Had their innocence been purer than alabaster or whiter than the driven snow they were probably well advised under existing circumstances in not remaining to take their trial.

Right or wrong, with good reason or without good reason, they went, and after various wanderings reached Rome, where they were received with no little honour. Neither, however, long survived their exile. . Tyrconnel died the following year, and Tyrone some eight years later, a sad, blind, broken-hearted man.

Nothing could have been more convenient for the Government than this departure. Under the circumstances, it meant, of course, a forfeiture of all their estates. Had the extent of territory which personally belonged to the two exiles alone been confiscated, the proceeding, no doubt, would have been perfectly legitimate. Whatever had led to it, the fact of their flight and consequent renouncement of allegiance was undeniable, and the loss of their estates followed almost as a matter of course. A far more sweeping measure than this, however, was resolved upon. The lawyers, under the direction of the Dublin Government, so contrived matters as to make the area forfeited by the two earls cover no less a space than six entire counties, all of which were escheated to the Crown, regardless of the rights of a vast number of smaller tenants and sub-proprietors against whom no plea of rebellion, recently at all events could be urged; a piece of injustice destined, as will be seen, to bear tragic fruit a generation later.

The plan upon which this new plantation was carried out was projected with the utmost care by the lawyers, the Irish Government, and the king himself. The former plantations in Munster were an acknowledged failure, the reason assigned being the huge size of the grants made to the undertakers. Many of these resided in England, and merely drew their rents, allowing Irish tenants to occupy the land. This mistake was now to be avoided. Only tracts that could be managed by a resident owner were to be granted, and from these the natives were to be entirely drawn. "As well," it was gravely stated, "for their greater security, as to preserve the purity of the English language."

The better to ensure this important result marriages were strictly forbidden between the native Irish and the settlers, and in order to avoid that ever-formidable danger the former were ordered to remove themselves and their belongings bodily into certain reserved lands set apart for them.

The person who took the most prominent part in this undertaking was the well-known Sir John Davis, a distinguished lawyer and writer, who has himself left us a minute account of his own and his colleagues' proceedings. That those proceedings should have aroused some slight excitement and dismay amongst the dispossessed owners was not, perhaps, astonishing, even to those engaged in it. In some instances, the proprietors even went the length of bringing lawyers from Dublin, to prove that their estates could not legally be forfeited through the attainder of the earls, and to plead, moreover, the king's recent proclamation which undertook to secure to the inhabitants their possessions. In reply to this, Sir John Davis and the other commissioners issued another proclamation. "We published," he says, "by proclamation in each county, what lands were to be granted to British undertakers, what to servitors, and what to natives, to the end that the natives should remove from the precincts allotted to the Britons, whereupon a clear plantation is to be made of English and Scottish without Irish." With regard to the rights of the king he is still more emphatic. "Not only," he says, "his Majesty may take this course lawfully, but he is bound in conscience to do so."

These arguments, and probably still more the evident

uselessness of any resistance, seem to have had their effect. The discomfited owners submitted sullenly, and withdrew to the tracts allotted to them. In Sir John Davis' own neat and incisive words, "The natives seemed not unsatisfied in reason, though they remained in their passions discontented, being grieved to leave their possessions to strangers, which they had so long after their manner enjoyed."

DOORWAY OF ST. CAEMIN'S CHURCH, INISMAIN, ARAN ISLES.

XXXII.

THE FIRST CONTESTED ELECTION.

IN 1613, it was resolved by the Government to summon an Irish Parliament, for the purpose of giving legality to their recent proceedings in Ulster, and also to pass an Act of formal attainder upon the two exiled earls.

The great difficulty felt by the executive was how to secure an adequate Protestant majority. Even after the recent large introduction of Protestants the great mass of the freeholders, and nearly all the burgesses in the towns were still Roman Catholics. In the Upper House, indeed, the nineteen Protestant bishops and five temporal lords who were Protestant, made matters safe. The House of Commons, therefore, was the rub. Carew and Sir John Davis set their wits energetically to this problem. The new towns, or rather agricultural forts, in Ulster were all converted into Corporations, and each given the power of returning two members. The Pale and the Leinster towns, though loyal, were nearly all Catholic. In the west, except at Athlone, there was "no hope," the president reported, "of any Protestants." From some of the other garrison towns better things were hoped for, still there was not a little alarm on the part of the Government that the numbers might still come short.

On the other side the Catholics were equally alive to the situation, and equally keen to secure a triumph. A belief prevailed, too, all over Ireland, that the object of summoning this Parliament was to carry out some sweeping act of confiscation, and this naturally added to the excitement. For the first time in Irish history a genuinely contested election took place. Both parties strained every nerve, both felt their future interests to depend upon the struggle. When at last all the members were collected it was found that the Government had a majority, though a narrow one, of twenty-four. Barely, however, had Parliament assembled, before a violent quarrel broke out over the election of a speaker; the Catholic party denouncing the irregularity by means of which many of the elections had been carried, and refusing therefore to consider themselves bound by the decision of the majority. Sir John Davis had been elected speaker by the supporters of the Government, but, during the absence of the latter in the division lobby, the recusants placed their own man, Sir John Everard, in the chair, and upon the return of the others a hot scuffle ensued between the supporters of the two Sir Johns, each side vehemently supporting the claims of its own candidate. In the end, "Mr. Treasurer and Mr. Marshall, two gentlemen of the best quality," according to a "Protestant declaration" sent to England of the whole occurrence, "took Sir John Davis by the arms, and lifting him from the ground, placed him in the chair upon Sir John Everard's lap, requiring the latter to come forth of the chair; which, he obstinately refusing, Mr. Treasurer, the Master of the Ordinance, and others, whose places were next the chair, laid their hands gently upon him, and removed him out of the chair, and placed Sir John Davis therein."

The gravity with which we are assured of the gentleness of these proceedings is delightful. The recusants, with Sir John Everard at their head, departed we are further told "in most contentious manner" out of the House. Being asked why they did not return, they replied that "Those within the House are no House, and the Speaker is no Speaker; but we are the House, and Sir John Everard is our Speaker."[1]

Not being able to be otherwise settled, the quarrel was at last referred to the king, and representatives of both sides went to England to plead their cause. In the end twelve of the new elections were found to have been so illegally carried that they had perforce to be cancelled, but Sir John Davis was at the same time confirmed in the Speakership.

After this delay the House at last got to work. A formal Act of attainder was passed upon Tyrone, Tyrconnel, and some of the other Ulster landowners. Every portion of Ireland was next made into shireland, and the last remnants of the Brehon law abolished. Upon the other hand, the statutes of Kilkenny was at length and finally repealed. Henceforth English and Irish were alike to be admitted to plead their own cause in the courts of law.

[1] Lodges, "Desiderata Curiosa Hibernica," pp. 410-411.

XXXIII.

OLD AND NEW OWNERS.

THE zeal for Irish colonization had by no means subsided after the Ulster settlement had been established; on the contrary, it was the favourite panacea of the hour, especially in the eyes of the king himself. After one such resounding success, why, it was asked, not extend so evident a blessing to the rest of Ireland? "A commission to inquire into defective titles" was set on foot, whose duty it was to collect evidence as to the condition of estates, and to inquire into the titles of owners. The pipe rolls in Dublin and the patents, kept in the Tower of London were alike eagerly ransacked, and title flaws found to be discoverable with the most delightful facility. There was a strong feeling too about this time in England that something good was to be made of Ireland. When tens of thousands of acres were to be had almost for the asking, who could be so slow or so mean-spirited as to hang back from doing so.

Something like a regular stampede of men ambitious to call themselves undertakers, began to cross over from the larger to the smaller island. Nor was the Government anxious to check this spirited impulse. In Wexford alone over 60,000 acres had been discovered by the lawyers to belong to the king, and of these a large portion were now settled with English undertakers. In Longford, Leitrim, Wicklow, and many other parts of Leinster, it was the same. Even where the older proprietors were not dispossessed heavy fines were levied in return for fresh grants. No proof of recent surrender or former agreement was allowed to count, and so ingeniously was the whole scheme carried out, and so inextricable was the jungle of legal technicalities in which it was involved, that what in reality was often sheer confiscations sounded like the most equitable of judicial arrangements.

The case of the Connaught landowners is particularly characteristic, and as space dwindles rapidly, may serve as an example of the rest. Nearly all the Connaught gentry, native and Norman alike, had surrendered their estates either to Elizabeth or to her father, and had received them back again upon new terms. Legal transfer, however, was so little understood, and the times were so rough and wild, that few had received patents, and title-deeds were all but unknown. In James I.'s reign this omission was rectified and patents duly made out, for which the landowners paid a sum little short of £30,000, equal to nearly £300,000 at the present day. These new patents, however, by an oversight of the clerks in Chancery, were neglected to be enrolled, and upon this plea fresh ones were called for, and fresh fees had to be paid by the landowners. Further it was announced that owing to the omission — one over which the owners, it is clear, had no control—all the titles had become defective, and all the lands had lapsed to the Crown. The other three provinces having by this time received plantations, the Connaught landowners were naturally not slow to perceive the use that might be made of so awkward a technical flaw. To appeal against the manifest injustice of the decision was of little avail, but a good round sum of money into the king's own hands was known to rarely come amiss. They agreed accordingly to offer him the same sum that would have fallen to his share had the plantations been carried out. This was accepted and another £10,000 paid, and the evil day thus for a while, but only, as will be seen, for a while averted.

Charles's accession awakened a good many hopes in Ireland, the Catholic party especially flattering themselves that a king who was himself married to one of their faith would be likely to show some favour to his Catholic subjects. In this they found their mistake, and an attempt to open a Catholic college in Dublin was speedily put down by force. In other directions a certain amount of leniency was, however, extended to recusants, and Lord Falkland, who a few years before had succeeded Sir Oliver St. John as deputy, was a man of conspicuous moderation and tolerance. In 1629, however, he resigned, worn out like so many others before and after him by the difficulties with which he had to contend, and not long afterwards a man of very different temperament and widely different theories of government came to assume the reins.

XXXIV.

STRAFFORD.

IN 1632, Wentworth—better known as Strafford—arrived in Ireland, prepared to carry out his motto of "Thorough." Only three years before, he had been one of the foremost orators in the struggle for the Petition of Right. The dagger of Fenton had turned him from an impassioned patriot and constitutionalist into a vehement upholder of absolutism. His revolt had been little more than a mask for his hostility to the hated favourite Buckingham, and when Buckingham's murder cleared the path to his ambition, Wentworth passed, apparently without a struggle, from the zealous champion of liberty to the yet more zealous champion of despotic rule.

He arrived in Ireland as to a conquered country, and proceeded promptly to act upon that understanding. His chief aim was to show that a parliament, properly managed, could be made not a menace, but a tool in the hand of the king. With this end he summoned an Irish one immediately upon his arrival, and so managed the elections that Protestants and Catholics should nearly equally balance one another. Upon its assembling, he ordered

THOMAS WENTWORTH, EARL OF STRAFFORD, 1641.

peremptorily that a subsidy of £100,000, to cover the
debts to the Crown, should be voted. There would,
he announced, be a second session, during which
certain long-deferred "graces" and other demands
would be considered. The sum was obediently voted,
but the second session never came. The parliament
was abruptly dissolved by the deputy, and did not
meet again for nearly four years.

The Connaught landlords were the next whom he
took in hand. We have seen in the last chapter that
they had recently paid a large sum to the Crown, in
order to ward off the dangers of a plantation. This
did not satisfy Wentworth. Their titles were again
called into question. He swept down in person into
the province, with the commissioners of plantations
at his heels; discovered, to his own complete satisfaction, that *all* the titles of all the five western counties
were defective, and that, as a natural consequence, all
lapsed to the Crown. The juries of Mayo, Sligo,
and Roscommon were overawed into submission, but
the Galway jury were obstinate, and refused to dispossess the proprietors. Wentworth thereupon took
them back with him to Dublin, summoned them
before the Court of the Castle Chamber, where they
were sentenced to pay a fine of £4,000 each, and the
sheriff £1000, and to remain in prison until they had
done so. The unfortunate sheriff died in prison.
Lord Clanricarde, the principal Galway landlord, died
also shortly afterwards, of anxiety and mortification.
The others submitted, and were let off by the triumphant deputy with the surrender, in some cases, of
large portions of their estates, in others of heavy fines.

By these means, and others too long to enter into here, he contrived to raise the annual Irish revenue to a surplus of £60,000, with part of which he proceeded to set on foot and equip an army for the king of 10,000 foot and 1,000 horse, ready to be marched at a moment's notice. This part of the programme was intended as a menace less against Ireland than England. Charles was to be absolute in both islands, and, to be so, his Irish subjects were to help him to coerce his English ones.

Let us, however, be just. Strafford was a born tyrant—worse, he was the champion of an absolutism of the most odious type conceivable, one which, if successful, would have been a death-blow to English liberty. But he was also a born ruler. No petty tyrants flourished under his sway. His hand was like iron upon the plunderers, the pluralists, the fraudulent officials, gorged with their ill-gotten booty What he did, too, he did well. If he struck, he could also protect. He ruthlessly suppressed the infant woollen trade, believing that it might in time come to be a rival to the English one, but he was the founder of the linen trade, and imported Flemish weavers to teach it, and the best flax-seed to sow in the fields. He cleared the sea of the pirates who swarmed along the coasts, and had recently burnt the houses and carried off the inhabitants of several villages. The king's authority once secured he was anxious to secure to the mass of the people, Catholic as well as Protestant, a just and impartial administration of the law. No one in Ireland, he was resolved, should tyrannize except himself.

JACOBUS USSERIUS, ARCHIEPISCOPUS ARMACHANUS,
TOTIUS HIBERNIÆ PRIMAS

He and Laud, the primate, were close allies, and both were bent upon bringing the Church of Ireland to an absolute uniformity with that of England, and, with this object, Wentworth set a Court of High Commission to work to root out the Presbyterian ministers and to suppress, as far as possible, dissent. The Irish bishops and episcopalian clergy were, with hardly an exception, Low Churchmen, with a leaning to Calvinism, and, upon these also his hand was heavy. His regard for the Church by no means stood in his way either in his dealings with individual churchmen. He treated the Primate Ussher—one of the most venerated names in all Irish history—with marked contempt; he rated the Bishop of Killaloe upon one occasion like a dog, and told him that "he deserved to have his rochet pulled over his ears;" boasting afterwards, to his correspondent, of how effectually he had "warmed his old sides."

In another letter to Laud, we get a graphic and rather entertaining account of his dealings with Convocation. The Lower House, it seems, had appointed a select committee, which had drawn up a book of canons upon the lines of what were known as the "Nine Articles of Lambeth." Wentworth was furious. "Instantly," he says, "I sent for Dean Andrews, that reverend clerk, who sat, forsooth, in the chair at this committee, and required him to bring along the aforesaid book of canons; this he obeyed, . . . but when I came to open the book, I confess I was not so much moved since I came into Ireland. I told him certainly not a Dean of Limerick, but an Ananias had sat in the chair at that committee, and sure

I was that Ananias had been there in spirit if not in body."[1]

The unhappy Ananias naturally submitted at once to the terrible deputy, and, although Archbishop Ussher and most of the bishops defended the attacked canons, Wentworth carried his point by a sheer exercise of power. Throwing the list of canons already drawn out aside, he drew up another of his own composition, and forced the Convocation to accept it. "There were some hot spirits, sons of thunder, amongst them," he tells Laud boastfully, "who moved that they should petition me for a free synod, but, in fine, they could not agree among themselves who should put the bell about the cat's neck, and so this likewise vanished."[2] The cat, in truth, was a terrible one to bell!

But the career of the master of Ireland was nearing its end. By the beginning of 1640 the Scotch were up in arms, and about to descend in force upon England. The English Puritans, too, were assuming a hostile attitude. Civil war was upon the point of breaking out. Charles summoned Wentworth over in hot haste from Ireland, and it was decided between them that the newly-organized Irish forces were to be promptly employed against the Scotch rebels. With this purpose Wentworth—now with the long-desired titles of Earl of Strafford and Lord-Lieutenant of Ireland—hurried back to make the final arrangements. Fresh subsidies were obtained from the ever-subservient Irish parliament; more recruits

[1] Earl of Strafford's "Letters and Despatches," vol. i. p. 342.
[2] Ibid.

were hastily summoned, and came in readily; the army was put under the command of the young Earl of Ormond, and Strafford once more returned to England. He did so only to find all his calculations upset. A treaty had been made in his absence with the Scots; the Long Parliament had assembled, and the fast-gathering storm was about to break in thunder over his own head. He was impeached. Witness after witness poured over from Ireland, all eager to give their evidence. Representatives even of the much-aggrieved Connaught landlords—though their wrongs did not perhaps count for much in the great total—were there to swell the tide. He was tried for high treason, condemned and executed. In England the collapse of so great and so menacing a figure was a momentous event. In Ireland it must have seemed as the very fall of Lucifer himself!

SHRINE OF ST. PATRICK'S BELL.

XXXV.

'FORTY-ONE.

STRAFFORD'S fall and death would alone have rendered this year, 1641, a memorable one in Irish history. Unhappily it was destined to be made yet more so; few years, indeed, in that long, dark bead-roll are perhaps as memorable, both from what it brought forth at the time, and, still more, from what was afterwards to follow from it.

The whole country, it must be remembered, was in a state of the wildest and most irrepressible excitement. The fall of such a ruler as Strafford—one under whose iron will it had for years lain as in a vice—would alone have produced a considerable amount of upheaval and confusion. The army collected by him, and mainly recruited by Catholics, was regarded with strong disfavour both by Irish Protestants and by the English Parliament, and Charles, much against his will, had been forced to disband it, and the arms had been stored in Dublin Castle. The men, however, remained, and among the leading Irish as well as English royalists there was a strong desire that they should be kept together, so as to serve if required in the fast nearing struggle.

Nor was this all. Strafford's persecution of the Presbyterians had done its work, and the feeling between them and the Irish Church party had been greatly embittered. Amongst the Catholics, too, the most loyal even of the gentry had been terror-stricken by his confiscations. No one knew how long his property would remain his own, or upon what pretence it might not next be taken from him. Add to these the long-gathering passion of the dispossessed clans in the north, and that floating element of disaffection always ready to stir, and it will be seen that the materials for a rebellion were ready laid, and needed only a spark to ignite them.

As usually happens in rebellions the plans of the more prudent were thwarted by the impetuosity of the more violent spirits. While Ormond, Antrim, and the barons of the Pale were communicating with the king, and considering what were the best steps to take, a plot had been formed without them, and was now upon the point of exploding.

Two men, Rory or Roger O'Moore, one of the O'Moores of Leix, and Sir Phelim O'Neill, a connection of the Tyrones, were its main movers, and were joined by Lord Maguire, a youth of about twenty-two, Hugh McMahon, the Bishop of Clogher, and a few other gentlemen, belonging chiefly to the septs of the north. The plan was a very comprehensive one. They were to seize Dublin Castle, which was known to be weakly defended; get out the arms and powder, and redistribute them to the disbanded troops; at the same time, seize all the forts and garrison towns in the north; turn all the Protestant settlers adrift—though it was at first stipulated without killing or otherwise injuring them—take possession of all the country houses, and make all who declined to join in the rising prisoners.

Never, too, was plot more nearly successful. October the 23rd was the day fixed, and up to the very evening before no hint of what was intended had reached the Lords Justices. By the merest chance, and by an almost inconceivable piece of carelessness on the part of the conspirators, it was divulged to a man called Conolly, a Presbyterian convert, who went straight and reported it to Sir William Parsons. The latter at first declined to believe in it, but, Conolly persisting in his story, steps were taken to strengthen the defences. The guard was doubled; Lord Maguire and Hugh McMahon were arrested at daybreak next morning; the rest, finding that their stroke had missed, fled with their followers.

If this part of the rising failed, the other portions, unhappily, were only too successful. The same day the Protestant settlers in Armagh and Tyrone, unsuspicious of any danger, were suddenly set upon by a horde of armed or half-armed men, dragged out of their houses, stripped to the skin, and driven, naked and defenceless, into the cold. No one dared to take them in, every door was shut in their faces, and though at first no actual massacre seems to have been intended, hundreds perished within the first few days of exposure, or fell dead by the roadside of famine and exhaustion.

Sir Phelim O'Neill—a drunken ruffian for whom even the most patriotic historian finds it hard to say a redeeming word—was here the ringleader. On the same day—the 23rd of October—he got possession of the fort of Charlemont, the strongest position in the new plantation, by inviting himself to dinner with Lord Caulfield, the governor, and suddenly seizing him prisoner. Dungannon, Mountjoy, and several of the other forts, were also surprised and taken. Enniskillen, however, was saved by its governor, Sir William Cole, and Derry, Coleraine, and Carrickfergus, had also time fortunately to shut their gates, and into these as many of the terrified settlers as could reach them crowded.

These were few, however, compared to those who could find no such haven of refuge. Sir Phelim O'Neill, mad with excitement, and intoxicated with the sudden sense of power, hounded on his excited and undisciplined followers to commit every conceivable act of cruelty and atrocity. Disappointed by the failure of the more important part of the rising, and furious at the unsuccess of his attempts to capture the defended towns, he turned like a bloodhound upon those unfortunates who were within his grasp. Old Lord Caulfield was murdered in Sir Phelim's house by Sir Phelim's own foster-brother; Mr. Blaney, the member for Monaghan, was hanged; and some hundreds of the inhabitants of Armagh, who had surrendered on promise of their lives, were massacred in cold blood. As for the more irregular murders committed in the open field upon helpless, terrified creatures, powerless to defend themselves, they are too numerous to relate, and there is happily no purpose to be gained in repeating the harrowing details. The effect produced by the condition of the survivors upon those who saw them arrive in Dublin and elsewhere—spent, worn out, frozen with cold, creeping along on hands and knees, and all but at the point of death—was evidently ineffaceable, and communicates itself vividly to us as we read their descriptions.

The effect of cruelty, too, is to produce more cruelty; of horrors like these to breed more horrors; till the very earth seems covered with the hideous brood, and the most elementary instincts of humanity die away under their poisonous breath. So it was now in Ireland. The atrocities committed upon one side were almost equalled, though not upon so large a scale by the other. One of the first actions performed by a Scotch force, sent over to Carrickfergus by the king, was to sally out like demons and mercilessly slaughter some thirty Irish families living in Island Magee, who had nothing whatever to say to the rising. In Wicklow, too, Sir Charles Coote, sent to suppress a disturbance amongst the O'Byrnes and O'Tooles, perpetrated atrocities the memory of which still survives in the region, and which, for coldblooded, deliberate horror almost surpass those committed in the north. The spearing by his soldiery of infants which had hardly left the breast he himself openly avowed, and excused upon the plea that if allowed to survive they would grow up to be men and women, and that his object was to extirpate the entire brood.

Here and there a faint gleam falls upon the blackened page. Bedell, the Bishop of Kilmore, who had won the reverence even of his fiercest opponents, was allowed to remain free and undisturbed in the midst of the worst scenes of carnage and outrage ; and when a few months later he died, was followed weeping to the grave by many who had been foremost in the work of horror. As to the number of those who actually perished, either from exposure, or by the hands of assassins, it has been so variously estimated that it seems to be all but impossible to arrive at anything like exact statistics. The tale was black enough as it really stood, but it was made blacker still by rumour and exaggeration. The real number of the victims grew to tenfold in the telling. Four thousand murdered swelled to forty thousand ; and eight thousand who died of exposure, to eighty thousand. Even now every fresh historian sets the sum total down at a different figure. Take it, however, at the very lowest, it is still a horrible one. Let us shut our eyes and pass on. The history of those days remains in Carlyle's words, " Not a picture, but a huge blot : an indiscriminate blackness, one which the human memory cannot willingly charge itself with ! "

XXXVI.

THE WATERS SPREAD.

So far the rising had been merely local. It was now to assume larger dimensions. Although shocked at the massacre, and professing an eager desire to march in person to punish its perpetrators, Charles' chief aim was really that terms should be made with the leaders, in order that their troops might be made available for service in England.

In Dublin courts-martial were being rapidly established. All Protestants were given arms; all strangers were ordered to quit the city on pain of death; Sir Francis Willoughby was given the command of the castle; Sir Charles Coote made military governor of the city. Ormond was anxious to take the field in the north before the insurrection spread further, before they had time, as he said, to "file their pikes." This the Lords Justices however refused to allow. They were waiting for orders from the English Parliament, with which they were in close alliance, and were perfectly willing to let the revolt spread so that the area of confiscated lands might be the greater.

None of the three southern provinces had as yet risen.

in the Pale the Anglo-Norman families were warm in their expressions of loyalty, and appealed earnestly to the Lords Justices to summon a parliament, and to distribute arms for their protection. This last was refused, and although a parliament assembled it was instantly prorogued, and no measures were taken to provide for the safety of the well-disposed. Early in December of the same year Lords Fingal, Gormanstown, Dunsany, and others of the principal Pale peers, with a large number of the local gentry, met upon horseback, at Swords, in Meath, to discuss their future conduct. The opposition between the king and Parliament was daily growing fiercer. The Lords Justices were the nominees of Parliament; to revolt against them was not, therefore, it was argued, to revolt against the king. Upon December 17th they met again in yet larger numbers, upon the hill of Crofty, where they were met by some of the leaders of the north. Rory O'Moore,—a man of no little address, who was personally clear of the worst stain of the massacres, and who had lately issued a proclamation declaring that he and his followers were in arms, not against Charles, but the Parliament—was the principal speaker on this occasion, and his arguments appear to have decided the waverers. They agreed unanimously to throw in their lot with their co-religionists. From that moment the rising had become a national one. The whole island was soon in arms. Munster followed Leinster, and Connaught shortly afterwards followed Munster. Lords Thomond, Clanricarde, and a few others stood out, but by the end of the year, with the exception of Dublin, Drogheda, Cork, Galway, Enniskillen, Derry, and some few other towns, all Ireland was in the hands of the rebels.

Even then the Lords Justices seem to have but little realized the gravity of the crisis. They occupied their time chiefly in preparing indictments, and cheerfully calculating the fast-growing area of land open to confiscation. In vain Ormond entreated to be allowed to proceed against Sir Phelim O'Neill. They steadily declined to allow him to leave the neighbourhood of Dublin.

The northern rising had by this time nearly worn itself out by its own excesses. Sir Phelim's efforts to take Drogheda were ludicrously unavailing, and he had been forced to take his ragged rabble away without achieving anything. Regarded as an army it had one striking peculiarity — there was not a single military man in it! Sir Phelim himself had been bred to the law; Rory O'Moore was a self-taught insurgent who had never smelt powder. They had no arms, no officers, no discipline, no organization of any kind; what was more, the men were deserting in all directions. In the south there was no one either to take the command. The new levies were willing enough to fight, but there was no one to show them how. The insurrection seemed in a fair way of dying out from sheer want of leadership.

Suddenly reinforcements arrived in two directions almost at the same time. Owen O'Neill—better known as Owen Roe—an honourable and gallant man, who had served with much distinction upon the Continent, landed in Donegal, accompanied by about a hundred French-Irish officers. He instantly took the command of the disorganized and fast-dissolving northern levies; superseded the incompetent Sir Phelim, who from that moment fell away into contempt and impotence; suppressed all disorders, and punished, as far as possible, those who had been foremost in the work of blood, expressing at the same time his utter detestation of the horrors which had hitherto blackened the rising.

Almost at the same moment Colonel Preston, a brother of Lord Gormanstown, and an officer who had also served with credit in the European wars, landed in the south, bringing with him a store of ammunition and field artillery, and between four and five hundred exiled Irish officers. The two forces thereupon began to assume a comparatively organized appearance. Both, however, were so far perfectly independent of each other, and both openly and avowedly hostile to the king.

To effect a union between these northern and southern insurgents a meeting was summoned at Kilkenny in October, 1642, consisting of over two hundred Roman Catholic deputies, nearly all the Irish Roman Catholic bishops, many of the clergy, and some fourteen peers. A council was formed of which Lord Mountgarret was appointed President. Owen Roe O'Neill was at the same time confirmed in the command of the northern forces, and Colonel Preston in that of the southern. The war was declared to be a Catholic one, to be known henceforward as the Catholic Confederacy, and between old Irish and Anglo-Irish there was to be no difference.

Charles's great aim was now to persuade the Confederates to unite with one another in his support. The chief difficulty was a religious one. The Kilkenny Council stood out for the restoration of the Catholic Church in all its original privileges. This, for his own sake—especially in the then excited state of feeling in England—Charles dared not grant, neither would Ormond abet him in doing so. Between the latter and the Catholic peers there was, however, a complete understanding, while between him and the Dublin Lords Justices there was an all but complete breach.

The King decided upon a *coup de main*. He dismissed the Lords Justices, and ordered several of the more Puritan members of the Privy Council to be tried for treason. The result was a rapid exodus of nearly the whole governing body to England. Early in 1644 Ormond was made Lord-deputy, and a truce of a year was entered into with the Confederates. Only the extravagance of the latter's demands now stood in the way of a complete union.

XXXVII.

CIVIL WAR.

THE passionate excitement which the news of the Ulster massacre had awakened in England seems to have deepened, rather than diminished, as time went on, and the details became more known. Nothing that has happened within living memory can be even approximately compared to it, though, perhaps, those who are old enough to remember the sensations awakened by the news of the Indian Mutiny will be able most nearly to realize the wrath and passionate desire of revenge which filled every Protestant breast. That the circumstances of the case were not taken into consideration was almost inevitable. Looking back with calmer vision—though even now a good deal of fog and misconception seems to prevail upon the subject—we can see that some such outbreak was all but inevitable; might have been, indeed ought to have been, foreseen. A wildly-excitable population driven from the land which they and their fathers had held from time immemorial, confined to a narrow and, for the most part, a worthless tract; seeing others in possession of these "fat lands" which they still regarded as their own—exiled to make room for planters of another race and another faith—what, in the name of sense or reason, was to be expected except what happened? That the very instant protection was withdrawn the hour for retribution would be felt to have struck. The unhappy Protestant colonists were absolutely guiltless in the matter. They were simply the victims, as the earlier proprietors had been the victims before them. The wrongs that had been wrought thirty years earlier by Sir John Davis and the Dublin lawyers had been wiped out in their unoffending blood.

This point is so important to realize, and the whole rising has so often been described as a purely religious and fanatical one, that it is worth dwelling upon it a minute or two longer. It was a rising, unquestionably, of a native Roman Catholic community against an introduced Protestant one, and the religious element, no doubt, counted for something—though it is not easy to say for how much—in the matter. In any case it was the smallest least vital part of the long gathered fury which resulted in that deed of vengeance. The rising was essentially an agrarian one— as almost every Irish rising has been before and since—and the fact that the two rival creeds found themselves face to face was little more than a very unfortunate accident. Could the plantations of James the First's time have been formed exclusively of English or Scotch Roman Catholics, we have no reason, and certainly no right to conclude that the event would have been in any way different, or that the number of those slaughtered would have been reduced by even a single victim.

It was not, however, to be expected that the English Protestants of that day would realize this. It is not always fully realized even yet. The heat awakened by that ruthless slaughter, that merciless driving away of hundreds of innocent women and children, the natural pity for the youth and helplessness of many of the victims has lasted down to our own time. Even to us the outrage is a thousand-fold more vivid than the provocation which led to it. How much more then to the English Protestants of that day? To them it was simply a new massacre of St. Bartholomew; an atrocity which the very amplest and bloodiest vengeance would still come far short of expiating.

It is easy to see that any negotiation with those implicated in a deed which had produced so widespread a feeling of horror was a proceeding fraught with peril to the royal cause. Anger does not discriminate, and to the Protestants of England, North and South, old Irish, and Anglo-Irish, honourable gentlemen of the Pale, and red-handed rebels of Ulster, were all alike guilty. Nor was this Charles's only difficulty. The Confederates declined to abate a jot of their terms. The free exercise of the Catholic religion, an independent Irish parliament, a general pardon, and a reversal of all attainders were amongst their conditions, and they would not take less. These Ormond dared not agree to. Had he done so every Protestant in Ireland, down to his own soldiery, would have gone over in a body to the Parliament. He offered what he dared, but the Irish leaders would listen to no compromise. They knew the imminence of the situation as well as he did, and every fresh royal defeat, the news of which reached Ireland, only made them stand out the firmer.

Charles cut the knot in his own fashion. Tired of Ormond's discretion and Ormond's inconvenient sense of honour, he secretly sent over Edward Somerset, Earl of Glamorgan, to make terms with the Confederates, who, excited at finding themselves the last hope and mainstay of an embarrassed king stood out for higher and higher conditions. The Plantation lands were to be given back: full and free pardon was to be granted to all; Mass was to be said in all the churches. To these terms and everything else required, Glamorgan agreed, and the Confederates, thereupon, agreed to despatch a large force, when called upon to do so, to England, and in the meantime to make sham terms with Ormond, keeping him in the dark as to this secret compact.

It was not long a secret. Ormond seems to have had some suspicions of it from the beginning, and an incident which presently occurred made suspicion certainty. The town of Sligo had been captured by the parliamentary troops under Coote, and in October, 1645, an attempt was made to recapture it by a party of Irish under a fighting prelate, the Roman Catholic Archbishop of Tuam. In the struggle which ensued the Archbishop was killed, and upon his body was found a copy of the secret treaty which was straightway despatched by Coote to London.

It awakened a sensation hardly less than that with which the news of the massacre itself had been received. It was the one thing still wanting to damage the royal cause. Charles, it is true, denied it stoutly, and the English royalists tried to accept the denial. The Irish ones knew better. Ormond, whose own honour was untouched, did what he could to save his king's. The Confederates, however, admitted it openly, and Glamorgan, after suffering a short and purely fictitious imprisonment, remained in Ireland to carry out his master's orders.

The already crowded confusion of the scene there had lately been added to by a new actor. Rinucini, Archbishop of Fermo, had been despatched by Pope Innocent X. as his nuncio, and at once threw himself into the struggle. To him it narrowed itself to one point. The moment, he felt, had now come for the re-establishment of the Catholic religion in Ireland, and if possible for its union with one of the Catholic Powers of Europe, and in order to achieve this object, his great aim was to hinder, if possible, anything like a reconciliation between the Catholic insurgents and the king.

Meanwhile, peace had been made in England. Charles was a prisoner, and the final acts of that drama in which he plays so strangely mixed a part were shortly to be enacted. In Ireland there was no pretence at peace. On the contrary, it was only then that hostilities seem really to have been carried on with vigour. At a battle fought upon June 4, 1646, near Benturb, Owen O'Neill had defeated Munroe and his Scottish forces with great slaughter, and from that moment the whole north was in his power. In the south Rinucini was rushing from town to town and pulpit to pulpit, fiercely arousing all the Catholic animosity of the country against both English parties alike. In this he was supported by Owen O'Neill, who, with his victorious army, hastened south to meet him. Together the chief and the legate marched in September of the same year into Kilkenny; took possession of the Council Chamber; flung the Moderates assembled there, including old Lord Mountgarret and the rest of the Council, into prison. Ormond was in Dublin, helpless to meet this new combination. No orders came from England. The royal cause seemed to be hopelessly lost. All Ireland was swarming with the troops of the insurgents. Lord Inchiquin, who had for a while declared for the king, had now gone over to the Parliament. O'Neill and the legate's army was daily gathering strength. It needed but a little more energy on their part and Dublin itself, with all its helpless crowd of fugitives, must fall into their hands.

In this dilemma Ormond came to a resolution. To throw in his lot with Rinucini and the rebels of the north, stained as the latter were in his eyes with innocent blood, was impossible. Even had they been disposed to combine heartily with him for the royal cause he could hardly have done so; as it was there was barely a pretence of any such intention. If Charles could effect his escape and would put himself in their hands, then, indeed, they said they would support him. In that case, however, it would have been as king of Ireland rather than England. Ormond could not and would not stoop to any such negotiations. He wrote to the English Parliament offering to surrender Dublin into their hands, and to leave the country. The offer was accepted, and a month later he had relinquished the impossible post, and joined the other escaped Royalists in France.

XXXVIII.

THE CONFUSION DEEPENS.

THE indescribable confusion of aims and parties in Ireland begins at this point to take even more rapid and perplexing turns. That "poor panther Inchiquin," as one of his opponents derisively calls him, who had already made one bound from king to Parliament, now, upon some fresh offence, bounded back again, and made overtures to Preston and the Moderates. Rinucini, whose only policy was to hinder any union between the Catholics and Royalists, thereupon fled to O'Neill, and together they opposed the Moderates tooth and nail. The latter were now seriously anxious to make terms with the Royalists. The king's trial was beginning, and his peril served to consolidate all but the most extreme. Ormond himself returned late in 1648 from France; Prince Rupert arrived early the following year with a small fleet of ships off Kinsale, and every day brought crowds of loyal gentlemen to Ireland as to a final vantage ground upon which to try a last desperate throw for the royal cause.

In Dublin the command, upon Ormond's surrender, had been given by the Parliament to Colonel Michael

Jones, a Puritan officer, who had greatly distinguished himself in the late war. The almost ludicrously involved state into which things had got is seen by the fact that Jones, though himself the leader of the Parliamentary forces, struck up at this juncture a temporary alliance with O'Neill, and instructed Monk who was in the north, to support him. The king's death brought all the Royalists, and most of the more moderate rebels into line at last. Rinucini, feeling that whatever happened, his project of a separate Ireland had become impossible, fled to Italy. Even O'Neill, finding that his alliance with Jones was not prospering, and that the stricter Puritans declined with horror the bare idea of holding any communication with him or his forces, gave in his adhesion. Old Irish and Anglo-Irish, Protestant and Catholic, North and South, all at last were in arms for the king.

The struggle had thus narrowed itself. It was now practically between Dublin, commanded by Jones, the Parliamentary general, upon one side, and all Ireland under Ormond and the now united Confederates on the other. Cromwell, it was known, was preparing for a descent upon Ireland, and had issued liberal offers of the forfeited Irish lands to all who would aid him in the enterprise. He had first, however, to land, and there was nowhere that he could do so excepting at Dublin or Londonderry. All the efforts therefore of the Royalists were concentrated upon taking the capital before it became the starting-point of a new campaign. Marching hastily from Kilkenny, Ormond established himself at a place called Baggotrath, near Rathmines, and close to the

JAMES, DUKE OF ORMOND.
(From an engraving by White, after a picture by Kneller.)

walls of the town. Two nights after his arrival he sent forward a body of men under Colonel Purcell to try and effect a surprise. Jones, however, was on the alert; drove Purcell back, and, following him with all the men at his command, fell upon Ormond's camp, where no proper watch was being kept. The surprise was thus completely reversed. Six thousand of the confederate troops were killed or forced to surrender, and Ormond, with the remainder, had to fall back upon Kilkenny.

The battle of Baggotrath does not figure amongst the more famous battles of this period, but it was certainly the turning-point of the Irish campaign. With his crippled forces, Ormond was unable again to take the field, and Jones was therefore left in undisputed possession of Dublin. A week later, in August, 1649, Cromwell had landed there with 12,000 troops at his back.

XXXIX.

CROMWELL IN IRELAND.

CROMWELL had hardly set foot upon Irish soil before he took complete control of the situation. The enterprise, in his own eyes and in those of many who accompanied him, wore all the sacred hue of a crusade. "We are come," he announced, solemnly, upon his arrival in Dublin, "to ask an account of the innocent blood that hath been shed, and to endeavour to bring to an account all who, by appearing in arms, shall justify the same."

Three thousand troops, the flower of the English cavaliers, with some of the Royalists of the Pale—none of whom, it may be said, had anything to say to the Ulster massacres—had been hastily thrown by Ormond into Drogheda, under Sir Arthur Ashton, a gallant Royalist officer; and to Drogheda, accordingly in September Cromwell marched. Summoned to yield, the garrison refused. They were attacked, and fought desperately, driving back their assailants at the first assault. At the second, a breach was made in the walls, and Ashton and his force were driven into the citadel. "Being thus entered," Cromwell's despatch to the Parliament runs, "we refused them quarter. I believe we put to the sword the whole number of the defendents. I do not think thirty escaped. Those that did are in safe custody for the Barbadoes. . . . I wish," he adds, a little later in the same despatch, "all honest hearts may give the glory of this to God alone."

From Drogheda, the Lord-General turned south to Wexford. Here an equally energetic defence was followed by an equally successful assault, and this also by a similar drama of slaughter. "There was lost of the enemy," he himself writes, "not many less than two thousand; and, I believe, not twenty of yours from first to last." The soldiers, he goes on to say, "got a very good booty in this place." Of "the former inhabitants . . . most of them are run away, and many of them killed in this service. It were to be wished that some honest people would come and plant here."[1]

The grim candour of these despatches needs no comment. We see the whole situation with that vividness which only a relation at first hand ever gives. The effect of these two examples was instantaneous. Most of the other towns surrendered upon the first summons. The Irish army fell back in all directions. An attempt was made to save Kilkenny, but after a week's defence it was surrendered. The same thing happened at Clonmel, and within a few months of his arrival nearly every strong place, except Waterford and Limerick, were in the Lord-General's hands.

That Cromwell, from his own point of view, was justified in these proceedings, and that he held him-

[1] "Cromwell's Letters and Speeches"—Carlyle.

self—even when slaughtering English Royalists in revenge for the acts of Irish rebels—a divinely-appointed agent sent to execute justice upon the ungodly, there can be little doubt. As regards ordinary justice his conduct was exemplary. Unlike most of the armies that had from time to time ravaged Ireland, he allowed no disorder. His soldiers were forbidden by proclamation to plunder, and were hanged, "in ropes of authentic hemp," as Carlyle remarks, when they did so. The merciless slaughter of two entire garrisons is a hideous deed, and a deed, too, which appeals with peculiar force to the popular imagination. As compared to many acts perpetrated from time to time in Ireland, it seems, if one examines it coolly, to fade into comparative whiteness, and may certainly be paralleled elsewhere. A far deeper and more ineffaceable stain rests—as will be seen in another chapter—upon Cromwell's rule in Ireland; one, moreover, not so readily justified by custom or any grim necessities of warfare.

The final steps by which the struggle was crushed out were comparatively tedious. Cromwell's men were attacked by that "country sickness" which seems at that time to have been inseparable from Irish campaigns. Writing from Ross in November, he says, "I scarce know one officer amongst us who has not been sick." His own presence, too, was urgently required in England, so that he was forced before long to set sail, leaving the completion of the campaign in the hands of others.

In the Royalist camp, the state of affairs was meanwhile absolutely desperate. The Munster colonists had gone over almost to a man to the enemy. The "panther Inchiquin" had taken another bound in the same direction. The quarrels between Ormond and the old Irish party had grown bitterer than ever. The hatred of the extreme Catholic party towards him appears to have been if anything rather deeper than their hatred to Cromwell, and all the recent disasters were charged by them to his want of generalship. The young king had been announced at one moment to be upon the point of arriving in person in Ireland. "One must go and die there, for it is shameful to live elsewhere!" he is reported to have cried, with a depth of feeling very unlike his usual utterances. He got as far as Jersey, but there paused. Ireland under Cromwell's rule was not exactly a pleasant royal residence, and, on the whole, he appears to have thought it wiser to go no further.

His signature, a year later, of the Covenant, in return for the Scotch allegiance, brought about a final collapse of the always thinly cemented pact in Ireland. The old Catholic party thereupon broke wholly away from Ormond, and after a short struggle he was again driven into exile. From this time forward, there was no longer a royal party of any sort left in the country.

Under Hugh O'Neill, a cousin of Owen Roe, who —fortunately, perhaps, for himself—had died shortly after Cromwell's arrival, the struggle was carried on for some time longer. As in later times, Limerick was one of the last places to yield. Despite the evident hopelessness of the struggle, Hugh O'Neill and his half-starved men held it with a courage which awoke admiration even amongst the Cromwellians. When it was surrendered the Irish officers received permission to take service abroad. Galway, with a few other towns and castles, which still held out, now surrendered. The eight years' civil war was at last over, and nothing remained for the victors to do but to stamp out the last sparks, and call upon the survivors to pay the forfeit.

ST. COLUMBA'S ORATORY, KELLS.

XL.

CROMWELL'S METHODS.

THE total loss of life during those weary eight years of war and anarchy has been estimated at no less than six hundred thousand lives, and there seems to be no reason to think that these figures are exaggerated. Whereas in 1641 the population of Ireland was nearly one and a half millions, at the end of 1649 it was considerably under one. More than a third, therefore, of the entire population had disappeared bodily.

Nor were the survivors left in peace to bind up their wounds and mourn their slain. In England, once the fighting was over, and the swords sheathed, there was little desire to carry the punishment further; and the vanquished were, for the most part, able to retire in more or less melancholy comfort to their homes. In Ireland the reverse was the case. There the struggle had been complicated by a bitterness unknown elsewhere, and had aroused a keen and determined thirst for vengeance, one which the cessation of hostilities only seemed to stimulate into greater vehemence.

The effect, especially amongst the Puritans, of the

Ulster massacres, far from dying out, had grown fiercer and bitterer with every year. Now that the struggle was over, that Ireland lay like an inert thing in the hands of her victors, her punishment, it was resolved, should begin. Had that punishment fallen only on the heads of those who could be proved to have had any complicity in that deed of blood there would not have been a word to say. Sir Phelim O'Neill was dragged from the obscurity to which ever since the coming of Owen Roe he had been consigned, tried in Dublin, and hanged—with little regret even from his own side. Lord Mayo, who had taken a prominent part in the rising, and was held responsible for a horrible massacre perpetrated at Shrule Bridge, near Tuam, was shot in Connaught. Lord Muskerry was tried, and honourably acquitted. Other trials took place, chiefly by court-martial, and though some of these appear to have been unduly pressed, on the whole, considering the state of feelings that had been awakened, it may be allowed that so far stern justice had not outstepped her province.

It was very different with what was to follow. An enormous scheme of eviction had been planned by Cromwell which was to include all the native and nearly all the Anglo-Irish inhabitants of Ireland, with the exception of the humblest tillers of the soil, who were reserved as serfs or servants. This was a scheme of nothing less than the transportation of all the existing Catholic landowners of Ireland, who, at a certain date, were ordered to quit their homes, and depart in a body into Connaught, there to inhabit a narrow desolate tract, between the Shannon and the sea, destitute, for the most part, of houses or any accommodation for their reception; where they were to be debarred from entering any walled town, and where a cordon of soldiers was to be stationed to prevent their return. May 1, 1654, was the date fixed for this national exodus, and all who after that date were found east of the appointed line were to suffer the penalty of death.

The dismay awakened when the magnitude of this scheme burst upon the unhappy country may easily be conceived. Delicate ladies, high-born men and women, little children, the old, the sick, the suffering —all were included in this common disaster; all were to share alike in this vast and universal sentence of banishment. Resistance, too, was hopeless. Everything that could be done in the way of resistance had already been done, and the result was visible. The Irish Parliament had ceased to exist. A certain number of its Protestant members had been transferred by Cromwell to the English one,—thus anticipating the Union that was to come a century and a half later. The whole government of the country was at present centred in a board of commissioners, who sat in Dublin, and whose direct interest it was to hasten the exodus as much as possible.

For the new owners, who were to supplant those about to be ejected, were ready and waiting to step into their places. The Cromwellian soldiers who had served in the war had all received promises of grants of land, and their pay, now several years due, was also to be paid to them in the same coin. The intention was, that they were to be marched down regiment by regiment, and company by company, to ground already chosen for them by lot, then and there disbanded, and put into possession. A vast Protestant military colony was thus to be established over the whole of the eastern provinces. In addition to these an immense number of English speculators had advanced money upon Irish lands, and were now eagerly waiting to receive their equivalent.

As the day drew nearer, there arose all over Ireland a wild plea for time, for a little breathing time before being driven into exile. The first summons had gone out in the autumn, and had been proclaimed by beat of drum and blast of trumpet all over the country, and as the 1st of May began to approach the plea grew more and more urgent. So evident was the need for delay that some, even among the Parliamentarians, were moved to pity, and urged that a little more time might be granted. The command to "root out the heathen" was felt to be imperative, but even the heathen might be allowed a little time to collect his goods, and to provide some sort of a roof to shelter him in this new and forlorn home to which he was being sent.

It happened, too, that some of the first batches of exiles were ordered into North Clare, to a district known as the Burren, whose peculiarity is that what little soil is to be found there has collected into rifts below the surface, or accumulated into pockets of earth at the feet of the hills, leaving the rest of the surface sheer rock, the very streams, whose edges would otherwise be green, being mostly carried underground. The general appearance of the region has been vividly described by one of the commissioners engaged in carrying out this very act of transplantation, who, writing back to Dublin for further instructions, informs his superiors that the region in question did not possess "water enough to drown a man, trees enough to hang a man, or earth enough to bury a man." It may be conceived what an effect such a region, so described, must have had upon men fresh from the fertile and flourishing pasture-lands of Meath and Kildare. Many turned resolutely back, preferring rather to die than to attempt life under such new and hopeless conditions, and stern examples had to be made before the unwilling emigrants were at last fairly got underweigh.

Yet even such exile as this was better than the lot of some. The wives and families of the Irish officers and soldiers who had been allowed to go into foreign service, had, of necessity, been left behind, and a considerable number of these, the Government now proceeded to ship in batches to the West Indies to be sold as slaves. Several thousand women, ladies and others, were thus seized and sold by dealers, often without any individual warrant, and it was not until after the accidental seizure of some of the wives of the Cromwellian soldiers that the traffic was put under regulations. Cromwell's greatness needs no defence, but the slaughter of the garrisons of Drogheda and Wexford, reckoned amongst the worst blemishes upon that greatness, pales beside such an act as this; one which would show murkily even upon the blackened record of an Alva or a Pizarro.

Slowly the long trains of exiles began now to

FAILURE OF THE EVICTION SCHEME. 271

pour out in all directions. Herds of cattle, horses laden with furniture, with food, with all the everyday necessities of such a multitude accompanied them. All across that wide limestone plain, which covers the centre of Ireland, innumerable family groups were to be seen slowly streaming west. There were few roads, and those few very bad. Hardly a wheeled conveyance of any sort existed in the country. Those who were too weak to walk or to ride had to be carried on men's backs or in horse litters. The confusion, the misery, the cold, the wretchedness may be conceived, and always behind, urging them on, rebuking the loiterers, came the armed escort sent to drive them into exile—Puritan seraphs, with drawn swords, set to see that none returned whence they came!

Nor was there even any marked satisfaction amongst those who inherited the lands and houses thus left vacant. Many of the private soldiers who had received bonds or debentures for their share of the land, had parted with them long since, either to their own officers or to the traffickers in such bonds, who had sprang up by hundreds, and who obtained them from the needy soldiers often for a mere trifle. Sharp-sighted speculators like Dr. Petty, by whom the well-known Survey of Ireland was made, acquired immense tracts of land at little or no outlay. Of those soldiers, too, who did receive grants of land many left after a while. Others, despite all regulations to the contrary, married Irish wives, and their children in the next generation were found to have not only become Roman Catholics, but to be actually unable to speak a word of English. Many, too, of the dispossessed proprietors, the younger ones especially, continued to hang about, and either harassed the new owners and stole their goods, or made friends with them, and managed after a while to slip back upon some excuse into their old homes. No sternness of the Puritan leaven availed to hinder the new settlers from being absorbed into the country, as other and earlier settlers had been absorbed before them; marrying its daughters, adopting its ways, and becoming themselves in time Irishmen. The bitter memory of that vast and wholesale act of eviction has remained, but the good which it was hoped would spring from it faded away almost within a generation.

XLI.

THE ACT OF SETTLEMENT.

CROMWELL was now dead, and after a very short attempt at government his son Richard had relinquished the reins and retired into private life. Henry Cromwell, who had for several years been Lord-Lieutenant in Ireland, and had won no little liking by his mild and equable rule, also honourably resigned at the same time, and left. Coote, on the other hand, and Broghill, both of whom had acquired immense estates under the Cromwellian rule, were amongst the foremost to hail the Restoration, and to secure their own interests by being eager to welcome the king. Such secular vicars of Bray were not likely to suffer whatever king or government came uppermost.

To the exiled proprietors, who had fought for that king's father and for himself, it naturally seemed that the time had come for their sufferings and exile to end. Now that the king had been restored to his own again, they who had been punished for his sake should also, they thought, in fairness, again enjoy what had been theirs before the war.

Charles's position, it must be acknowledged, was a very difficult one. Late found as it was, the loyalty

HENRY CROMWELL, LORD-LIEUTENANT FROM 1657 TO 1660.
(*From a Mezzotint.*)

of Coote, Broghill, and others of their stamp had been eminently convenient, as without it the army in Ireland would hardly have returned to its allegiance. To deprive them of what they had acquired was felt to be out of the question, and the same argument applied, with no little force, to many of the other newly-made proprietors. The feeling, too, against the Irish Catholics was far from having died out in England, and anything like a wholesale ejection of the new Protestant settlers for their benefit, would have been very badly received there.

On the other hand, decency and the commonest sense of honour required that something should be done. Ormond, who had been made a duke, was at once reinstated in his own lands, with a handsome additional slice as a recompense for his services. A certain number of other great proprietors and lords of the Pale, a list of whom was rather capriciously made out, were also immediately reinstated. For the rest, more tardy and less satisfactory justice was to be meted.

A Court of Claims was set up in Dublin to try the cases of those who claimed, during the late war, to have been upon the king's side. Those who could prove their entire innocence of the original rebellion were to be at once reinstated; those, on the other hand, who were in arms before '49, or who had been at any time joined to the party of Rinucini, or had held any correspondence, even accidentally, with that party, were to be excluded, and if they had received lands in Connaught might stay there and be thankful.

A wearisome period of endless dispute, chicanery,

and wrangling followed this decision. As the soldiers and adventurers were only to be dispossessed in case of a sufficiency of reserved lands being found to compensate them, it followed that the fewer of the original proprietors that could prove their loyalty the better for the Government. At the first sitting of the Court of Claims the vast majority of those whose cases were tried were able thus to prove their innocence; and as all these had a claim to be reinstated, great alarm was felt, and a clamour of indignation arose from the new proprietors, at which the Government, taking alarm, made short work of many of the remaining claims, whereupon a fresh, and certainly not less reasonable, clamour was raised upon the other side.

The end of the long-drawn struggle may be stated in a few words. The soldiers, adventures, and debenture holders agreed at length to accept two-thirds of their land, and to give up the other third, and on this arrangement, by slow degrees, the country settled down. As a net result of the whole settlement we find that, whereas before '41 the Irish Roman Catholics had held two-thirds of the good land and all the waste, after the Restoration they held only one-third in all, and this, too, after more than two millions of acres previously forfeited had been restored to them.

XLII.

OPPRESSION AND COUNTER OPPRESSION.

No class of the community suffered more severely from the effects of the Restoration than the Presbyterians of Ulster. The church party which had returned to Ireland upon the crest of the new wave signalized its return by a violent outburst of intolerance directed not so much against the Papists as the Nonconformists. Of the 300,000 Protestants, which was roughly speaking the number calculated to be at that time in Ireland, fully a third were Presbyterians, another 100,000 being made up of Puritans and other Nonconformists, leaving only one-third Churchmen. Against the two former, but especially against the Presbyterians, the terrors of the law were now put in force. A new Act of Uniformity was passed, and armed with this, the bishops with Bramhall, the Primate, at their head, insisted upon an acceptance of the Prayer-book being enforced upon all who were permitted to hold any benefice, or to teach or preach in any church or public place.

The result was that the Presbyterians were driven away in crowds from Ireland. Out of seventy ministers in Ulster, only eight accepted the terms and were ordained; all the remainder were expelled, and their flocks in many cases elected to follow them into exile.

This persecution was the more monstrous that no hint or pretext of disloyalty was urged against them. They had been planted in the country as a defence and breakwater against the Roman Catholics, and now the same intolerance which had, in a great measure forced the latter to rebel, was in its turn being brought to bear upon them.

The Roman Catholics, on the other hand, now found themselves indulged to a degree that they had not experienced for nearly a century. The penal laws at the special instance of the king were suspended in their favour. Many of the priests returned, and were allowed to establish themselves in their old churches. They could not do so, however, without violent alarm being awakened upon the other side. The Irish Protestants remonstrated angrily, and their indignation found a vehement echo in England. The '41 massacre was still as fresh in every Protestant's mind as if it had happened only the year before, and suspicion of Rome was a passion ready at any moment to rise to frenzy.

The heir to the Crown was a Papist, and Charles was himself strongly, and not unreasonably suspected of being secretly one also. His alliance with Louis XIV. was justifiably regarded with the utmost suspicion and dislike by all his Protestant subjects. It only wanted a spark to set this mass of smouldering irritation and suspicion into a flame.

That spark was afforded by the murder of Sir

Edmondbury Godfrey, under circumstances which were at first believed to point to its having been committed by Papists. A crowd of perjured witnesses, with Titus Oates at their head, sprang like evil birds of the night into existence, ready to swear away the lives of any number of innocent men. The panic flew across the Channel. Irish Roman Catholics of all classes and ages were arrested and flung into prison. Priests who had ventured to return were ordered to quit the country at once. Men of stainless honour, whose only crime was their faith, were on no provocation seized and subjected to the most ignominious treatment, and in several instances put to death.

The case of Dr. Plunkett, the Roman Catholic Archbishop of Armagh, a man whom even Protestants regarded with the utmost reverence, is the most notorious of these. Upon a ridiculous charge of being implicated in a wholly mythical French descent, he was dragged over to London, summarily sentenced, convicted, and hung, drawn, and quartered. Although the most eminent, he was only one, however, of the victims of this most insane of panics. Reason seemed to have been utterly lost. Blood and blood alone could satisfy the popular craving, and victim after victim was hurried, innocent but unpitied, to his doom.

At last the tide stayed. First slackened, then suddenly—in Ireland at least—reversed itself, and ran almost as recklessly and as violently as ever, only in the opposite direction. In 1685 Charles died, and James now king, resolved with hardly an attempt at further concealment to carry out his own long-cherished plans. From the beginning of his reign his private determination seems to have been to make Ireland a stronghold and refuge for his Roman Catholic subjects, in order that by their aid he might make himself independent both of England and the Parliament, and so carry out that despotism upon which his whole narrow, obstinate soul was inflexibly set.

His first step was to recall the Duke of Ormond, whom Charles had left as Viceroy, and to appoint in his place two Lords Justices, Lord Granard and the Primate Boyle, who were likely, he believed, to be more malleable. All tests were to be immediately done away with. Catholicism was no longer to be a disqualification for office, and Roman Catholics were to be appointed as judges. A more important change still, the army was to be entirely remodelled; Protestant officers were to be summarily dismissed, and Roman Catholic ones as summarily put in their places.

Such sweeping changes could not, even James found, be carried out all at once. The Lords Justices were next dismissed, and his own brother-in-law, Lord Clarendon, sent over as Lord-Lieutenant. He in turn proving too timid, or too constitutional, his place was before long filled by Richard Talbot, a fervent Catholic, but a man of indifferent public honour and more than indifferent private character. Talbot was created Earl of Tyrconnel, and arrived in 1686 avowedly to carry out the new policy.

From this point the stream ran fast and strong. The recent innovations, especially the re-organization of the army, had naturally caused immense alarm amongst the whole Protestant colony. A petition drawn out by the former proprietors and forwarded to the king against the Act of Settlement had made them tremble also for their estates, and now this new appointment came to put a climax to their dismay. What might not be expected they asked in terror, under a man so unscrupulous and so bigoted, with an army, too, composed mainly of Roman Catholics at his back to enforce his orders? The departure of Clarendon was thus the signal for a new Protestant exodus. Wild reports of a general massacre, one which was to surpass the massacre of '41, flew through the land. Terrified people flocked to the sea-coast and embarked in any boat they could find for England. Those that remained behind drew themselves together for their own defence within barricaded houses, and in the towns in the north, especially in Enniskillen and Londonderry, the Protestant inhabitants closed their gates and made ready to withstand a siege.

Meanwhile in Dublin sentences of outlawry were fast being reversed, and the estates of the Protestants being restored in all directions to their former proprietors. The charters of the corporate towns were next revoked, and new (by preference Catholic) aldermen and mayors appointed by the viceroy. All Protestants were ordered to give up their arms by a certain day, and to those who did not, "their lives and goods," it was announced, "should be at the mercy and discretion of the soldiers." These soldiers, now almost exclusively Catholic, lived at free quarters upon the farms and estates of the Protestants. "Tories," lately out "upon their keeping," with prices upon their heads, were now officers in the king's service. The property of Protestants was seized all over the country, their houses taken possession of, their sheep and cattle slaughtered by hundreds of thousands. All who could manage to escape made for the north, where the best Protestant manhood of the country had now gathered together, and was standing resolutely in an attitude of self-defence.

In England, William of Orange had meanwhile landed in Torbay, and James had fled precipitately to France. Tyrconnel, who seems to have been unprepared for this event, hesitated at first, undecided what to do or how matters would eventually shape themselves. He even wrote to William, professing to be rather favourable than otherwise to his cause, a profession which the king, who was as yet anything but firm in his own seat, seems to have listened to with some belief, and General Richard Hamilton was sent over by him to negotiate matters with the viceroy.

The passions awakened on both sides were far too strong however, for any such temporizing. Louis XIV. had received James upon his flight with high honour, and his return to the throne was believed by his own adherents to be imminent. In England, especially in London, the excitement against the Irish Catholics was prodigious, and had been increased by the crowd of Protestant refugees who had recently poured in. The Irish regiments brought to England by James had been insultingly disbanded, and their officers put under arrest. "Lilibullero," the anti-Catholic street song, was sung by thousands of excited lips. Lord Jefferies, who embodied in his own person all that the popular hatred most detested in his master's rule, had been dragged to prison amid the threatening howls of the populace. The "Irish night," during which—though without the faintest shadow of reason—the London citizens had fully believed an Irish mob to be in the act of marching upon the town, with the set purpose of massacring every Protestant man, woman, and child in it, had worked both town and nation to the highest possible pitch of excitement. In Ireland too the stream had gone too far and too fast to turn back. The minority and the majority stood facing one another like a pair of pugilists. The Protestants, whose property had been either seized or wasted, were fast concentrating themselves behind Lough Foyle. Thither Tyrconnel sent Richard Hamilton—who, deserting William, had thrown himself upon the other side—with orders to reduce Londonderry before aid could arrive from England. To James himself Tyrconnel wrote, urging him to start for Ireland without delay. Though unprepared at present to furnish soldiers, Louis was munificent in other respects. A fleet of fourteen men-of-war, with nine smaller vessels, was provided. Arms, ammunition, and money without stint were placed at the command of the exile, and a hundred French officers with the Count d'Avaux, one of the king's most trusted officials, as envoy, were sent to accompany the expedition. On March 12, 1689, James II. landed at Kinsale.

XLIII.

WILLIAM AND JAMES IN IRELAND.

JAMES'S appearance in Ireland was hailed with a little deserved burst of enthusiasm. As a king, as a Catholic, and as a man in deep misfortune, he had a triple claim upon the kindly feeling of a race never slow to respond to such appeals. All along the road from Cork to Dublin the people ran out out in crowds to greet him with tears, blessings, and cries of welcome. Women thronged the banks along the roadsides, and held up their children to see him go by. Flowers—as to the poor quality of which it was hardly worth Lord Macaulay's while, by the way, to speak so disparagingly—were offered for his acceptance, or strewn under his feet. Every mark of devotion which a desperately poor country could show was shown without stint. Accompanied by the French ambassador, amid a group of English exiles, and advancing under a waving roof of flags and festoons, hastily improvised in his honour, the least worthy of the Stuarts arrived in Dublin, and took up his residence at the castle.

His sojourn there was certainly no royal bed of roses! The dissensions between his English and his

Irish followers were not only deep, but ineffaceable. By each the situation was regarded solely from the standpoint of his own country. Was James to remain in Ireland and to be an Irish king? or was he merely to use Ireland as a stepping-stone to England? Between two such utterly diverse views no point of union was discoverable.

In the interests of his own master, D'Avaux, the French envoy, strongly supported Tyrconnel and the Irish leaders. The game of France was less to replace James on the English throne than to make of Ireland a permanent thorn in the side of England. With this view he urged James to remain in Dublin, where he would necessarily be more under the direct control of the parliament. James, however declined this advice, and persisted in going north, where he would be within a few hours' sail of Great Britain. Once Londonderry had fallen (and it was agreed upon all hands that Londonderry could not hold out much longer), he could at any moment cross to Scotland, where it was believed that his friends would at once rally around him.

But Londonderry showed no symptoms of yielding. In April, 1689, James appeared before its walls, believing that he had only to do so to receive its submission. He soon found his mistake. Lundy, its governor, was ready indeed to surrender it into his hands, but the townsfolk declined the bargain, and shut their gates resolutely in the king's face. Lundy escaped for his life over the walls, and James, in disgust, returned to Dublin, leaving the conduct of the siege in the hands of Richard Hamilton, who was afterwards superseded in the command by De Rosen, a Muscovite in the pay of France, who prosecuted it with a barbarity unknown to the annals of civilized warfare.

The tale of that heroic defence has been so told that it need assuredly never, while the world lasts, be told again. Suffice it then that despite the falseness of its governor, the weakness of its walls, the lack of any military training on the part of its defenders; despite the treacherous dismissal of the first ships sent to its assistance; despite the long agony of seeing other ships containing provisions hanging inertly at the mouth of the bay; despite shot and shell without, and famine in its most grisly forms within—despite all this the little garrison held gallantly on to the "last ounce of horse-flesh and the last pinch of corn." At length, upon the 105th day of the siege, three ships, under Kirke's command, broke through the boom in the channel, and brought their freights in safety to the starved and ghastly defenders, gathered like ghosts, rather than human beings, upon the quay, Three days later De Rosen broke up his camp, and moved off in disgust, leaving behind him the little city, exhausted but triumphant, having saved the honour of its walls, and won itself imperishable fame.

While all this was going on in the north, James, in Dublin, had been busily employed in deluging the country with base money to supply his own necessities, with the natural result of ruining all who were forced to accept it. At the same time the Parliament under his nominal superintendence had settled down to the congenial task of reversing most of the earlier Acts, and putting everything upon an entirely new footing. It was a Parliament composed, as was natural, almost wholly of Roman Catholics, only six Protestants having been returned. Its first task was to repeal Poynings Act, the Act, which, it will be remembered, was passed in Henry VII.'s reign, binding it in dependence upon the English Parliament. Its next to establish freedom of worship, giving the Roman Catholic tithes to the priests. So far no objections could reasonably be raised. Next, however, followed the question of forfeitures. The hated Act of Settlement, upon which all property in Ireland was now based, was set aside, and it was setted that all lands should revert to their former proprietors. Then followed the punishment of the political adversaries. "The hugest Bill of attainder," says Mr. Green, "the world has seen," was hastily drawn up and passed. By its provisions over 2,240 persons were attained, and everything that they possessed vested in the king. Many so attained were either women or young children, indeed a large proportion of the names seem to have been inserted at haphazard or from some merely momentary feeling of anger or vindictiveness.

These Acts were perhaps only what is called natural, but it must be owned that they were also terribly unfortunate. Up to that date those directly penal laws against Catholics which afterwards disfigured the statute book were practically unknown. A Catholic could sit in either Irish House of Parliament; he could inherit lands, and bequeath them to whom he would; he could educate his children how and where he liked. The terror planted in the breast of the Protestant colony by that inoperative piece of legislation found its voice in the equally violent, but unfortunately not equally inoperative, passed Acts by them in the hour of *their* triumph. Acts, by means of which it was fondly hoped that their enemies would be thrown into such a position of dependence and humiliation that they could never again rise up to be a peril.

In the north a brilliant little victory had meanwhile been won by the Enniskillen troops under Colonel Wolseley, at Newtown Butler, where they attacked a much larger force of the enemy and defeated them, killing a large number and driving the rest back in confusion. William was still detained in England, but had despatched the Duke of Schomberg with a considerable force. Schomberg's men, were mostly raw recruits, and the climate tried them severely. He arrived in the autumn, but not venturing to take the field, established himself at Dundalk, where his men misbehaved and all but mutinied, and where, a pestilence shortly afterwards breaking out, swept them away in multitudes.

On both sides, indeed, the disorganization of the armies was great. Fresh reinforcements had arrived for James, under the Comte de Lauzan, in return for which an equal number of Irish soldiers under Colonel Macarthy had been drafted for service to France. In June, 1690, William himself landed at Carrickfergus with an army of 35,000 men, composed of nearly every nationality in Europe—Swedes, Dutch, Swiss, Batavians, French Huguenots, Finns, with about 15,000 English soldiers. He came up to James's army upon the banks of the Boyne, about twenty miles from Dublin, and here it was that the turning battle of the campaign was fought.

This battle James watched at a discreet distance from the hill of Donore. The Irish foot, upon whom the brunt of the action fell, were untrained, indifferently armed, and had never before been in action; their opponents were veterans trained in European wars. They were driven back, fled, and a considerable number of them slaughtered. The Irish cavalry stood firm, but their valour was powerless to turn the day. Schomberg was killed, but William remained absolute and undisputed master of the field.

At the first shock of reverse James flew down the hill and betook himself to Dublin. He arrived there foaming and almost convulsed with rage. "Madam, your countrymen have run away!" was his gracious address to Lady Tyrconnel. "If they have, sire, your Majesty seems to have won the race," was that lady's ready retort.

The king's flight was without reason or measure. As before in England, so now, he seemed to pass in a moment from insane self-confidence to an equally insane panic. He fled south, ordering the bridges to be broken down behind him; took boat at Waterford, and never rested until he found himself once more safe upon French soil.

His flight at least left the field clear for better men. Patrick Sarsfield now took the principal command, and prosecuted the campaign with a vigour of which it had hitherto shown no symptoms. Sarsfield is the one redeeming figure upon the

Jacobite side. His gallant presence sheds a ray of chivalric light upon this otherwise gloomiest and least attractive of campaigns. He could not turn defeat to victory, but he could, and did succeed in snatching honour out of that pit into which the other leaders, and especially his master, had let it drop. Brave, honourable, upright, "a gentleman of eminent merit," is praise which even those least inclined to favour his side of the quarrel bestow upon him without stint.

William, now established in Dublin, issued a proclamation offering full and free pardon to all who would lay down their arms. He was genuinely anxious to avoid pushing the struggle to the bitter end, and to hinder further bloodshed. Though deserted by their king, and fresh from overwhelming defeat, the Irish troops showed no disposition, however, of yielding. Athlone, Galway, Cork, Kinsale, and Limerick still held out, and behind the walls of the last named the remains of James's broken army was now chiefly collected. Those walls, however, were miserably weak, and the French generals utterly scouted the possibility of their being held. Tyrconnel, too, advised a capitulation, but Sarsfield insisted upon holding the town, and the Irish soldiers—burning to wipe out the shame of the Boyne—supported him like one man. William was known, to be moving south to the attack, and accordingly Lauzan and Tyrconnel, with the rest of the French troops moved hastily away to Galway, leaving Sarsfield to defend Limerick as he could.

They had hardly left before William's army appeared in sight with the king himself at their head, and drew up before the walls. A formidable siege train, sent after him from Dublin, was to follow in a day or two. Had it arrived it would have finished the siege at once. Sarsfield accordingly slipped out of the town under cover of night, fell upon it while it was on its way through the Silvermine Hills in Tipperary, killed some sixty of the men who were in charge, and filling the cannons with powder, burst them with an explosion which startled the country round for miles, and the roar of which is said to have reached William in his camp before Limerick.

This brilliant little feat delayed the siege. Nevertheless it was pressed on with great vigour. Two more guns were obtained, several of the outworks carried, and a breach began to show in the ramparts. It was now autumn, the rainy season was setting in, and William's presence was urgently wanted in England. After another violent attempt, therefore, to take the town, which was resisted with the most desperate valour, the very women joining in the fight, and remaining under the hottest fire, the besiegers drew off, and William shortly afterwards sailed for England, leaving the command in the hands of Ginkel, the ablest of his Dutch generals.

This first siege of Limerick is in many respects a very remarkable one, and bears a close analogy to the yet more famous siege of Londonderry. To give the parallel in Lord Macaulay's words—"The southern city," he says "was, like the northern city, the last asylum of a Church and of a nation. Both places were crowded by fugitives from all parts of Ireland. Both places appeared to men who had made a regular study of the art of war incapable of resisting an enemy. . . . In both cases, religious and patriotic enthusiasm struggled unassisted against great odds ; in both cases, religious and patriotic enthusiasm did what veteran warriors had pronounced it absurd to attempt."

In Galway, meanwhile, violent quarrels had broken out. The French troops were sick, naturally enough, of the campaign, and not long afterwards sailed for France. Their places were taken later on by another body of French soldiers under General St. Ruth. St. Ruth was a man of cold, disdainful temperament, but a good officer. He at once set to work at the task of restoring order and getting the army into a condition to take the field. Early in the spring Ginkel had collected his army in Mullingar ready to march to the assault of Athlone, the ancient Norman fortress, upon the bank of the Shannon, which was here spanned by a single bridge. Upon Ginkel's advance this bridge was broken down, and the besieged and besiegers were separated therefore by the breadth of the river. After an unsuccessful attempt to repair the breach the Dutch general resolved to ford the latter. As it happened the water was unusually low, and although St. Ruth with a large force was at the time only a mile away, he, unaccountably, made no attempt to defend the ford. A party of Ginkel's men waded or swam across in the dark, caught the broken end of the bridge, and held it till it was repaired. This done, the whole English army poured across the river.

The struggle was now narrowing fast. Leaving Athlone Ginkel advanced to Ballinasloe, so well-known now from its annual sheep fairs. The country here is all but a dead flat, but the French general took advantage of some rising ground on the slope of which stood the ruined castle of Aughrim. Here the Irish were posted by him in force, one of those deep brown bogs which cover so much of the surface of Galway lying at their feet and surrounding them upon two sides.

The battle which broke at five o'clock the next morning was a desperate one. Roused at last from his coldness St. Ruth appealed in the most moving terms to the officers and men to fight for their religion, their liberties, their honour. His appeal was gallantly responded to. A low stone breast-work had been raised upon the hillside in front of the Irish, and against this Ginkel's veterans again and again advanced to the attack, and again and again were beaten back, broken and, in one instance, chased down the hill on to the plain. St. Ruth broke into vehement enthusiasm. "The day," he cried, waving his hat in the air, "is ours, gentlemen!" A party of Huguenot cavalry, however, were presently seen to be advancing across the bog so as to turn the flank of the Irish army. It seemed to be impossible that they could get through, but the ground was firmer than at first appeared; and some hurdles thrown down in front of them formed a sort of rude causeway. St. Ruth flew to the point of danger. On his way he was struck by a cannon ball which carried off his head, and the army was thus left without a general. Sarsfield was at some distance with the reserve. There was no one to give any orders. The breast-work was carried.

The Irish fought doggedly, retreating slowly from enclosure to enclosure. At last, left to themselves, with no one to direct or support them, they broke and fled down the hill. Then followed a hideous butchery. Few or no prisoners were taken, and the number of the slain is stated to have been "in proportion to the number engaged greater than in any other battle of that age." An eye-witness who looked from the hill the next day said that the country for miles around was whitened with the naked bodies of the slain. It looked, he remarked with grim vividness, like an immense pasture covered with flocks of sheep!

INITIAL LETTER FROM THE BOOK OF KELLS.

XLIV.

THE TREATY OF LIMERICK.

NOTHING was now left but Limerick. Galway had yielded immediately after the day of Aughrim, its garrison claiming and obtaining the right of marching out with all the honours of war. Tyrconnel was dying, and had long lost, too, what little reputation he had ever had as a soldier. Sarsfield, however, stood firm to the last. Fresh reinforcements were hoped for from France, but none came until too late to be of any use. The town was again invested and besieged. An English fleet held the mouth of the Shannon so as to prevent any relief from coming to its aid. From the middle of August to the end of September the siege went on, and the walls, always weak, were riddled with shot and shell. Still it showed no symptoms of submission. Ginkel, who was in command of William's army, dreaded the approach of autumn, and had instructions from his master to finish the campaign as rapidly as possible, and with this end in view to offer good and honourable terms to the Irish. An armistice accordingly was agreed to for three days, and before the three days ended the famous " Articles of Limerick" were drawn up and signed by Sarsfield on the one hand, and the Lords Justices, who had just arrived in camp from Dublin, on the other.

The exact purport of these articles, and the extent to which they were afterwards mutilated and perverted from their original meaning has been hotly disputed, and is too large and complicated a question to enter into here at any length. Suffice it to say, that they engaged that the Roman Catholics of Ireland should enjoy the same privileges as they had previously enjoyed in the reign of Charles II.; that they should be free to follow the same trades and professions as before the war, and that all who were in arms, having a direct commission from King James, "with all *such as were under their protection*," should have a free pardon and be left in undisputed ownership of their lands and other possessions.

It is over the clause placed in italics that controversy has waxed fiercest. That it was in the first draft is admitted; that it was not in the document itself is equally certain. Had it been intentionally or accidentally excluded? is the question. William's own words were that it had been "casually omitted by the writer." The evidence seems clear, yet historians, who on other matters would hardly question his accuracy, seem to think that in this instance he was mistaken. That his own mind was clear on the point there can be little doubt, seeing that he made the most honourable efforts to get the clause in question carried into effect. In this he failed. Public opinion in England ran furiously against the Irish Catholics, and the Parliament absolutely refused to ratify it.

The essential clause was accordingly struck out, and the whole treaty soon became an absolute dead letter.

On the other hand, the military one, which was drawn up at the same time and signed by the two generals, was carried honourably into effect. By its terms it was agreed that such Irish officers and soldiers as desired to go to France should be conveyed there, and in the meantime should remain under the command of their own officers. Ginkel made strenuous efforts to enlist the Irish troops in his master's service. Few, however, agreed to accept his offer. A day was fixed for the election to be made, and the Irish troops were passed in review. All who would take service with William were directed to file off at a particular spot; all who passed it were held to have thrown in their lot with France. The long procession was watched with keen interest by the group of generals looking on, but the decision was not long delayed. The vast majority unhesitatingly elected exile, only about a thousand agreeing to take service with William.

The most piteous part of the story remains. Sarsfield, with the soldiers under him who had elected to go to France, withdrew into Limerick, and the next day proceeded to Cork, where they were to embark. The news had, in the meanwhile, spread, and the roads were covered with women rushing to see the last of husbands, brothers, sons. Wives, mothers, and children followed the departing exiles to the water's edge, imploring with cries of agony not to be left behind. In the extremity of his pity Sarsfield proclaimed that his soldiers might take their wives and families with them to France. It was found utterly impossible, however, to do so, since no transport could be provided for such a multitude. Room was found for a few families, but the beach was still crowded with those who had perforce to be left behind. As the boats pushed off the women clung desperately to them, and several, refusing to let go, were dragged out of their depth and drowned. A wild cry went up as the ships began to move. The crowd rushed frantically along the shore from headland to headland, following them with their eyes as long as they remained in sight. When the last ship had dropped below the horizon, and the dull autumn dusk had settled down over sea and shore, they dispersed slowly to their desolate homes. Night and desolation must indeed have seemed to have settled down for good upon Ireland.

XLV.

THE PENAL CODE.

WE are now upon the brink of a century as full of strange fortunes for Ireland as any that had preceded it, but in which those fortunes were destined to take a widely different turn. In the two preceding ones revolts and risings had, as we have seen, been the rule rather than the exception. In this one from the beginning down to within a couple of years of its close when a rebellion—which, in most impartial historians' opinion, might with a little care have been averted—broke the peace of the century, hardly a symptom of any disposition to appeal to arms is discoverable. Two great Jacobite risings convulsed England ; the American revolt, so fraught with momentous consequences, was fought and carried, but Ireland never stirred. The fighting element was gone. It was in France, in Spain, in the Low Countries —scattered over half the battlefields of Europe. The country which gave birth to these fighters was quiet ; a graveyard quiet, it may be said, but still significant, if only by contrast with what had gone before.

One advantage which the student of this century has over others is that it has been made the subject of a work which enables us to thread our way through its mazes with what, in comparison to other periods may be called ease. In his "History of the Eighteenth Century" Mr. Lecky has done for the Ireland of one century what it is much to be desired some one would hasten to do for the Ireland of all. He has broken down a barrier of prejudice so solid and of such long standing that it seemed to be invulnerable, and has proved that it is actually possible to be just in two directions at once—a feat no previous historian of Ireland can be said to have even attempted. This work, the final volume of which has not yet appeared, so completely covers the whole ground that it seems to afford an excuse for an even more hasty scamper over the same area than the exigencies of space have elsewhere made inevitable.

The task to which both the English and the Irish Parliaments now energetically addressed themselves was—firstly, the undoing of the Acts passed in the late reign; secondly, the forfeiture of the estates of those who had taken the losing side in the late campaign; thirdly, the passing of a series of Acts the aim of which was as far as possible to stamp out the Roman Catholic religion altogether, and in any case to deprive it of any shadow or semblance of future political importance.

To describe at length the various Acts which make up what is known as the Penal code—"a code impossible," as Mr. Lecky observed in an earlier work, " for any Irish Protestant whose mind is not wholly perverted by religious bigotry, to look back at without shame and indignation," would take too long. It will be enough, therefore, if I describe its general purport, and how it affected the political and social life of that century upon which we are now entering.

In several respects it not a little resembled what is nowadays known as "boycotting," only it was boycotting inflicted by the State itself. As compared with some of the enactments passed against Protestants in Catholic countries, it was not, it must be said, sanguinary, but its aim seemed to be to make life itself intolerable; to reduce the whole Catholic population to the condition of pariahs and outcasts. No Papist might possess a horse of the value of over £5; no Papist might carry arms; no Papist might dispose as he chose of his own property; no Papist might acquire any landed freehold; no Papist might practise in any of the liberal professions; no Papist might educate his sons at home, neither might he send them to be educated abroad. Deeper wrong, more biting and terrible injury even than these, it sowed bitter strife between father and son, and brother and brother. Any member of a family, by simply turning Protestant, could dispossess the rest of that family of the bulk of the estate to his own advantage. Socially, too, a Papist, no matter what his rank, stood below, and at the mercy of, his Protestant neighbours. He was treated by the executive as a being devoid, not merely of all political, but of all social rights, and only the numerical superiority of the members of the persecuted creed can have enabled them to carry on existence under such circumstances at all.

For it must be remembered (and this is one of its worst features) that those placed under this monstrous ban constituted the vast majority of the whole country.

In Burke's memorable words, "This system of penalty and incapacity has for its object no small sect or obscure party, but a very numerous body of men, a body which comprehends at least two-thirds of the whole nation; it amounts to two million eight hundred thousand souls—a number sufficient for the constituents of a great people."[1] "The happiness or misery of multitudes," he adds in another place, "can never be a thing indifferent. A law against the majority of the people is in substance a law against the people itself; its extent determines its invalidity; it even changes its character as it enlarges its operation; it is not particular injustice, but general oppression, and can no longer be considered as a private hardship which might be borne, but spreads and grows up into the unfortunate importance of a national calamity."

As was natural under the circumstances, many feigned conversions took place, that being the only way to avoid been utterly cut adrift from public life. For by a succession of enactments, not only were the higher offices and the professions debarred to Roman Catholics, but they were even prohibited —to so absurd a length can panic go—from being sheriffs, jurymen, constables, or even gamekeepers. "Every barrister, clerk, attorney, or solicitor," to quote again Burke, "is obliged to take a solemn oath not to employ persons of that persuasion; no, not as hackney clerks, at the miserable salary of seven shillings a week." It was loudly complained of many years later, that men used to qualify for taking

[1] "Tracts on the Popery Laws."

the oaths required upon being admitted as barristers or attorneys by attending church and receiving a sacramental certificate on their road to Dublin. Others, to save their property from confiscation, sacrificed their inclinations, often what they held to be their hopes of salvation, to the exigencies of the situation, and nominally embraced Protestantism. Old Lady Thomond, for instance, upon being reproached by some stricter co-religionist for thus imperilling her soul, asked with quick scorn whether it was not better that one old woman should burn than that the Thomonds should lose their own. The head of the house would thus often present himself or herself at the parish church, while the other members of the family kept to the old faith, and the chaplain, under the name of the tutor or secretary, celebrated mass in the harness-room or the servants' hall.

To the credit of Irish Protestants it may be said that, once the first violence of fanaticism had died out, there was little attempt to enforce the legal enactments in all their hideous atrocity. According to the strict letter of the law, no Roman Catholic bishop, archbishop, or other dignitary; no monk, nun, or member of any religious fraternity, could set foot in Ireland; and any one who harboured them was liable at the third offence to confiscation of all his goods. A list of parish priests was also drawn up and certified, and their names entered, and when these had died no others were by law allowed to come, any so doing being liable to the penalties of high treason. As a matter of fact, however, they came with very little hindrance, and the succession was steadily kept up from the Continent. The attempt to stamp out a religion by force proved to be the most absolute of failures, although, as no rule is without its exception, it must be added that in England, where exactly the same penal laws were in force, and where the number of Roman Catholics was at the beginning of the century considerable, they dwindled by the end of it almost to the point of extinction. In Ireland the reverse was the case. The number of Roman Catholics, according to the most trustworthy statistics, increased rather than diminished under the Penal code, and there were many more conversions from Protestantism to Catholicism than there were the other way.

This, no doubt, was in great measure due to the neglect with which the scattered Protestant communities were treated, especially in the south and west. The number of Protestant clergymen was extremely small, as many as six, seven, and even ten livings being frequently held by a single individual, and of these many were absentees, and their place filled by a curate. Thus—isolated in a vast Roman Catholic community, often with no church of their own within reach—the few Protestants drifted by a natural law to the faith of their neighbours. On the emphatic and angry testimony of Archbishop Boulter, we know that conversions from Protestantism to Catholicism were in his time extremely common amongst the lower orders. By law, too, no marriage between a Protestant and Catholic was recognizable, yet there were many such, and the children in most cases seem to have reverted to the elder faith.

"TIGER" ROCHE, A FAMOUS IRISH DUELIST, BORN IN DUBLIN 1729.

The best side of all this for the Catholics showed itself in that feeling of devotion and fealty to their own faith which persecution rarely fails to awaken, and for which the Roman Catholics of Ireland, high and low alike, have always been honourably distinguished. The worst was that this sense of being under an immoveable ban sapped at all the roots of manliness and honourable ambition. Amongst the well-to-do classes the more spirited of the young men went abroad and enlisted under foreign banners. The rest stayed at home, and fell into an idle, aimless, often disreputable, fashion of existence. The sense of being of no account, mere valueless items in the social hive, is no doubt answerable for a good deal of all this. Swift assures us that in his time the Catholic manhood of Ireland were of no more importance than its women and children; of no more importance, he adds in another place, than so many trees. With a patience pathetic in so essentially impatient a race, both priests and people seem to have settled down after awhile into a sort of desperate acceptance of the inevitable. So complete indeed was their submission that towards the close of the century we find the English executive, harassed and set at nought by its own Protestant colonists, turning by a curious nemesis to the members of this persecuted creed, whose patience and loyalty three quarters of a century of unexampled endurance seemed to have gone far to prove

XLVI.

THE COMMERCIAL CODE.

ALL power, place, and authority had thus once more swung round into the hands of the Protestant colony—"The Protestant Ascendency," as it came after a while to be called. They alone had seats in Parliament, they alone, until near the end of the century, were competent to vote. Taxes were collected over the whole island, but only Protestants had a voice in their disposal. All the parliamentary struggles of this century, it must clearly be understood, were struggles between Protestants and Protestants, and the different political parties, " patriotic " and others, were parties formed exclusively amongst the Protestants themselves. Protestantism was not only the privileged, but it was also the polite, creed ; the creed of the upper classes, as distinguished from the creed of the potato-diggers and the turf-cutters ; a view of the matter of which distinct traces may even yet be discovered in Ireland.

If Protestants, as compared with their Roman Catholic brethren, were happy, the Protestant colony was very far from being allowed its own way, or permitted to govern itself as it thought fit. Although avowedly kept as her garrison, and to preserve her own power in Ireland, England had no notion of allowing it equal advantages with herself, or of running the smallest risk of its ever coming to stand upon any dangerous footing of equality. The fatal theory that it was the advantage of the one country that the other should be kept poor, had by this time firmly taken root in the minds of English statesmen, and to it, and to the unreasonable jealousy of a certain number of English traders, the disasters now to be recorded were mainly due.

Cromwell had placed English and Irish commerce upon an equal footing. Early in Charles II.'s reign an Act had however been passed to hinder the importation of Irish cattle into England, one which had struck a disastrous, not to say fatal, blow at Irish agricultural interests. Then as now cattle was its chief wealth, and such a prohibition meant nothing short of ruin to the landowners, and through them to all who depended upon them. So far Irish ports were open, however, to foreign countries, and when the cattle trade ceased to be profitable, much of the land had been turned by its owners into sheepwalks. There was a large and an increasing demand for Irish wool upon the Continent, in addition to which a considerable number of manufacturers had of late started factories, and an energetic manufacture of woollen goods was going on, and rapidly becoming the principal form of Irish industry. The English traders, struck by this fact, were suddenly smitten with panic. The Irish competition, they declared, were reducing their gains, and they cried loudly, therefore, for legislative protection. Their prayer was granted. In 1699, the last year of the century, an Act was passed forbidding the export of Irish woollen goods, not to England alone, but to *all* other countries.

The effect of this Act was instantaneous and startling. The manufacturers, who had come over in large numbers, left the country for the most part within six months, never to return again. A whole population was suddenly thrown out of employment. Emigration set in, but, in spite of the multitude that left, famine laid hold of many of those who remained. The resources of the poorest classes are always so low in Ireland that a much less sweeping blow than this would at any time have sufficed to bring them over the verge of starvation.

Another important result was that smuggling immediately began on an enormous scale. Wool was now a drug in the legitimate market, and woollen goods had practically no market. A vast contraband trade sprang swiftly up upon the ruins of the legitimate one. Wool, which at home was worth only 5d. or 6d. a lb., in France fetched half-a-crown. The whole population, from the highest to the lowest, flung themselves energetically on the side of the smugglers. The coast-line was long and intricate; the excise practically powerless. Wool was packed in caves all along the south and south-west coast, and carried off as opportunity served by the French vessels which came to seek it. What was meant by nature and Providence to have been the honest and open trade of the country was thus forced to be carried on by stealth and converted into a crime. It alleviated to some degree the distress, but it made Law seem more than ever a mockery, more than ever the one arch-enemy against which every man's hand might legitimately be raised.

Even this, if bad enough, was not the worst. The worst was that this arbitrary Act—directed, it must be repeated, by England, not against the Irish natives, but against her own colonists—done, too, without there being an opportunity for the country to be heard in its own defence—struck at the very root of all enterprise, and produced a widespread feeling of hopelessness and despair. Since this was the acknowledged result of too successful rivalry with England, of what use, it was openly asked, to attempt any new enterprise, or what was to hinder the same fate from befalling it in its turn? The whole relationship of the two islands, even where no division of blood or creed existed, grew thus to be strained and embittered to the last degree; the sense of hostility and indignation being hardly less strong in the latest arrived colonist than in the longest established. "There was scarce an Englishman," says a writer of the time, "who had been seven years in the country, *and meant to remain there*, who did not become averse to England, and grow into something of an Irishman." All this must be taken into account before those puzzling contradictions and anomalies which make up the history of this century can ever be properly realized.

XLVII.

MOLYNEUX AND SWIFT.

THE early half of the eighteenth century is such a very dreary period of Irish history that there is little temptation to linger over it. Two men, however, stand out conspicuously against this melancholy background, neither of whom must be passed over without a few words.

The first of these was William Molyneux, the "Ingenious Molyneux," as he was called by his contemporaries, a distinguished philosopher, whose life was almost exclusively devoted to scientific pursuits. Molyneux is, or ought to be, a very interesting figure to any one who cares, even slightly, about Ireland. He was one of the chief founders of the Philosophical Association in Dublin, which was the parent both of the present Dublin Society and of the Royal Irish Academy. He was also a Fellow of the Royal Society, and a friend of John Locke, with whom he constantly corresponded. Both his letters, and those of his brother, Dr. Thomas Molyneux, show the most vivid and constant interest in everything connected with the natural history of Ireland. Now it is a moving bog, which has scared the natives in its neighbourhood out of their senses; now, again, some great find of Irish elks, or some tooth of a mammoth which has been unearthed, and it is gravely discussed how such a "large-bodied beast" could have been transported over seas, especially to a country where the "Greeks and Romans never had a footing," and where therefore the learned Mr. Camden's theory, that the elephants' bones found in England were the remains of those "brought over by the Emperor Claudius," necessarily falls to the ground. Both the brothers Molyneux belong to a band of Irish naturalists whose numbers are, unfortunately, remarkably limited. Why it should be so is not easily explained, but so it is. When Irish archæology is mentioned, the names of Petrie, of Wilde, of Todd, of Graves, and, last but not least, of Miss Margaret Stokes spring to the mind. Irish geologists, with Sir Richard Griffiths at their head, show as good a record as those of any other country, but the number of Irish naturalists whose fame has reached beyond a very narrow area is small indeed. This is the less accountable as, though scanty as regards the number of its species, the natural history of Ireland is full of interest, abounding in problems not even yet fully solved: the very scantiness of its fauna being in one sense, an incentive and stimulus to its study, for the same reason that a language which is on the point of dying out is often of more interest to a philologist than one that is in full life and vigour.

This, however, is a digression, and as such must be forgiven. Returning to the arena of politics, Molyneux's chief claim to remembrance rests upon a work published by him in favour of the rights of the Irish

Parliament in the last year but one of the seventeenth century, only seven years therefore after the treaty of Limerick.

As one of the members of the Dublin University he had every opportunity of judging how the grasp which the English Parliament maintained by means of the obsolete machinery of Poynings' Act was steadily throttling and benumbing all Irish enterprise. In 1698 his famous remonstrance, known as "The Case of Ireland being bound by Act of Parliament made in England," appeared, with a dedication to King William. It at once created an immense sensation, was fiercely condemned as seditious and libellous by the English Parliament, by whom, as a mark of its utter abhorrence, it was condemned to be burned by the common hangman.

Few things will give a clearer idea of the extraordinarily exasperated state of politics at the time than to read the remonstrance which produced so tremendous a storm. Take, for example, the words with which the earlier portion of it closes, and which are worth studying, if only for the impressive dignity of their style, which not a little foreshadows Burke's majestic prose :—

"To conclude, I think it highly inconvenient for England to assume this authority over the kingdom of Ireland. I believe there will need no great arguments to convince the wise assembly of English senators how inconvenient it may be to England to do that which may make the lords and the people of Ireland think that they are not well used, and may drive them to discontent. The laws and liberties of England were granted above five hundred years ago to the people of Ireland, upon their submission to the Crown of England, with a design to keep them in the allegiance of the king of England. How consistent it may be with true policy to do that which the people of Ireland may think an invasion of their rights and liberties, I do most humbly submit to the Parliament of England to consider. They are men of great wisdom, honour, and justice, and know how to prevent all future inconveniences. We have heard great outcries, and deservedly, on breaking the edict of Nantes, and other stipulations. How far the breaking our constitution, which has been of five hundred years standing exceeded these, I leave the world to judge."

In another place Molyneux vindicates the dignity of a Parliament in words of singular force and moderation :—

"The rights of Parliament should be preserved sacred and inviolable wherever they are found. This kind of government, once so universal all over Europe, is now almost vanished amongst the nations thereof. Our king's dominions are the only supporters of this most noble Gothic constitution, save only what little remains may be found thereof in Poland. We should not therefore make so light of that sort of legislature, and, as it were, abolish it in one kingdom of the three wherein it appears, but rather cherish and encourage it wherever we meet it." [1]

[1] "The Case of Ireland being bound by Acts of Parliament made in England." By William Molyneux, Esq., Dublin.

For a remonstrance so dignified, couched in language so respectful, burning by the common hangman seems a hard lot. The disgrace, if such it was, does not appear to have very deeply penetrated its author, who pursued the even tenour of his way, and the same year paid a visit to his friend John Locke, on the return journey from which visit he unfortunately caught a chill, from the effects of which he died the following October. After his death the momentary stir which his eloquence had created died out, as the circles left by the falling of a stone die out upon some stagnant pool, until nearly a quarter of a century later a much more violent splash again aroused attention, and a far less pacific exponent of Irish abuses than Molyneux sprang fiercely into the turmoil.

Jonathan Swift had been eleven years Dean of St. Patrick's before he produced those famous letters which have left their mark so indelibly upon the course of Irish politics. Swift's part in this Stygian pool of the eighteenth century is rather a difficult one to explain. He was not in any sense an Irish champion, indeed, objected to being called an Irishman at all, and regarded his life in Ireland as one of all but unendurable banishment. He was a vehement High Churchman, and looked upon the existing penal proscription under which the Catholics lay as not merely desirable, but indispensable. At the same time it would be quite untrue to suppose, as is sometimes done, that he merely made a cat's-paw of Irish politics in order to bring himself back into public notice. He was a man of intense and even passionate sense of justice, and the state of affairs in

DEAN SWIFT.
(From an engraving by Fourdinier after Jervis.)

the Ireland of his day, the tyranny and political dishonesty which stalked in high places, the degradation and steadily-increasing misery in which the mass of the people were sunk, were enough to lash far less scathing powers of sarcasm than he possessed to their highest possible pitch of expression.

The cause that drew forth the famous Drapier letters—why Swift chose to spell the word *draper* with an *i* no one has ever explained—appears at first sight hardly worthy of the occasion. Ireland wanted a copper coinage, and Walpole, who was then the Prime Minister, had given a patent for the purpose to a person called Wood, part of the profits of which patent were to go to the Duchess of Kendal, the king's mistress. There seems no reason to think that the pennies produced by Wood were in any way inferior to the existing English ones, and Sir Isaac Newton—who was at the time Master of the Mint—declared that, if anything, they were rather better. The real wrong, the real insult, was that the patent was granted by the Minister without reference to the Lord-Lieutenant, to the Irish Parliament, or to any single human being in Ireland. It was a proof the more of that total indifference with which the interests of Ireland were regarded, and it was upon this score that Swift's wrath exploded like a bomb.

The line he chose to take was to attack the patent, not as a monstrous job—which undoubtedly it was— but from the point of view of the value of the pennies. Assuming the character of a tradesman, he adjured all classes of the community, down to the very beggars, not to be induced to accept them. Assured them that for the benefit of Mr. Wood, "a mean man, a hardware dealer," every human being in Ireland was about to be deliberately robbed and ruined. His logic sounded unanswerable to the ignorant. His diatribes produced the most extraordinary effect. A terrific panic set in, and so overwhelming was the sensation that the Ministers in the end found it necessary to cancel the patent, and suspend the issue of Wood's halfpence. For the first time in Irish history public opinion, unsupported by arms, had carried its point: an epoch of vast importance in the history of every country.

That Swift knew perfectly well that the actual value of the copper coinage was not a matter of profound importance may be taken for granted, and so far his conduct is certainly not justifiable on any very strict rule of ethics. If the pennies were of small importance, however, there were other things that were of more. Little of a patriot as he was, little as he was supposed, or supposed himself, to care for Ireland or Irishmen, his wrath burnt fiercely at what he saw around him. He saw, too, his own wrongs, as others have done before and since, "writ large" in the wrongs of the country, and resented them as such. With his keen, practical knowledge of men, he knew, moreover, how thick was that medium, born of prejudice and ignorance, through which he had to pierce—a medium through which nothing less pointed than the forked lightnings of his own terrible wit could have found its way. Whatever his motives were, his success at least is indisputable. High Churchman as he was, vehement anti-papist as he was, he became from that moment, and remained to the hour of his death, beyond all question the most popular man in Ireland and his name was ever afterwards upon the lips of all who aspired to promote the best interests and prosperity of their country.

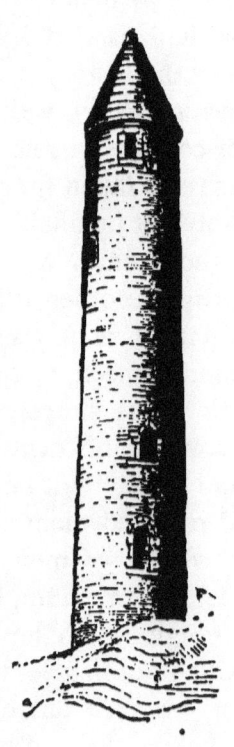

XLVIII.

HENRY FLOOD.

THE forty years which follow may be passed rapidly over. They were years of absolute tranquillity in Ireland, but beyond that rather negative praise little of good can be reported of them. Public opinion was to all practical purposes dead, and the functions of Parliament were little more than nominal. Unlike the English one, the Irish Parliament had by the nature of its constitution, no natural termination, save by a dissolution, or by the death of the sovereign. Thus George the Second's Irish Parliament sat for no less than thirty-three years, from the beginning to the end of his reign. The sessions, too, had gradually come to be, not annual as in England, but biennial, the Lord-Lieutenant spending as a rule only six months in every two years in Ireland. In his absence all power was vested in the hands of the Lords Justices, of whom the most conspicuous during this period were the three successive archbishops of Armagh, namely, Swift's opponent Boulter, Hoadly, and Stone, all three Englishmen, and devoted to what was known as the "English interest," who governed the country by the aid of a certain number of great

PHILIP Earl of CHESTERFIELD.

Delightful task! to rear the tender thought,
To teach the young idea how to shoot,
To pour the fresh instruction o'er the mind,
To breathe th'enlivening spirit, and to fix
The generous purpose in the glowing breast. *Thomson.*

LORD LIEUTENANT FROM 1745 TO 1754.

Irish borough-owners, or Undertakers, who "undertook" to carry on the king's business in consideration of receiving the lion's share of the patronage, which they distributed amongst their own adherents. Of these borough-owners Lord Shannon was the happy possessor of no less than sixteen seats, while others had eight, ten, twelve, or more, which were regularly and openly let out to hire to the Government. Efforts were from time to time made by the more independent members to curtail these abuses, and to recover some degree of independence for the Parliament, but for a long time their efforts were without avail, and owing to the nature of its constitution, it was all but impossible to bring public opinion to bear upon its proceedings, so that the only vestige of independence shown was when a collision occurred between the selfish interests of those in whose hands all power was thus concentrated.

About 1743 some stir began to be aroused by a succession of statements published by Charles Lucas, a Dublin apothecary, in the *Freeman's Journal*, a newspaper started by him, and in which he vehemently denounced the venality of Parliament, and loudly asserted the inherent right of Ireland to govern itself, a right of which it had only been formally deprived by the Declaratory Act of George I.[1] So unequivocal was his language that the grand jury of Dublin at last gave orders for his addresses to be burnt, and in 1749 a warrant was issued for his apprehension, whereupon he fled to England, and did not return until many years later, when he was at once

---

[1] English Statutes, 6 Geo. c. 5.

elected member for Dublin. His speeches in the House of Commons seem never to have produced an effect at all comparable with that of his writings, but he gave a constant and important support to the patriotic party, which had now formed itself into a small but influential opposition under the leadership of Henry Flood.

Flood and Grattan are by far the two greatest of those orators and statesmen whose eloquence lit up the debates of the Irish House of Commons during its brief period of brilliancy, and as such will require, even in so hasty a sketch as this, to be dwelt upon at some length. Since a good deal of the same ground will have to be gone over in succeeding chapters, it seems best to explain here those points which affected them personally, and to show as far as possible in what relationship they stood one to the other.

Henry Flood was born near Kilkenny in 1732, and was the son of the Chief Justice of the King's Bench. At sixteen he went to Trinity College, Dublin, and afterwards to Oxford. In 1759 he entered the Irish Parliament as member for Kilkenny, and at once threw himself vehemently upon the popular side, his first speech being an attack upon the Primate Stone. As an orator his style appears to have been laboured, and his speeches brim over in all directions with forced illustrations and metaphors, but his powers of argument and debate were remarkably strong. For about ten years he waged a continual struggle against the Government, urging especially a limitation to the duration of Parliament and losing no opportunity of asserting its claims to independence, or of attacking

RIGHT HON. HENRY FLOOD.
(*After a drawing by Comerford.*)

the pension list, which under the system then prevailing grew steadily from year to year. Upon reform he also early fixed his attention, although, unlike Grattan, he was from the beginning to the end of his life steadily hostile to all proposals for giving the franchise to the Catholics.

During the viceroyalty of Lord Townshend, who became Lord-Lieutenant in 1767, an Octennial Bill was passed limiting the duration of Parliament to eight years, but this momentary gleam of better things was not sustained; on the contrary, corruption was, under his rule, carried even further than it had been before. Under the plea of breaking the power of the borough-owners, he set himself deliberately to make the whole Parliament subservient to Government, thus practically depriving it of what little vestige of independence it still possessed. A succession of struggles took place, chiefly over Money Bills, the more independent members, under Flood's leadership, claiming for the Irish House of Commons the complete control of the national purse, a claim as uniformly resisted by the Government. Though almost invariably defeated on a division in the end the opposition were to a great degree successful, and in 1773 the hated viceroy was re-called.

This was the moment at which Flood stood higher in his countrymen's estimation than was ever again the case. He was identified with all that was best in their aspirations, and no shadow of self-seeking had as yet dimmed the brightness of his fame. It was very different with his next step. Lord Townshend was succeeded by Lord Harcourt, whose administration at first promised to be a shade more liberal and less corrupt than that of his predecessors. Of this administration Flood, to his own misfortune, became a member. What his motives were it is rather difficult to say. He was a rich man, and therefore had no temptation to sell or stifle his opinions for place. Whatever they were, it is clear, from letters still extant, that he not only accepted but solicited office. He was made Vice-Treasurer, a post hitherto reserved for Englishmen, at a salary of £3,500 a year.

Although, as Mr. Lecky has pointed out, no actual stain of dishonour attaches to Flood in consequence of this step, there can be no doubt that it was a grave error, and that he lived to repent it bitterly. For the next seven years not only was he forced to keep silence as regards all those points he had previously advocated so warmly, but, as a member of the Government, he actually helped to uphold some of the most damaging of the restraints laid upon Irish trade and prosperity. Upon the outbreak of the America war a two years' embargo was laid upon Ireland, and a force of 4,000 men raised and despatched to America at its expense. The state of defencelessness in which this left the country led, as will be seen in a succeeding chapter, to a great volunteer movement, in which all classes and creeds joined enthusiastically. Flood was unable to resist the contagion. His voice was once again heard upon the liberal side. He flung away the trammels of office, surrendered his large salary, and returned to his old friends. He never, however, regained his old place. A greater man had in the meanwhile risen to the front, and in Henry Grattan

Irish aspiration had found its clearest and strongest voice.

This was a source of profound mortification to Flood, and led eventually to a bitter quarrel between these two men—patriots in the best sense both of them. Flood tried to outbid Grattan by pushing the concessions won from England in the moment of her difficulty yet further, and by making use of the volunteers as a lever to enforce his demands. This Grattan honourably, whether wisely or not, resisted, and the Parliament supported his resistance. After an unsuccessful attempt to carry a Reform Bill, Flood retired, to a great degree, from Irish public life, and not long afterwards succeeded in getting a seat in the English Parliament. His oratory there proved a failure. He was "an oak of the forest too great and old," as Grattan said, "to be transplanted at fifty." This failure was a fresh and a yet more mortifying disappointment, and his end was a gloomy and somewhat obscure one, but he will always be remembered with gratitude as one of the first who in the Irish Parliament lifted his voice against those restrictions under which the prosperity of the country lay shackled and all but dead.

XLIX.

HENRY GRATTAN.

"GREAT men," wrote Sydney Smith, sixty years ago in an article in *The Edinburgh Review*, "hallow a whole people, and lift up all who live in their time. What Irishman does not feel proud that he lived in the days of Grattan? Who has not turned to him for comfort from the false friends and open enemies of Ireland? Who did not remember him in the days of its burnings, wastings, and murders?"

Grattan is, indeed, pre-eminently the Irish politician to whom other Irish politicians—however diverse their views or convictions—turn unanimously with the common sense of admiration and homage. Two characteristics—usually supposed in Ireland to be inherently antagonistic—met harmoniously in him. He was consistently loyal and he was consistently patriotic. From the beginning to the end of his career his patriotism never hindered him either from risking his popularity whenever he considered duty or the necessities of the case required him to do so; a resolution which more than once brought him into sharp collision with his countrymen, on one occasion even at some little risk to himself.

RIGHT HON. HENRY GRATTAN, M.P.
(*From an engraving by Godby after Pope.*)

In 1775 he entered Parliament—sixteen years, therefore, later than Flood—being brought in by his friend Lord Charlemont. The struggle with America was then beginning, and all Grattan's sympathies went with those colonists who were battling for their own independence. His eloquence from the moment it was first heard produced an extraordinary effect, and when the volunteer movement broke out he threw himself heartily into it, and availed himself of it to press in the Irish Parliament for those measures of free trade and self-government upon which his heart was set. When the first of these measures was carried, he brought forward the famous Declaration of Rights, embodying the demand for independence, a demand which, in the first instance, he had to defend almost single-handed. Many of his best friends hung back, believing the time to be not yet ripe for such a proposal. Even Edmund Burke—the life-long and passionate friend of Ireland—cried out in alarm "Will no one speak to that madman? Will no one stop that madman Grattan?" The madman, however, went on undismayed. His words flew like wildfire over the country. He was supported in his motion by eighteen counties, by addresses from the grand juries, and by resolutions from the volunteers. By 1782, the impulse had grown so strong that it could no longer be resisted. An address in favour of Grattan's Declaration of Rights was carried enthusiastically in April by the Irish Parliament, and so impressed was the Government by the determined attitude of the country that, by the 27th of May the Viceroy was empowered to announce the concurrence of the English legislature. The Declaratory Act of George I. was then repealed by the English Parliament. Bills were immediately afterwards passed by the Irish one embodying the Declaration of Rights, also a biennial Mutiny Act, and an Act validating the marriage of Dissenters, while, above all, Poynings' Act, which had so long fettered its free action, was once for all repealed.

This was the happiest moment of Grattan's life. The country, with a burst of spontaneous gratitude, voted him a grant of £100,000. This sum he declined, but in the end was persuaded, with some reluctance, to take half. A period of brief, but while it lasted unquestionable prosperity spread over the country. In Dublin, public buildings sprang up in all directions; a bright little society flourished and enjoyed itself; trade too prospered to a degree never hitherto known. Between England and Ireland, however, the commercial restrictions were still in force. The condition of the Irish Catholics, though latterly to some degree alleviated, was still one of all but unendurable oppression. Reform, too, was as far off as ever, and corruption had increased rather than diminished, owing to the greatly increased importance of the Parliament. In 1789 an unfortunate quarrel sprang up between the two legislatures over the appointment of a Regent, rendered necessary by the temporary insanity of George III., and this difference was afterwards used as an argument in favour of a legislative Union. In 1793 a measure of half-emancipation was granted, Roman Catholics being admitted to vote, though not to sit in Parliament, an anomalous distinction giving power to the ignorant, yet still keeping the fittest men out of public life. Upon the arrival of Lord Fitzwilliam as Viceroy in 1795, it was fervently believed that full emancipation was at last about to be granted, and Grattan brought in a Bill to that effect. These hopes, as will presently be seen, were destined to be bitterly disappointed. Lord Fitzwilliam was recalled, and from that moment Grattan was doomed to stand helplessly by and watch the destruction of that edifice which he had spent his whole life to erect and strengthen. The country grew more and more restless, and it was plain to all who could read the signs of the times that, unless discontent was in some way allayed, a rebellion was sure to break out. In 1798 this long foreseen calamity occurred, but before it did so, Grattan had retired heart-broken and despairing into private life.

He re-emerged to plead, vehemently but fruitlessly, against the Union which was passed the following spring. As will be seen, when we reach that period the fashion in which that act was carried made it difficult for an honourable man, however loyal—and no man, it must be repeated, was more steadily loyal than Henry Grattan—to give it his support. He believed too firmly that Ireland could work out its own destiny best by the aid of a separate Parliament, and to this opinion he throughout his life clung. In his own words, "The two countries from their size must stand together—united *quoad* nature—distinct *quoad* legislation."

In 1805 he became a member of the English Parliament, where unlike Flood, his eloquence had almost as much effect as in Ireland, and where he was regarded by all parties with the deepest respect and regard. His heart, however, remained firmly anchored to its old home, and all his recollections in his old age centred around these earlier struggles. He died in 1820, and was buried in Westminster Abbey. One more quotation from Sydney Smith sums up the man for us in a few words: "The highest attainments of human genius were within his reach, but he thought the noblest occupation of a man was to make other men happy and free, and in that straight line he kept for fifty years, without one side-look, one yielding thought, one motive in his heart which might not have laid open to the view of God or man." A generation which produced two such men as Henry Grattan and Edmund Burke might well be looked back to by any country in the world as the flower and crown of its national life. There have not been many greater or better in the whole chequered history of the human race.

L.

THE IRISH VOLUNTEERS.

THE revolt of the English Colonies in America, although it evoked no disloyalty, had a strong and unforeseen influence upon the equally English colony in Ireland. It would have been strange had it not done so. The circumstances of the two colonies —looking at Ireland merely in that light—were in many respects all but identical. If England could tax America without the consent of its representatives, then, equally it could tax Ireland, in which case the long struggles lately waged by Flood, Grattan, and others in the Irish Parliament over Money Bills would be definitely decided against it. Compared to Ireland, America indeed had little to complain of. The restrictions which held back Irish commerce still existed in almost all their pristine force. The woollen trade, save for some very trifling home consumption, was practically dead; even the linen trade, which had been promised encouragement, had hitherto hardly received any. Bounties had been offered, on the contrary, to English woollen manufacturers, and duties levied on Irish sail-cloth, which had effectually put a stop to that important branch of the trade. Another cause had also affected commerce seriously. The manufacturers of the north, were almost to a man Presbyterian, and the laws against Presbyterians had been pressed with almost as much severity as against Catholics. Under the rule of Archbishops Boulter, Hoadly, and Stone, who had in succession governed the country, the Test Act had been employed with a suicidal severity, which had driven thousands of industrious men to join their brethren in America, where they could worship in peace, and where their presence was before long destined to produce a formidable effect upon the impending struggle.

The whole condition of the country was miserable in the extreme. Agriculture was at the lowest possible ebb. The Irish farmers, excluded from the English and all foreign markets, were reduced to destitution. Land was offered at fourteen and twelve years' purchase, and even at those prices found no buyers. Many of the principal landowners were absentees, and though the rents themselves do not seem as a rule to have been high, the middlemen, by whom the land was commonly taken, ground the wretched peasants under them to powder with their exactions. While everything else was thus steadily shrinking, the pension list was swelling until it stood not far short of £100,000. The additional troops recently raised in Ireland had been sent to America, and their absence had left the country all but defenceless. In 1779, an attempt was made to carry out a levy of militia, in which Prostestants only were to be enrolled, and an Act passed for the purpose. It failed utterly, for so miserably bankrupt was the condition of the Irish Government, that it was found impossible to collect money to pay the men, and the scheme in consequence had to be given up.

It proved, however, to be the parent of a really successful one. In the same year a volunteer movement sprang into sudden existence. Belfast had been left empty of troops, and was hourly in fear of a French descent, added to which it was harassed by the dread of a famous pirate of the period, called Paul Jones. Under these circumstances its citizens resolved to enrol themselves for their own defence. The idea, once started, flew through the country like wild-fire. The old fighting spirit sprang to sudden life at the cry to arms. After three-quarters of a century of torpor all was stir and animation. In every direction the gentry were enrolling their tenants, the sons of the great houses officering the corps and drilling their own retainers. Merchants, peers, members of Parliament all vied with one another, and in a few months' time nearly 60,000 men had been enrolled.

Although a good deal alarmed at the rapidity of this movement, the Government could not very well refuse to let the country arm in its own defence, and 16,000 stand of arms, which had been brought over for the projected militia, were after a while distributed. The greatest pride was felt in the completeness and perfection of the equipments. Reviews were held, and, for once, national sentiment and loyalty seemed to have struck hands.

Hardly, too, were the volunteers enrolled before it began to be felt what a power was thus conferred

JAMES CAULFIELD, EARL OF CHARLEMONT, COMMANDER OF THE IRISH VOLUNTEERS.
(*From an etching after a picture by Hogarth.*)

upon that party which had so long pleaded in vain for the relief of Ireland from those commercial disabilities under which it still laboured. Although the whole tone of the volunteers was loyal, and although their principal leader, Lord Charlemont, was a man of the utmost tact and moderation, it was none the less clear that an appeal backed by 60,000 men in arms acquired a weight and momentum which no previous Irish appeal had ever even approached.

In October of the same year Parliament met, and an amendment to the address was moved by Grattan, demanding a right of free export and import. Then Flood rose in his place, still holding office, and proposed that the more comprehensive words Free Trade should be adopted. It was at once agreed to and carried unanimously. Next day the whole House of Commons went in a body to present the address to the Lord-Lieutenant, the volunteers lining the streets and presenting arms as they went by.

The Government were startled. Lord Buckinghamshire, the Lord-Lieutenant, wrote to England to say that the trade restrictions must be repealed, or he would not answer for the consequences. Lord North, the Prime Minister, yielded, and a Bill of repeal were brought in, allowing Ireland free export and import to foreign countries and to the English Colonies. When the news reached Dublin, the utmost delight and excitement prevailed. Bonfires were lit, houses in Dublin illuminated, the volunteers fired salvoes of rejoicing, and addresses of gratitude were forthwith forwarded to England.

The next step in the upward progress has been

already partially described in the chapter dealing with Grattan. At the meeting of Parliament in 1782, the Declaration of Rights proposed by him was passed, and urgently pressed upon the consideration of the Government. The moment was exceptionally favourable. Lord North's Ministry had by this time fallen, after probably the most disastrous tenure of office that had ever befallen any English administration. America had achieved her independence, and England was in no mood for embarking upon fresh struggle with another of her dependencies. In Ireland the Ulster volunteers had lately met at Dungannon, and passed unanimous resolutions in favour of Grattan's proposal, and their example had been speedily followed all over Ireland. The Whig Ministry, now in power, was known to be not unfavourable to the cause which the Irish patriots had at heart. A Bill was brought forward and carried, revoking the recent Declaratory Acts which bound the Irish Parliament, and giving it the right to legislate for itself. Poynings' Act was thereupon repealed, and a number of independent Acts, as already stated, passed by the now emancipated Irish Parliament. The legislative independence was an accomplished fact.

The objects of the volunteers' existence was now over. The American war was at an end, the independence of the Parliament assured, and it was felt therefore, by all moderate men, that it was now time for them to disband. Flood, who had now again joined the patriotic party, was strongly opposed to this. He pressed forward his motion for "simple repeal," and was supported by Lord Bristol, the Bishop of Derry, a scatter-brained prelate, who had been bitten by a passion for military glory, and would have been perfectly willing to see the whole country plunged into bloodshed. A better and more reasonable plea on Flood's part was that reform was the crying necessity of the hour, and ought to be carried while the volunteers were still enrolled, and the effect already produced by their presence was still undiminished. Grattan also desired reform, but held that the time for carrying it was not yet ripe. A vehement debate ensued, and bitter recriminations were exchanged. A convention of volunteers was at the moment being held in Dublin, and Flood endeavoured to make use of their presence there to get his Reform Bill passed. This the House regarded as a menace, and after a violent debate his Bill was thrown out. There was a moment during which it seemed as if the volunteers were about to try the question by force of arms. More prudent counsels, however, prevailed, and, greatly to their credit, they consented a week later to lay down their arms, and retire peaceably to their own homes.

LI.

DANGER SIGNALS.

THE significant warnings uttered by Flood and others against the danger of postponing reform until the excitement temporarily awakened upon the subject had subsided and the volunteers disbanded, proved, unfortunately, to be only too well justified. Where Flood, however, had erred, had been in failing to see that a reform which left three-fourths of the people of the country unrepresented, could never be more than a reform in name. This error Grattan never made. During the next ten or twelve years, his efforts were steadily and continually directed to obtaining equal political power for all his fellow-countrymen alike. Reform was indeed the necessity of the hour. The corruption of Parliament was increasing rather than diminishing. From 130 to 140 of its members were tied by indissoluble knots to the Government, and could only vote as by it directed. Most of these were the nominees of the borough-owners; many held places or enjoyed pensions terminable at the pleasure of the king, and at the smallest sign of insubordination or independence instant pressure was brought to bear upon them until they returned to their obedience.

Although free now to import and export from the rest of the world no change with regard to Ireland's commercial intercourse with Great Britain had as yet taken place. In 1785, a number of propositions were drawn up by the Dublin Parliament, to enable the importation of goods through Great Britain into Ireland, or *vice versa*, without any increase of duty. These propositions were agreed to by Pitt, then Prime Minister, and were brought forward by him in the English House of Commons. Again, however, commercial jealousy stepped in. A number of English towns remonstrated vehemently; one petition despatched to the House alone bearing the signature of 80,000 Lancashire manufacturers. "Greater panic," it was said at the time, "could not have been expressed had an invasion been in question." The result was, that a number of modifications were made to the propositions, and when returned to Ireland, so profoundly had they been altered, that the patriotic party refused to accept them, and although when the division came on, the Government obtained a majority it was so small that the Bill was allowed to drop, and thus the whole scheme came to nothing.

Outside Parliament, meanwhile, the country was in a very disturbed state. Long before this local riots and disturbances had broken out, especially in the south. As early as 1762, secret societies, known under the generic name of Whiteboys, had inspired terror throughout Munster, especially in the counties of Cork, Limerick, and Tipperary. These risings, as

RIGHT HON. EDMUND BURKE.
(*From an engraving by Jones after Romney.*)

has been clearly proved by Mr. Lecky, had little, if any, connection with either politics or religion. Their cause lay, as he shows, on the very surface, in the all but unendurable misery in which the great mass of the people were sunk.

Lord Chesterfield, one of the few Lord-Lieutenants who had really attempted to understand Ireland, had years before spoken in unmistakeable language on this point. Subletting was almost universal, three or four persons standing often between the landowner and the actual occupier, the result being that the condition of the latter was one of chronic semi-starvation. So little was disloyalty at the root of the matter, that in a contemporary letter, written by Robert Fitzgerald, the Knight of Kerry, it is confidently asserted that, were a recruiting officer to be sent to the district, the people would gladly flock to the standard of the king, although, he significantly adds, " it seems to me equally certain that if the enemy effects a landing within a hundred miles of these people, they will most assuredly join them."[1]

The tithe system was another all but unendurable burden, and it was against the tithe proctors that the worst of the Whiteboy outrages were committed. That these outrages had little directly to say to religion is, however, clear, from the fact that the tithe system was nearly as much detested by the Protestant landowners as by their tenants. In the north risings of a somewhat similar character had broken out chiefly amongst Protestants of the lower classes,

[1] " History of England in the Eighteenth Century," vol. iv. p. 340.

who gathered themselves into bands under the name of "Oak boys" and "Steel boys." The grievances of which they complained being, however, for the most part after a while repealed, they gradually dispersed, and were heard of no more. In the south it was otherwise, and the result has been that Whiteboy conspiracies continued, under different names, to be a terror to the country, and have so continued down to our own day.

As long as the volunteers remained embodied there was an all but complete cessation of these local disturbances, but upon their disbandment they broke out with renewed force. Many too of the volunteers themselves, who, although disbanded, retained their arms, began to fall under new influences, and to lose their earlier reputation. "What had originally," in Grattan's words, "been the armed property of Ireland, was becoming its armed beggary." A violent sectarian spirit, too, was beginning to show itself afresh, although as yet chiefly amongst the lowest and most ignorant classes. A furious faction war had broken out in the North of Ireland, between Protestants and Roman Catholics. The former had made an association known as the "Peep-of-day boys," to which the latter had responded by one called the "Defenders." In 1795 a regular battle was fought between the two, and the "Defenders" were defeated with the loss of many lives. The same year saw the institution of Orange Lodges spring into existence, and spread rapidly over the north. Amongst the more educated classes a strongly revolutionary feeling was beginning to spread, especially in Belfast. The passionate sympathy of the Presbyterians for America had awakened a vehemently republican spirit, and the rising tide of revolution in France, found a loudly reverberating echo in Ireland, especially amongst the younger men. In 1791 in Belfast, the well-known "Society of United Irishmen" came into existence and its leaders were eager to combine this democratic movement in the north with the recently reconstructed Roman Catholic committee in Dublin. All these, it is plain, were elements of danger which required careful watching. The one hope, the one necessity, as all who were not blinded by passion or prejudice saw plainly, lay in a reformed Parliament— one which would represent, no longer a section, but the whole community. To combine to procure this, and to sink all religious differences in the common weal, was the earnest desire of all who genuinely cared for their country, whether within or without the Parliament. Of this programme, the members even of the United Irishmen were, in the first instance, ardent exponents, and their demands, ostensibly at least, extended no further. In the words of the oath administered to new members, they desired to forward " an identity of interests, a communion of rights, and a union amongst Irishmen of all religious persuasions, without which every reform in Parliament must be partial, not national, inadequate to the wants, delusive to the wishes, and insufficient for the freedom and happiness of the country."

LII.

THE FITZWILLIAM DISAPPOINTMENT.

THE eagerness shown at this time by the principal Irish Protestants to give full emancipation to their Roman Catholic countrymen is eminently creditable to them, and stands in strong relief to the bitterness on both sides, both in earlier and latter times. By 1792 there seems to have been something almost like unanimity on the subject. What reads strangest perhaps to our ears, 600 Belfast Protestant householders warmly pressed the motion on the Government. In a work, published six years earlier, Lord Sheffield, though himself opposed to emancipation, puts this unanimity in unmistakable words. "It is curious," he says, "to observe one-fifth or one-sixth of a nation in possession of all the power and property of the country, eager to communicate that power to the remaining four-fifths, which would, in effect, entirely transfer it from themselves."

The generation to which Flood, Lucas, and Lord Charlmont had belonged, and who were almost to a man opposed to emancipation, was fast passing away, and amongst the more independent men of the younger generation there were few who had not been won over

("A man of importance.")
THE EARL OF MOIRA.
By Gillray.

to Grattan's view of the matter. In England, too, circumstances were beginning to push many, even of those hitherto bitterly hostile to concession, in the same direction. The growing terror of the French Revolution had loosened the bonds of the party, and the hatred which existed between the Jacobins and the Catholic clerical party, inclined the Government to extend the olive branch to the latter in hopes of thereby securing their support. Pitt was personally friendly to emancipation, and in December, 1792, a deputation of five delegates from the Catholic convention in Dublin was graciously received by the king himself, and returned under the impression that all religious disabilities were forthwith to be abolished. Next month, January, 1793, at the meeting of the Irish Parliament, a Bill was brought in giving the right of voting to all Catholic forty-shilling freeholders, and throwing open also to Catholics the municipal franchise in the towns. Although vehemently opposed by the Ascendency, this Bill, being supported by the Opposition, passed easily and received the royal assent upon April 9th.

It was believed to be only an instalment of full and free emancipation soon to follow. In 1794, several of the more moderate Whigs, including Edmund Burke and Lord Fitzwilliam, left Fox, and joined Pitt. One of the objects of the Whig members of this new coalition was the admission of Irish Roman Catholics to equal rights with their Protestant fellow-countrymen. To this Pitt at first demurred, but in the end agreed to grant it subject to certain stipulations, and Lord Fitzwilliam was accordingly appointed Lord-Lieutenant, and arrived in Ireland in January, 1795.

His appointment awakened the most vehement and widely expressed delight. He was known to be a warm supporter of emancipation. He was a personal friend of Grattan's, and a man in whom all who had the interests of their country at heart believed that they could confide. He had himself declared emphatically that he would "never have taken office unless the Roman Catholics were to be relieved from every disqualification." He was received in Dublin with enthusiastic rejoicings. Loyal addresses from Roman Catholics poured in from every part of Ireland. Large supplies were joyfully voted by the Irish Parliament, and, although he reported in a letter to the Duke of Portland that the disaffection amongst the lower orders was very great, on the other hand the better educated of the Roman Catholics were loyal to a man. For the moment the party of disorder seemed indeed to have vanished. Grattan, though he refused to take office, gave all the great weight of his support to the Government, and obtained leave to bring in an Emancipation Bill with hardly a dissentient voice. The extreme Jacobine party ceased apparently for the moment to have any weight in the country. Revolution seemed to be scotched, and the dangers into which Ireland had been seen awhile before to be rapidly hastening, appeared to have passed away.

Suddenly all was changed. On February 12th, leave to bring in a Bill for the admission of Roman Catholics to Parliament was moved by Grattan. On February 9th, a letter reached Lord Fitzwilliam from

Pitt, which showed that some changes had taken place in the intentions of the Government, but no suspicion of the extent of those changes was as yet entertained. On February 23rd, however, the Duke of Portland wrote, "by the king's command," authorizing Lord Fitzwilliam to resign. The law officers and other officials who had been displaced were thereupon restored to their former places. Grattan's Bill was hopelessly lost, and all the elements of rebellion and disaffection at once began to seethe and ferment again.

What strikes one most in studying these proceedings is the curious folly of the whole affair! Why was a harbinger of peace sent if only to be immediately recalled? Why were the hopes of the Roman Catholics, of the whole country in fact, raised to the highest pitch of expectation, if only that they might be dashed to the ground? Pitt no doubt had a very difficult part to play. George III. was all his life vehemently opposed to the admission of Roman Catholics to Parliament. Two of the officials whom Fitzwilliam had dismissed, Cooke, the Under Secretary of State, and Beresford, the Chief Commissioner of Customs, were men of no little influence, and Beresford, immediately upon his arrival in England had had a personal interview with the king. That Pitt knew how critical was the situation in Ireland is certain. He was not, however, prepared to resign office, and short of that step it was impossible to bring sufficient pressure to bear upon the king's obstinacy. His own preference ran strongly towards a Union of the two countries, and with this end in view, he is often accused of having been cynically indifferent as to what disasters and horrors Ireland might be destined to wade through to that consummation. This it is difficult to conceive ; nevertheless, there can be no doubt that the rising of four years later dated from this decision, and was almost as directly due to it as if the latter had been planned with that object.

From this point the stream runs darkly and steadily to the end. Lord Fitzwilliam's departure was regarded by Protestants and Catholics alike as a national calamity. In Dublin shops were shut; people put on mourning, and his carriage was followed to the boat by lamenting crowds. Grattan's Bill was of course lost, and the exasperation of the Catholics rendered tenfold by the disappointment. " The demon of darkness," it was said, " could not have done more mischief had he come from hell to throw a fire-brand amongst the people."

Henceforward the Irish Parliament drops away into all but complete insignificance. After two or three abortive efforts to again bring forward reform, Grattan gave up the hopeless attempt, and retired broken-hearted from public life. The " United Irishmen," in the first instance an open political body, inaugurated and chiefly supported by Protestants, now rapidly changed its character. Its leaders were now all at heart republicans, and thoroughly impregnated with the leaven of the French Revolution. It was suppressed and apparently broken up by the Government in 1795, but was almost immediately afterwards reconstructed and re-organized upon an immense scale. Every member was bound to take an oath of secrecy, and its avowed object had become the erection by force of a republican form of Government in Ireland. The rebellion was bound to come now, and only accident could decide how soon.

RIGHT HON. EDMUND BURKE.
(*From a sketch from life.*)

LIII.

'NINETY-EIGHT.

IT was not long delayed. The Society of United Irishmen had now grown to be little more than a mere nest of Jacobinism, filled with all the turbulent and disaffected elements afloat in the whole country. Of this society Wolfe Tone was the creator, guide, and moving spirit. Any one who wishes to understand the movement rather as it originally took shape than in the form which it assumed when accident had deprived it of all its leaders, should carefully study his autobiography. As he reads its transparent pages, brimful of all the foolish, generous enthusiasms of the day, he will find it not a little hard, I think, to avoid some amount of sympathy with the man, however much he may, and probably will, reprobate the cause which he had so at heart.

Amongst the other leaders of the rising were Lord Edward Fitzgerald, a brother of the Duke of Leinster, Arthur O'Connor, a nephew of Lord Longueville, Thomas Addis Emmett, elder brother of the better known Robert Emmett—whose attempted rebellion in 1803, was a sort of postscript to this earlier one—and the two Sheare brothers. Compared to Wolfe Tone, however, all these were mere amateurs in insurrection, and pale and shadowy dabblers in rebellion. Lord Edward was an amiable warm-hearted visionary, high-minded and gallant, but without much ballast, and to a great degree under the guidance of others. The mainspring of the whole movement, as has been seen, was Protestant and Northern, and now that all hope of constitutional reform was gone, it was resolved to appeal openly to force and to call in the aid of the enemies of England to assist in the coming struggle.

Insane as the idea appears, looked back at from this distance, it evidently was not viewed in the same light by those at hand. England and France, it must be remembered, were at fierce war, and a descent upon the Irish coast was then, as afterwards by Napoleon, regarded as a natural and obvious part of the aggressive policy of the latter. In the summer of 1796 Lord Edward Fitzgerald went to Paris to open negotiations with the French Directory, and there met Wolfe Tone, who had been induced some time before to leave Ireland in order to avoid arrest. Lord Edward's Orleanist connection proving a bar to his negotiations, he left Paris, and the whole of the arrangements devolved into the latter's hand. He so fired Carnot, one of the Directory, and still more General Hoche, with a belief of the feasibility of his scheme of descent, that, in December of the same year a French fleet of forty-three vessels containing fifteen thousand troops were actually despatched under Hoche's command, Wolfe Tone being on board of one of them, which vessels, slipping past the English fleet in the Channel, bore down upon

THEOBALD WOLFE TONE.
(*From a lithograph after a sketch by Hullmandel.*)

the Irish coast, and suddenly appeared off Cape Clear.

All Ireland was thrown into the wildest panic. There were only a small body of troops in the south and not a war-ship upon the coast. The peasantry of the district, it is true, showed no disposition to rise, but for all that had the French landed, nothing could have hindered them from marching upon the capital. But—" those ancient and unsubsidised allies of England upon which English ministers depend as much for saving kingdoms as washerwomen for drying clothes," —the winds again stood true to their ancient alliance. The vessel with Hoche on board got separated from the rest of the fleet, and while the troops were waiting for him to arrive a violent gale accompanied with snow suddenly sprang up. The fleet moved on to Bear Island, and tried to anchor there, but the storm increased, the shelter was insufficient, the vessels dragged their anchors, were driven out to sea and forced to return to Brest. The ship containing Hoche had before this been forced to put back to France, and so ended the first and by far the most formidable of the perils which threatened England under this new combination.

One very unfortunate result of the narrowness of this escape was that the Irish Executive—stung by the sense of their own supineness, and utterly scared by the recent peril—threw themselves into the most violent and arbitrary measures of repression. The Habeas Corpus Act had already been suspended, and now martial law was proclaimed in five of the northern counties at once. The committee of the

United Irishmen was seized, the office of their organ *The Northern Star* destroyed, and an immense number of people hurried into gaol. What was much more serious throughout the proclaimed districts, the soldiery and militia regiments which had been brought over from England were kept under no discipline, but were allowed to ill-use the population almost at their own discretion. Gross excesses were committed, whole villages being in some instances plundered and the people turned adrift, while half hangings, floggings and picketings, were freely resorted to to extort confessions of concealed arms.

Against these measures—so calculated to precipitate a rising, and by which the innocent and well-disposed suffered no less than the guilty—Grattan, Ponsonby, and other members of the Opposition protested vehemently. They also drew up and laid before the House a Bill of reform which, if passed, would, they pledged themselves, effectually allay the agitation and content all but the most irreconcilable. Their efforts, however, were utterly vain. Many of the members of the House of Commons were themselves in a state of panic, and therefore impervious to argument. The motion was defeated by an enormous majority, a general election was close at hand, and feeling the fruitlessness of further struggle Grattan, as already stated, refused to offer himself for re-election, and retired despairingly from the scene.

The commander-in-chief, Lord Carhampton and his subordinate General Lake were the two men directly responsible for the misconduct of the troops in Ireland. So disgraceful had become the license allowed that loud complaints were made in both the English Houses of Parliament, in consequence of which Lord Carhampton was recalled and Sir Ralph Abercromby sent in his place. He more than endorsed the worst of the accounts which had been forwarded. "Every cruelty that could be committed by Cossacks or Calmucks," he states, "has been committed here." "The manner in which the troops have been employed would ruin," he adds, "the best in Europe." He at once set himself to change the system, to keep the garrison in the principal towns, and to forbid the troops acting except under the immediate direction of a magistrate. The Irish Executive however was in no mood to submit to these prudent restrictions. Angry disputes broke out. Lord Camden, the Lord-Lieutenant, vacillated from side to side, and the end was that in April, 1797, Sir Ralph Abercromby indignantly resigned the command, which then fell into General Lake's hands, and matters again went on as before.

Meanwhile the failure of the French descent under Hoche, and the defeat of the Dutch fleet at the battle of Camperdown in the autumn of 1797, had determined Lord Edward Fitzgerald and the other chiefs of the executive committee to attempt an independent rising. Wolfe Tone was still in France, eagerly endeavouring to bring about a fresh expedition, so that their councils had not even the advantage of his guidance. The Government had full information of all their proceedings, being kept well informed by spies, several of whom were actually enrolled in

LORD EDWARD FITZGERALD.
(*After a picture by Hamilton.*)

the association. In March, 1798, a sudden descent was made upon the executive committee, which had met at the house of a man called Bond, and a number of delegates and several leaders arrested. Lord Edward, however, received warning and went into concealment, and it was while in hiding that he hastily concerted a scheme for a general rising, which was now definitely fixed to take place upon the 24th of May.

Only a few days before this date his hiding-place was betrayed to the Government by a man named Magan. A guard of soldiers was sent to arrest him, and a desperate struggle took place, in the course of which the captain of the guard was fatally stabbed, while Lord Edward himself received a bullet on the shoulder from the effects of which he shortly afterwards died in goal. Within a day or two of his arrest all the other leaders in Dublin were also seized and thrown into prison.

The whole of the executive committee were thus removed at one blow, and the conspiracy left without head. In estimating the hideous character finally assumed by the rising this fact must never be forgotten. The sickening deeds committed while it was at its height were committed by a mass of ignorant men, maddened by months of oppression, and deprived of their leaders at the very moment they most required their control.

In the meantime the 24th of May had come, and the rising had broken out. The non-arrival of the daily mail-coaches was to be the signal, and these were stopped and burnt by the insurgents in four different directions at once. In Kildare and Meath scattered parties of soldiers and yeomanry were attacked and killed, and at Prosperous the barracks were set on fire, and the troops quartered in it all burnt or piked. In Dublin prompt measures had been taken, and the more loyal citizens had enrolled themselves for their own defence, so that no rising took place there, the result being that the outlying insurgents found themselves isolated. In the north especially, where the whole movement had taken its rise, and where the revolutionists had long been organized, the actual rising was thus of very trifling importance, and the whole thing was easily stamped out within a week.

It was very different in Wexford. Here from the beginning the rising had assumed a religious shape, and was conducted with indescribable barbarity. Yeomanry corps and bodies of militia had been quartered in the county for months, and many acts of tyranny had been committed. These were now hideously avenged. Several thousand men and women, armed chiefly with pikes and scythes, collected together on the hill of Oulart under the guidance of a priest named Father John Murphy. They were attacked by a small party of militia from Wexford, but defeating them, burst into Ferns, where they burnt the bishop's palace, then hastened on to Enniscorthy, which they took possession of, and a few days afterwards appeared before the town of Wexford.

Here resistance was at first offered them by Colonel Maxwell, who was in command of the militia regiments. Nearly all the Roman Catholics, however under his orders deserted, the rest grew disorganized and fled, and the end was that the militia departed and the rebels took possession triumphantly of the town. It at once became the scene of horrible outrages. Houses were plundered; many of the Protestant citizens murdered; others dragged from their homes, and cruelly maltreated. Bagenal Harvey, a United Irishman and a Protestant, who had been imprisoned at Wexford by the Government, was released and elected general of the rebels. He found himself, however, utterly unable to control them. A camp had been formed upon Vinegar Hill, near Enniscorthy, and from it as a centre the whole district was overrun, with the exception of New Ross, where most of the available troops had been concentrated. The wretched Protestants, kept prisoners on Vinegar Hill, were daily taken out in batches, and slaughtered in cold blood, while at Scullabogue, after an unsuccessful attempt on the part of the rebels to take New Ross, the most frightful episode of the whole rising occurred; a barn containing over a hundred and eighty Protestant loyalists collected from the country round being set on fire, and all of them perishing in the flames.

In the meanwhile troops were rapidly arriving from Dublin. Arklow and New Ross had defended themselves gallantly, and the rebels had fallen back from them repulsed. Vinegar Hill was attacked upon June 21st by General Lake, and after a struggle the rebels fled precipitately, and were slaughtered in great numbers. The day before this Father Roche and the rebels under him were met outside Wexford and also put to flight after hard fighting. Inside the town a horrible butchery was the same day perpetrated by a body of ruffians upon over ninety Protestant prisoners, who were slaughtered with great cruelty upon the bridge leading to New Ross, and only the passionate intervention of a priest named Corrin hindered the deaths of many more.

With the recapture of Wexford and Vinegar Hill the struggle ended. Such of the rebels as had escaped the infuriated soldiery fled to hide themselves in Wicklow and elsewhere. Father Michael Murphy—believed by his followers to be bullet proof—had been already killed during the attack on Arklow. Father Roche was hung by Lake's order over the bridge at Wexford, the scene of the late massacres. So also was the unfortunate Bagenal Harvey, the victim rather than the accomplice of the crimes of others. Father John Murphy was caught and hung at Tallow, as were also other priests in different parts of the country. The rising had been just long enough, and just formidable enough, to awaken the utmost terror and the most furious thirst for vengeance, yet not formidable enough to win respect for itself from a military point of view. As a result the retribution exacted was terrible; the scenes of violence which followed being upon a scale which went far to cause even the excesses committed by the rebels themselves to pale into insignificance.

Two final incidents, either of which a few months earlier might have produced formidable results, brings the dismal story to an end. In August, just after the rising had been definitely stamped out, General Humbert with a little over a thousand French troops under his command landed at Killala, where he was joined, if hardly reinforced, by a wild mob of unarmed peasants. From Killala he advanced to Ballina, defeated General Lake, who was sent against him, and moved on to Sligo. Shortly afterwards, however, he found himself, after crossing the Shannon, confronted with an overwhelming force under Lord Cornwallis, who had recently succeeded Lord Camden, and held double offices of Lord-Lieutenant and Commander-in-chief. Yielding to the inevitable, Humbert surrendered at discretion, and he and his men were received with due courtesy as prisoners of war. The account given by the bishop of Killala who was kept prisoner while that town was occupied by the French, will be found to be extremely well worth reading.

The last scene of the drama brings Wolfe Tone appropriately back upon the gloomy stage. When General Humbert sailed for Killala a much larger French force under General Hardi had remained behind at Brest. In September this second detachment sailed, Wolfe Tone being on board the principal vessel called the *Hoche*. Outside Lough Swilly they were overtaken by an English squadron, and a desperate struggle ensued. The smaller French vessels escaped, but the *Hoche* was so riddled with shot and shell as to be forced to surrender, and was towed by the victors into Lough Swilly. Here the French officers including Wolfe Tone were hospitably entertained at dinner by Lord Cavan. While at table Tone was recognized by an old school friend, and was at once arrested and sent prisoner to Dublin. A court martial followed, and despite his own plea to be regarded as a French officer, and therefore, if condemned shot, he was sentenced to be hung. In despair he tried to kill himself in prison, but the wound though fatal, was not immediately so, and the sentence would have been carried rigorously out but for the intervention of Curran, who moved for a writ of Habeas Corpus on the plea that as the courts of law were then sitting in Dublin, a court martial had no jurisdiction. The plea was a mere technicality, but it produced the required delay, and Wolfe Tone died quietly in prison.

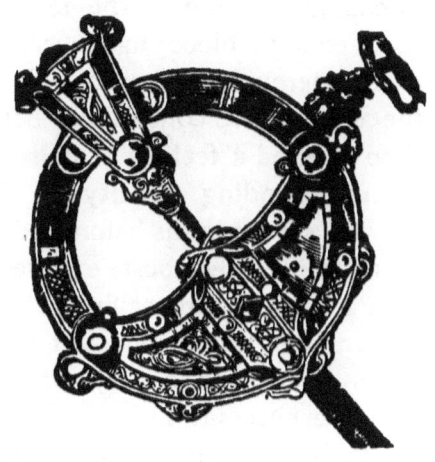

LIV.

THE UNION.

By the month of August the last sparks of the rebellion of '98 had been quenched. Martial law prevailed everywhere. The terror which the rising had awakened was finding its vent in violent actions and still more violent language, and Lord Cornwallis, the Lord-Lieutenant, was one of the few who ventured to say that enough blood had been shed, and that the hour for mercy had struck. The ferocity with which the end of the contest had been waged by the rebels had aroused a feeling of corresponding, or more than corresponding ferocity on the other side. That men who a few months before had trembled to see all whom they loved best exposed to the savagery of such a mob as had set fire to the barn at Scullaboge, or murdered the prisoners at Rossbridge, should have been filled with a fury which carried them far beyond the necessities of the case is hardly perhaps surprising, but the result was to hurry them in many instances into cruelties fully as great as those which they intended to avenge.

It was at this moment, while the country was still racked and bleeding at every pore from the effects of the recent struggle, that Pitt resolved to carry out his long projected plan of a legislative Union. Public opinion in Ireland may be said for the moment to have been dead. The mass of the people were lying crushed and exhausted by their own violence. Fresh from a contest waged with gun and pike and torch, a mere constitutional struggle had probably little or no interest for them. The popular enthusiasm which the earlier triumphs of the Irish Parliament had awakened had all but utterly died away in a fratricidal struggle. To the leaders of the late rebellion it was an object of open contempt, if not indeed of actual aversion. Wolfe Tone, the ablest man by far on the revolutionary side, had never wearied of pouring contempt upon it. In his eyes it was the great opponent of progress, the venal slave which had not only destroyed the chances of a successful outbreak, and whose endeavour had been to keep Ireland under the heel of her tyrant. To him the opposition as little deserved the name of patriot as the veriest place-men. Grattan, throughout his long and noble career had been as steadily loyal, and as steadily averse to any appeal to force as any paid creature of the Government. To men who only wanted to break loose from England altogether, to found an Irish republic as closely as possible upon the model then offered for their imitation in France, anything like mere constitutional opposition seemed not contemptible merely, but ridiculous.

This explains how it was that no great burst of public feeling—such as a few years before would have made the project of a Union all but impossible—

VIEW OF THE FOUR COURTS, DUBLIN, FINISHED THE YEAR OF THE UNION, 1800.

was now to be feared. Pitt had for a long time firmly fixed his mind upon it as the object to be attained. He honestly believed the existing state of things to be fraught with peril for England, and to have in it formidable elements of latent danger, which a war or any other sudden emergency might bring to the front. He knew too, undoubtedly, that no opportunity equally favourable for carrying his point was ever likely to recur again.

He accordingly now proceeded to take his measures for securing it with the utmost care, and the most anxious selection of agents. Two opposite sets of inducements were to be brought to bear upon the two contending factions. To the Protestants, fresh from their terrible struggle, the thought of a closer union with England seemed to promise greater protection in case of any similar outbreak. Irish churchmen too had been always haunted with a dread sooner or later of the disestablishment of their Church, and a union, it was argued, with a country where Protestants constituted the vast majority of the population, would render that peril for ever impossible, and it was agreed that a special clause to that effect should be incorporated in the Act of Union. To the Roman Catholics a totally different set of inducements were brought forward. The great bait was Emancipation, which they were privately assured would never be carried as long as the Irish Parliament existed, but might safely be conceded once it had ceased to exist. No actual pledge was made to that effect, but there was unquestionably an understanding, and Lord Castlereagh, the Chief Secretary, was untiring in his efforts to lull them into security upon this point.

So much discrepancy of statement still prevails upon the whole subject that it is extremely difficult to ascertain what really was the prevailing sentiment in Ireland at this time for and against the project of a Union. In Ulster the proposal seems certainly to have been all but unanimously condemned, and in Dublin, too, the opposition to it was vehement and unhesitating, but in other parts of the country it seems to have met with some support, especially in Galway and Tipperary. In January, 1799, Parliament met, and the proposal was brought forward in a speech from the throne, but encountered a violent opposition from all the remaining members of the patriotic party. Grattan, who had returned to Parliament for the express purpose, eloquently defended the rights of the Irish legislature, and was supported by Sir John Parnell, by Plunkett, and by all the more prominent members of the opposition. After a debate which lasted nearly twenty-two hours, a division was called, and the numbers were found to be equal; another fierce struggle, and this time the Government were beaten by five; thus the proposal for the time was lost.

Not for long though. Pitt had thoroughly made up his mind, and was bent on carrying his point to a successful issue. Most of those who had voted against the Union were dismissed from office, and after the prorogation of Parliament, the Government set to work with a determination to secure a majority before the next session. There was only one means of effecting this, and that means was now employed. Eighty-five boroughs—all of which were in the hands of private owners—would lose their members if a Union were passed, and all these, accordingly, it was resolved to compensate, and no less than a million and a quarter of money was actually advanced for that purpose, while for owners less easily reached by this means peerages, baronetcies, steps in the peerage, and similar inducements, were understood to be forthcoming as an equivalent.

It is precisely at this point that controversy grows hottest, and where it becomes hardest, therefore, to see a clear way between contending statements, which seem to meet and thrust one another, as it were at the very sword's point. That the sale of parliamentary seats—so shocking to our reformed eyes—was not regarded in the same light at the date of the Irish Union is certain, and in questions of ethics contemporary judgment is the first and most important point to be considered. The sale of a borough carried with it no more necessary reprobation then than did the sale of a man, say, in Jamaica or Virginia. Boroughs were bought and sold in open market, and many of them had a recognized price, so much for the current session, so much more if in perpetuity. We must try clearly to realize this, in order to approach the matter fairly, and, as far as possible, to put the ugly word "bribery" out of our thoughts, at all events not allow it to carry them beyond the actual facts of the case. Pitt, there is no question, had resolved to carry his point, but we have no right to assume that he wished to carry it by corrupt means, and the fact that those who opposed it were to be indemnified for their seats no less than those who promoted it, makes so far strongly in his favour.

On the other hand, the impression which any given transaction leaves upon the generation which has actually witnessed it is rarely entirely wrong, and that the impression produced by the carrying of the Irish Union—almost equally upon its friends and its foes —was, to put it mildly, unfavourable, few will be disposed to deny. Over and above this general testimony, we have the actual letters of those who were mainly instrumental in carrying it into effect, and it is difficult to read those of Lord Cornwallis without perceiving that he at least regarded the task as a repellent one, and one which as an honourable man he would gladly have evaded had evasion been possible. It is true that Lord Castlereagh, who was associated intimately with him in the enterprise, shows no such reluctance, but then the relative characters of the two men prevent that circumstance from having quite as much weight as it otherwise might.

The fact is that the whole affair is still enveloped in such a hedge of cross-statement and controversy, that in spite of having been eighty-seven years before the world, it still needs careful elucidation, and the last word upon it has certainly not yet been written. To attempt anything of the sort here would be absurd, so we must be content with simply following the actual course of events.

The whole of that memorable summer was spent carrying out the orders of the Prime Minister. The Lord-Lieutenant and the Chief Secretary travelled in

MARQUIS CORNWALLIS.
(Engraved by James Stow from an original drawing by S. D. Koster.)

person round Ireland to assist in the canvass, and before the Parliament met again the following January, they were able to report that they had succeeded. Grattan had been suffering from a severe illness, and was still almost too ill to appear. He came, however, and his wonted eloquence rose to the occasion. He appealed in the most moving and passionate terms against the destruction of the Parliament. Even then there were some who hoped against hope that it might be saved. At the division, however, the Government majority was found to be overwhelming, only a hundred members voting against it. The assent of the Upper House had already been secured, and was known all along to be a mere formality. And so the Union was carried.

How far it was or was not desirable at the time; how far it was or was not indispensable to the safety of both countries; to what extent Pitt and in a less degree those who acted under him were or were not blameworthy in the matter—are points which may be almost indefinitely discussed. They were not as blameworthy as they are often assumed to have been, but it is difficult honestly to see how we are to exonerate them from blame altogether. The theory that the end justifies the means has never been a favourite with honourable men, and some at least of the means by which the Union of Great Britain and Ireland was carried would have left fatal stains upon the noblest cause that ever yet inspired the breast of man. Early in the last century Ireland through her Parliament had herself proposed a legislative union, and England had rejected her appeal. Had it been accomplished then, or had it been brought about in the same fashion as that which produced the Union between Scotland and England, it might have been accepted as a boon instead of a curse, and in any case could have left no such bitter and rankling memories behind it. It is quite possible, and perfectly logical, for a man to hold that a Union between the two countries was and is to the advantage of both, and yet to desire that when it did come about it had been accomplished in almost any other conceivable way.

CRYPT OF CHRIST CHURCH CATHEDRAL.

LV.

O'CONNELL AND CATHOLIC EMANCIPATION.

ANOTHER century had now dawned, and, like the last, it was heralded in with great changes in Ireland. More than change, however, is needed for improvement. "*Plus ça change plus cést la même chose*" has been said of French politics, and is at least equally applicable to Irish ones. The Union had not brought union, and the years which followed it were certainly no great improvement on those that had preceded them. The growth of political institution is not so naturally stable in Ireland that the lopping down of one such institution tended to make the rest stronger or more healthy. It was a tree that had undoubtedly serious flaws, and whose growing had not been as perfect as it might have been, but it had admittedly borne some good fruit, and might have borne better had it been left alone. Anyhow it was gone, and the history of the next twenty-nine years is a confused and distracting medley of petty outbreaks—that in 1803 of which Robert Emmett was the leader being the most important—and of recurrent acts of repression, out of the monotonous welter of which one great

ROBERT EMMET.
(*From a stipple engraving by J. Heath.*)

figure presently rises like a colossus, till it comes to dominate the whole scene.

At a meeting of Catholic citizens in Dublin in 1800 to protest against the Union, Daniel O'Connell, then a young barrister of twenty-six, made his first public speech, and from that time forward his place as a leader may be said to have been fixed. A Catholic Association had some years earlier been formed, and of this he soon became the chief figure, and his efforts were continually directed towards the relief of his co-religionists. In 1815 a proposal had been made by the Government that Catholic Emancipation should be granted, coupled with a power of veto in the appointment of Catholic bishops, and to this compromise a considerable Catholic party was favourable. Richard Lalor Sheil—next to O'Connell by far the ablest and most eloquent advocate for Emancipation —supported it; even the Pope, Pius VII., declared that he felt "no hesitation in conceding it." O'Connell, however, opposed it vehemently, and so worked up public opinion against it that in the end he carried his point, and it was agreed that no proposal should be accepted which permitted any external interference with the Catholic Church of Ireland. This was his first decisive triumph.

O'Connell's buoyancy and indomitable energy imparted much of its own impulse to a party more dead and dispirited than we who have only known it in its resuscitated and decidedly dominant state can easily conceive. In 1823 a new Irish Catholic Association was set on foot, of which he was the visible life and soul. It is curious to note how little enthusiasm its proceedings seem at first to have awakened, especially amongst the priesthood. At a meeting on February 4, 1824, the necessary quorum of ten members running short, it was only supplied by O'Connell rushing downstairs to the book-shop over which the association met, and actually forcing upstairs two priests whom he accidently found there, and it was by the aid of these unwilling coadjutors that the famous motion for establishing the "Catholic rent" was carried. No sooner was this fund established, however, than it was largely subscribed for all over the country, and in a wonderfully short time the whole priesthood of Ireland were actively engaged in its service. The sums collected were to be spent in parliamentary expenses, in the defence of Catholics, and in the cost of meetings. In 1825 the association was suppressed by Act of Parliament, but was hardly dead before O'Connell set about the formation of another, and the defeat of the Beresfords at the election for Waterford in 1826 was one of the first symptoms which showed where the rising tide was mounting to.

It was followed two years later by a much more important victory. Although Catholics were excluded from sitting in Parliament the law which forbade their doing so did not preclude their being returned as members, and it had long been thought that policy required the election of some Catholic, if only that the whole anomaly of the situation might be brought into the full light of day. An opportunity soon occurred. Mr. Fitzgerald, the member for Clare, having accepted office as President of the Board of

Trade, he was obliged to appeal to his constituents for re-election, and O'Connell caught at the suggestion made to him of contesting the seat. His purpose had hardly been announced before it created the wildest excitement all over Ireland. The Catholic Association at once granted £5,000 towards the expenses, and £9,000 more was easily raised within a week. In every parish in Clare the priests addressed their parishioners from the altar, appealing to them to be true to the representative of their faith. After a vehement contest, victory declared itself unhesitatingly for O'Connell, who was found to have polled more than a thousand votes over his antagonist.

The months which followed were months of the wildest and most feverish excitement all over Ireland. O'Connell, though he used his "frank," did not present himself at the House of Commons. He devoted his whole time to organizing his co-religionists, who by this time may be said to have formed one vast army under his direction. In every parish the priests were his lieutenants. Monster meetings were held in all directions, and it may without exaggeration be said that hardly a Catholic man escaped the contagion. So universal a demonstration was felt to be irresistible. A sudden perception of the necessity for full and unqualified Emancipation sprang up in England. Even the Duke of Wellington bent his head before the storm. In the king's speech of February, 1829, a revision of the Catholic disabilities was advised. The following month the Catholic Relief Bill was carried through the House of Commons by a majority of 180, and received the royal assent on the 13th of April.

Thus the victory was won, and won too without a single shackling condition. It was won, moreover, by the efforts of a single individual, almost without support, nay, in several cases against the active opposition of some who had hitherto been its warmest advocates, a fact for which O'Connell's own violence was undoubtedly largely responsible. This seems to be the place to attempt an analysis of this extraordinary man, setting down the good and the evil each in their due proportion. The task, however, would in truth be impossible. For good or ill his figure is too massive, and would escape our half inch of canvas were we to try and set it there. The best description of him compressible in a few words is Balzac's — " He was the incarnation of an entire people." Nothing can be truer. Not only was he Irish of the Irish, but Celt of the Celts, every quality, every characteristic, good, bad, loveable, or the reverse which belongs to the type being found in him, only on an immense scale. To the average Irishman of his day he stands as Mont Blanc might stand were it set down amongst the Magillicuddy Reeks. He towers, that is to say, above his contemporaries not by inches, but by the head and shoulders. His aims, hopes, enthusiasms were theirs, but the effective, controlling power was his alone. He had a great cause, and he availed himself greatly of it, and to this and to the magnetic and all but magical influence of his personality, that extraordinary influence which he for so many years wielded is no doubt due.

DANIEL O'CONNELL, M.P.
(*From a pen-and-ink sketch by Doyle, in the Department of Prints and Drawings, British Museum.*)

Two points must be here set down, since both are of great importance to the future of Ireland, and for both O'Connell is clearly responsible—whether we regard them as amongst his merits or the reverse. He first, and as it has been proved permanently, brought the priest into politics, with the unavoidable result of accentuating the religious side of the contest and bringing it into a focus. The bitterness which three generations of the penal code had engendered only, in fact, broke out then. The hour of comparative freedom is often—certainly not alone in Ireland—the hour when the sense of past oppression first reveals itself in all its intensity, and that biting consciousness of being under a social ban which grew up in the last century is hardly even yet extinct there, and certainly was not extinct in O'Connell's time. Another, and an equally important effect, is also due to him. He effectually, and as it has proved finally, snapped that tie of feudal feeling which, if weakened, still undoubtedly existed, and which was felt towards the landlord of English extraction little less than towards the few remaining Celtic ones. The failings of the upper classes of Ireland of his day, and long before his day, there is no need to extenuate, but it must not in fairness be forgotten that what seems to our soberer judgment the worst of those failings — their insane extravagance, their exalted often ludicrously inflated notions of their own relative importance; their indifference to, sometimes open hostility to, the law—all were bonds of union and sources of pride to their dependants rather than the other way. It needed a yet stronger impulse—that of religious enthusiasm—to break so deeply rooted and inherent a sentiment. When that spark was kindled every other fell away before it.

As regards England, unfortunately, the concession of Emancipation was spoilt not merely by the sense that it was granted to force rather than to conviction, but even more to the intense bitterness and dislike with which it was regarded by a large proportion of English Protestants. A new religious life and a new sense of religious responsibility was making itself widely felt there. The eighteenth century, with its easy-going indifferentism, had passed away, and one of the effects of this new revival was unhappily to reawaken in many conscientious breasts much of the old and half-extinct horror of Popery, a horror which found its voice in a language of intolerance and bigotry which at the present time seems scarcely conceivable.

The years which followed were chiefly marked by a succession of efforts upon O'Connell's part to procure Repeal. An association which had been formed by him for this purpose was put down by the Government in 1830, but the next year it was reformed under a new name, and at the general election in 1831 forty members were returned pledged to support Repeal. The condition of Ireland was meanwhile miserable in the extreme. A furious tithe-war was raging, and many outrages had been committed, especially against tithe proctors, the class of men who were engaged in collecting the tax. Ribbon associations and other secret societies too had been spreading rapidly underground. Of such societies O'Connell was through life the implacable enemy. The events of 1798 and 1803 had left an indelible impression on his mind. The "United Irishmen," in his own words, "taught me that all work for Ireland must be done openly and above board." The end of the tithe struggle, however, was happily approaching. In 1838 an Irish Tithes Commutation Act was at last carried, and a land tax in the form of a permanent rent charge substituted.

Repeal was now more than ever the question of the hour, and to Repeal henceforward O'Connell devoted his entire energies. In 1840 the Loyal National Repeal Association was founded, and a permanent place of meeting known as Conciliation Hall established for it in Dublin. 1841, O'Connell had early announced, would be known henceforward as the year of Repeal, and accordingly he that year left England and went to Ireland, and devoted himself there to the work of organization. A succession of monster meetings were held all over the country, the far-famed one on Tara Hill being, as is credibly asserted, attended by no less than a quarter of a million of people. Over this vast multitude gathered together around him the magic tones of the great orator's voice swept triumphantly; awakening anger, grief, passion, delight, laughter, tears, at its own pleasure. They were astonishing triumphs, but they were dearly bought. The position was, in fact, an impossible one to maintain long. O'Connell had carried the whole mass of the people with him up to the very brink of the precipice, but how to bring them safely and successfully down again was more than even he could accomplish. Resistance he had always steadily denounced, yet every day his own words seemed to be bringing the inevitable moment of collision nearer and nearer. The crisis came on October the 5th. A meeting had been summoned to meet at Clontarf, near Dublin, and on the afternoon of the 4th the Government suddenly came to the resolution of issuing a proclamation forbidding it to assemble. The risk was a formidable one for responsible men to run. Many of the people were already on their way, and only O'Connell's own rapid and vigorous measures in sending out in all directions to intercept them hindered the actual shedding of blood.

His prosecution and that of some of his principal adherents was the next important event. By a Dublin jury he was found guilty, sentenced to two years imprisonment, and conveyed to prison, still earnestly entreating the people to remain quiet, an order which they strictly obeyed. The jury by which he had been condemned was known to be strongly biassed against him, and an appeal had been forwarded against his sentence to the House of Lords. So strong there, too, was the feeling against O'Connell, that little expectation was entertained of its being favourably received. Greatly to its honour, however, the sentence was reversed and he was set free. His imprisonment had been of the lightest and least onerous description conceivable; indeed was ironically described by Mitchell shortly afterwards as that of a man— "addressed by bishops, complimented by Americans, bored by deputations, serenaded by bands, comforted by ladies, half smothered by roses, half drowned in champagne.". The enthusiasm shown at his release was frantic and delirious. None the less those months in Richmond prison proved the death-knell of his power. He was an old man by this time; he was already weakened in health, and that buoyancy which had hitherto carried him over any and every obstacle never again revived. The "Young Ireland" party, the members of which had in the first instance been his allies and lieutenants, had now formed a distinct section, and upon the vital question of resistance were in fierce hostility to all his most cherished principles. The state of the country, too, preyed visibly upon his mind. By 1846 had begun that succession of disastrous seasons which, by destroying the feeble barrier which stood between the peasant and a cruel death, brought about a national tragedy, the most terrible perhaps with which modern Europe has been confronted. This tragedy, though he did not live to see the whole of it, O'Connell—himself the incarnation of the people—felt acutely. Deep despondency took hold of him. He retired, to a great degree, from public life, leaving the conduct of his organization in the hands of others. Few more tragic positions have been described or can be conceived than that of this old man —so loved, so hated, so reverenced, so detested—who had been so audaciously, triumphantly successful in his day, and round whom the shadows of night were now gathering so blackly and so swiftly. Despair was tightening its grip round the hearts of all Irishmen, and it found its strongest hold upon the heart of the greatest Irishman of his age. Nothing speaks more eloquently of the total change of situation than the pity and respectful consideration extended at this time to O'Connell by men who only recently had exhausted every possibility of vituperation in abuse of the burly demagogue. In 1847 he resolved to leave Ireland, and to end his days in Rome. His last public appearance was in the House of Commons, where an attentive and deeply respectful audience hung upon the faultering and barely articulate accents which fell from his lips. In a few deeply moving words he appealed for aid and sympathy for his suffering countrymen, and left the House; within a few months he had died at Genoa. Such a bare summary leaves necessarily whole regions of the subject unexplored, but, let the final verdict of history on O'Connell be what it may, that he loved his country passionately, and with an absolute disinterestedness no pen has ever been found to question, nor can we doubt that whatever else may have hastened his end it was the Famine killed him, almost as surely as it did the meanest of its victims.

LVI.

"YOUNG IRELAND."

THE camp and council chamber of the "Young Ireland" party was the editor's room of *The Nation* newspaper. There it found its inspiration, and there its plans were matured—so far, that is, as they can be said to have been ever matured. For an eminently readable and all things considered a wonderfully impartial account of this movement, the reader cannot do better than consult Sir Charles Gavan Duffy's "Four Years of Irish History," which has the immense advantage of being history taken at first hand, written that is by one who himself took a prominent part in the scenes which he describes.

The most interesting figure in the party had, however, died before those memorable four years began. Thomas Davis, who was only thirty at the time of his death in 1845, was a man of large gifts, nay, might fairly be called a man of genius. His poetry is, perhaps, too national to be appreciated out of Ireland, yet two, at least, of his ballads, " Fontenoy " and " The Sack of Baltimore," may fairly claim to compare with those of any contemporary poet. His prose writings, too, have much of the same charm, and, if he had no time to become a master of any of the subjects of which he treats, there is something infectious in the very spontaneousness and, as it were, untaught boyish energy of his Irish essays.

The whole movement in fact was, in the first instance, a literary quite as much as a political one. Nearly all who took part in it—Gavan Duffy, John Mitchell, Meagher, Dillon, Davis himself—were very young men, many fresh from college, all filled with zeal for the cause of liberty and nationality. The graver side of the movement only showed itself when the struggle with O'Connell began. At first no idea of deposing, or even seriously opposing the great leader seems to have been intended. The attempt on O'Connell's part to carry a formal declaration against the employment under any circumstances of physical force was the origin of that division, and what the younger spirits considered " truckling to the Whigs" helped to widen the breach. When, too, O'Connell had partially retired into the background, his place was filled by his son, John O'Connell, the "Head conciliator," between whom and the "Young Irelanders" there waged a fierce war, which in the end led to the indignant withdrawal of the latter from the Repeal council.

Before matters reached this point, the younger camp had been strengthened by the adhesion of Smith O'Brien, who, though not a man of much intellectual calibre, carried no little weight in Ireland. His age—which compared to that of the other members of his party, was that of a veteran—his rank and position as a county member, above all, his vaunted descent from

Brian Boroimhe, all made him an ally and a convert to be proud of. Like the rest he had no idea at first of appealing to physical force, however loudly an abstract resolution against it might be denounced. Resistance was to be kept strictly within the constitutional limits, indeed the very year of his junction with this the extreme left of the Repeal party, Smith O'Brien's most violent proceeding was to decline to sit upon a railway committee to which he had been summoned, an act of contumacy for which he was ordered by the House of Commons into the custody of the Sergeant-at-Arms, and committed to an extemporized prison, by some cruelly declared to be the coal-hole. "An Irish leader in a coal-hole!" exclaims Sir Charles Gavan Duffy, indignantly, can more unworthy statement be conceived? "Regullus in a barrel, however," he adds, rather grandly, "was not quite the last one heard of Rome and its affairs!"

In Ireland matters were certainly sad enough and serious enough without any such serio-comic incidents. Famine was already stalking the country with giant strides, and no palliative measures as yet proposed seemed to be of the slightest avail. Early in January, 1847, O'Connell left on that journey of his which was never completed, and by the middle of May Ireland was suddenly startled by the news that her great leader was dead.

The effect of his death was to produce a sudden and immense reaction. A vast revulsion of love and reverence sprang up all over the country; an immense sense of his incomparable services, and with it a vehement anger against all who had opposed him.

Upon the "Young Ireland" party, as was inevitable, the weight of that anger fell chiefly, and from the moment of O'Connell's death whatever claim they had to call themselves a national party vanished utterly. The men "who killed the Liberator" could never again hope to carry with them the suffrages of any number of their countrymen.

This contumely, to a great degree undeserved, naturally reacted upon the subjects of it. The taunt of treachery and ingratitude flung at them wherever they went stung and nettled. In the general reaction of gratitude and affection for O'Connell, his son John succeeded easily to the position of leader. The older members of the Repeal Association thereupon rallied about him, and the split between them and the younger men grew deeper and wider.

A wild, impracticable visionary now came to play a part in the movement. A deformed misanthrope, called James Lalor, endowed with a considerable command of vague, passionate rhetoric, began to write incentives to revolt in *The Nation.* These growing more and more violent were by the editor at length prudently suppressed. The seed, however, had already sown itself in another mind. John Mitchell is described by Mr. Justin McCarthy as "the one formidable man amongst the rebels of '48; the one man who distinctly knew what he wanted, and was prepared to run any risk to get it." Even Mitchell, it is clear, would never have gone as far as he did but for the impulse which he received from the crippled desperado in the background. Lalor was, in fact, a monomaniac, but this Mitchell seems to have failed to perceive. To him it was intolerable that any human being should be willing to go further and to dare more in the cause of Ireland than himself, and the result was that after awhile he broke away from his connection with *The Nation*, and started a new organ under the name of *The United Irishmen*, one definitely pledged from the first to the policy of action.

From this point matters gathered speedily to a head. Mitchell's newspaper proceeded to fling out challenge after challenge to the Government, calling upon the people to gather and to "sweep this island clear of the English name and nation." For some months these challenges remained unanswered. It was now, however, "'48," and nearly all Europe was in revolution. The necessity of taking some step began to be evident, and a Bill making all written incitement of insurrection felony was hurried through the House of Commons, and almost immediately after Mitchell was arrested.

Even then he seems to have believed that the country would rise to liberate him. The country, however, showed no disposition to do anything of the sort. He was tried in Dublin, found guilty, sentenced to fourteen years' transportation, and a few days afterwards put on board a vessel in the harbour and conveyed to Spike Island, whence he was sent to Bermuda, and the following April in a convict vessel to the Cape, and finally to Tasmania.

The other "Young Irelanders," stung apparently by their own previous inaction, thereupon rushed frantically into rebellion. The leaders — Smith O'Brien, Meagher, Dillon, and others — went about the country holding reviews of "Confederates," as they now called themselves, a proceeding which caused the Government to suspend the Habeas Corpus Act, and to issue a warrant for their arrest. A few more gatherings took place in different parts of the country, a few more ineffectual attempts were made to induce the people to rise, one very small collision with the police occurred, and then the whole thing was over. All the leaders in the course of a few days were arrested and Smith O'Brien and Meagher were sentenced to death, a sentence which was speedily changed into transportation. Gavan Duffy was arrested and several times tried, but the jury always disagreed, and in the end his prosecution was abandoned. The "Young Ireland" movement, however, was dead, and never again revived.

LVII.

THE FAMINE.

ALL the time the earlier of the foregoing scenes were being enacted, the famine had been drawing its python grasp tighter and tighter around the unhappy island. The first symptoms of the dread potato disease showed themselves in the autumn of 1845, and even that year there was much suffering, though a trifle to what was to follow. Many remedies were tried, both to stop the blight and save the crops, but all alike proved unavailing. The next year the potatoes seemed to promise unusually well, and the people, with characteristic hopefulness, believed that their trouble was over. The summer, however, was very warm and wet, and with August there came on a peculiarly dense white fog, which was believed by all who were in Ireland at the time to have carried the blight with it in its folds. Whether this was the case or not, there is no doubt that in a single fatal night nearly the whole potato crop over the entire country blackened, and perished utterly. Then, indeed, followed despair. Stupor and a sort of moody indifference succeeded to the former buoyancy and hopefulness. There was nothing to do; no other food was attainable.

The fatal dependence upon a single precarious crop had left the whole mass of the people helpless before the enemy.

Soon the first signs of famine began to appear. People were to be seen wandering about; seeking for stray turnips, for watercresses, for anything that would allay the pangs of hunger. The workhouses, detested though they were, were crammed until they could hold no single additional inmate. Whole families perished; men, women, and children lay down in their cabins and died, often without a sign. Others fell by the roadside on their way to look for work or seek relief. Only last summer, at Ballinahinch in Connemara, the present writer was told by an old man that he remembered being sent by his master on a message to Clifden, the nearest town, and seeing the people crawling along the road, and that, returning the same way a few hours later, many of the same people were lying dead under the walls or upon the grass at the roadside. That this is no fancy picture is clear from local statistics. No part of Ireland suffered worse than Galway and Mayo, both far more densely populated then than at present. In this very region of Connemara an inspector has left on record, having to give orders for the burying of over a hundred and thirty bodies found along the roads within his own district.

Mr. W. E. Forster, who, above all other Englishmen, deserved the gratitude of Ireland for his efforts during this tragic time, has left terrible descriptions of the scenes of which he was himself an eye-witness, especially in the west. " The town of Westport," he tells us in one of his reports, "was itself a strange and fearful sight, like what we read of in beleaguered cities; its streets crowded with gaunt wanderers, sauntering to and fro with hopeless air and hunger-struck look—a mob of starved, almost naked women around the poor-house clamouring for soup-tickets. Our inn, the head-quarters of the road engineer and pay clerks, beset by a crowd of beggars for work." In another place "the survivors," he says, "were like walking skeletons—the men gaunt and haggard, stamped with the livid mark of hunger; the children crying with pain; the women in some of the cabins too weak to stand. When there before I had seen cows at almost every cabin, and there were besides many sheep and pigs owned in the village. But now the sheep were all gone—all the cows, all the poultry killed—only one pig left; the very dogs which had barked at me before had disappeared—no potatoes; no oats."

One more extract more piteous even than the rest: "As we went along our wonder was not that the people died, but that they lived;. and I have no doubt whatever that in any other country the mortality would have been far greater; that many lives have been prolonged, perhaps saved, by the long apprenticeship to want in which the Irish peasant had been trained, and by that lovely touching charity which prompts him to share his scanty meal with his starving neighbour."

Of course all this time there was no lack of preventative measures. Large sums had been voted from the Treasury; stores of Indian corn introduced;

great relief works set on foot. An unfortunate fatality seemed, however, to clog nearly all these efforts. Either they proved too late to save life, or in some way or other to be unsuitable to the exigencies of the case. Individual charity, too, came out upon the most magnificent scale. All Europe contributed, and English gold was poured forth without stint or stay. Still the famine raged almost unchecked. The relief works established by the Government, with the best intentions possible, too often were devoted to the most curiously useless, sometimes even to actually harmful, objects. To this day "Famine roads" may be met with in the middle of snipe bogs, or skirting precipices where no road was ever wanted or could possibly be used. By the time, too, they were in full working order the people were, in many cases, too enfeebled by want and disease to work. For close upon the heels of the famine followed an epidemic hardly less fatal than itself. In the course of the two years that it raged over two hundred thousand people are said to have perished from this cause alone, and three times the number to have been attacked and permanently enfeebled by it.

In 1849 a Relief Act was passed which established soup kitchens throughout the unions, where food was to be had gratis by all who required it. Long before this similar kitchens had been privately set on foot, and men and women had devoted themselves to the work with untiring energy and the most absolute self-devotedness. Of these self-appointed and unpaid workers a large number shared the fate of those whom they assisted. Indeed, it is one of the most singular features of the time that not only old, or feeble, or specially sensitive people died, but strong men, heads of houses—not regarded as by any means specially soft-hearted—raised, too, by circumstances out of reach of actual hunger, died —just as O'Connell had died—of sheer distress of mind, and the effort to cope with what was beyond the power of any human being to cope with. In the single county of Galway the records of the times show—as may easily be verified—an extraordinary number of deaths of this type, a fact which alone goes far to disprove those accusations of heartlessness and indifference which have in some instances been too lightly flung.

After the famine followed ruin—a ruin which swept high and low alike into its net. When the poor rate rose to twenty and twenty-five shillings in the pound it followed that the distinction between rich and poor vanished, and there were plenty of instances of men, accounted well off, who had subscribed liberally to others at the beginning of the famine, who were themselves seeking relief before the end. The result was a state of things which has left bitterer traces behind it than even the famine itself. The smaller type of landowners, who for the most part had kindly relations with their tenants, were swept away like leaves before the great storm, their properties fell to their creditors, and were sold by order of the newly established Encumbered Estates Courts. No proposing purchaser would have anything to say to estates covered with a crowd of pauper tenants, and the result was a wholesale clearance, carried out usually by orders given by strangers at a distance, and executed too often with a disregard of humanity that it is frightful to read or to think of. Most of the people thus ejected in the end emigrated, and that emigration was under the circumstances their best hope few can reasonably doubt. Even here, however, misfortune pursued them. Sanitary inspection of emigrant ships was at the time all but unheard of, and statistics show that the densely crowded condition of the vessels which took them away produced the most terrible mortality amongst the already enfeebled people who crowded them, a full fifth of the steerage passengers in many cases, it is said, dying upon the voyage, and many more immediately after landing. The result of all this has been that the inevitable horrors of the time have been deepened and intensified by a sense of ill-usage, which has left a terrible legacy behind —one which may prove to be a peril to generations still unborn. Even where those who emigrated have prospered most, and where they or their sons are now rich men, they cling with unhappy persistency to the memory of that wretched past—a memory which the forty years which have intervened, far from softening, seem, in many cases, to have only lashed into a yet more passionate bitterness.

In Ireland itself the permanent effects of the disaster differed of course in different places and with different people, but in one respect it may be said to have been the same everywhere. Between the Ireland of the past and the Ireland of the present the Famine lies like a black stream, all but entirely blotting out and effacing the past. Whole phases of life, whole types of character, whole modes of existence and ways of thought passed away then and have never been renewed. The entire fabric of the country was torn to pieces and has never reformed itself upon the same lines again. After a while every-day life began again of course, as it does everywhere all over the world, and in some respects the struggle for existence has never since been quite so severe or so prolonged. The lesson of those two terrible years has certainly not been lost, but like all such lessons it has left deep scars which can never be healed. Men and women, still alive who remember the famine, look back across it as we all look back across some personal grief, some catastrophe which has shattered our lives and made havoc of everything we cared for. We, too, go on again after a while as if nothing had happened, yet we know perfectly well all the while that matters are not the least as they were before; that on the contrary they never can or will be.

LVIII.

THE LATEST DEVELOPMENT.

THE story of the last forty years must be compressed into a nutshell. The famine was over at last, but its effects remained. Nearly a million of people had emigrated, yet the condition of life for those remaining was far from satisfactory. The Encumbered Estates Act, which had completed the ruin of many of the older proprietors, pressed, in some respects, even more severely upon the tenants, a large number of whom found themselves confronted with new purchasers, who, having invested in Irish land merely as a speculation, had little other interest in it. In 1850 an attempt at a union of North and South was made, and a Tenant League Conference assembled in Dublin. Of this league the remnants of the "Young Ireland" party formed the nucleus, but were supplemented by others with widely different aims and intentions. Of these others the two Sadleirs, John and James, Mr. Edmund O'Flaherty, and Mr. William Keogh, afterwards Judge Keogh, were the most prominent. These with their adherents constituted the once famous "Brass Band" which for several years filled Parliament with its noisy declamations, and which posed as the specially appointed champion of Catholicism. In 1853 several of its members took office under Lord Aberdeen, but their course was not a long one. A bank kept in Ireland by the two Sadleirs broke, ruining an enormous number of people, and on investigation was found to have been fraudulently conducted from the very beginning. John Sadleir thereupon killed himself; his brother James was expelled from the House of Commons, and he and several others implicated in the swindle fled the country and never reappeared, and so the "Brass Band" broke up, amid the well-deserved contempt of men of every shade of political opinion.

After this succeeded a prolonged lull. Secret agitations, however, were still working underground, and as early as 1850 one known as the Phœnix organization began to collect recruits, although for a long time its proceedings attracted little or no attention.

In 1859 several of its members were arrested, and it seemed then to die down and disappear, but some years later it sprang up again with a new name, and the years 1866 and 1867 were signalized by the Fenian rising, or to put it with less dignity, the Fenian scare. With the close of the American War a steady backward stream of Americanized Irishmen had set in, and a belief that war between England and America was rapidly approaching had become an article of fervent faith with a large majority in Ireland. The Fenian plan of operation was a two-headed one. There was to be a rising in

Ireland, and there was to be a raid into Canada across the American frontier. Little formidable as either project seems now, at the time they looked serious enough, and had the strained relations then existing between England and America turned out differently, no one can say but what they might have become so. The Fenian organization, which grew out of the earlier Phœnix one, was managed from centres, a man called Stephens being the person who came most prominently before the world in the capacity of Head centre. In 1865 Stephens was arrested in Dublin, but managed to escape not long afterwards from Richmond prison by the aid of two confederates within its walls. The following May, 1866, a small body of Fenians crossed the Niagara river, but the United States authorities rigidly enforced the neutrality of the American frontier, and so the attempt perished. The same spring a rising broke out in Ireland, but it also was stamped with failure from its onset, and the famous snowstorm of that year finished the discomfiture of its adherents.

Two other Fenian demonstrations, not to mention an abortive project to seize Chester Castle, were shortly afterwards made in England. In 1867, some Fenian prisoners were rescued in Manchester, while on their way to gaol, and in the attempt to burst the lock of the van in which they were being conveyed a police officer named Brett, who was in charge of it, was accidentally shot. Five men were found guilty for this offence. One Macquire was proved to have been arrested by mistake, another Conder had the sentence commuted, but three—Allen, Larkin, and O'Brien—were hung.

Another Fenian exploit of a somewhat different character followed in December, 1867, when an attempt was made by some desperados belonging to the party to blow up the Clerkenwell House of Detention, in which two Fenian prisoners were then confined. Luckily for them, as it turned out, they were not in that part of the prison at the time, or the result of their would-be liberators' efforts would have simply been to kill them. As it was, twelve other people were either killed on the spot or died from its effects, and over a hundred were more or less badly wounded. For this crime six persons were put upon their trial, but only one was convicted and actually executed.

The next Irish event of any moment stands upon a curiously different platform, though there were not wanting suggestions that the two had an indirect connection as cause and effect. In 1868 the Liberal party came into power after the General Election with Mr. Gladstone as Prime Minister, and the session of 1869 saw the introduction of a Bill for the Disestablishment of the Irish Church. The controversies to which that measure gave rise are already quite out of date, and there is no need therefore to revive them. Few measures so vehemently opposed have produced less startling effects in the end. It neither achieved those great things hoped by its supporters, nor yet brought about the dire disasters so freely threatened by its opponents. To the Roman Catholics of Ireland the grievance of an alien State Church had, since the settlement of the tithe question, lapsed into being little more than a sentimental one, so that practically the measure affected them little. As an institution, however, the position of the Irish State Church was undoubtedly a difficult one to defend, the very same arguments which tell most forcibly for the State Church of England telling most forcibly against its numerically feeble Irish sister. Whatever the abstract rights or wrongs of the case it is pretty clear now that the change must have come sooner or later, and few therefore can seriously regret that it came when it did. The struggle was protracted through the entire session, but in the end passed both Houses of Parliament, and received the royal assent on July 26, 1869.

It was followed early the following year by the Irish Land Act, which was introduced into the House of Commons by Mr. Gladstone on February 15, 1870. This Act has been succinctly described as one obliging all landlords to do what the best landlords did spontaneously, and this perhaps may be accepted as a fairly accurate account of it. Owing to the fact of land being practically the only commodity of value, there has always been in Ireland a tendency to offer far more for it than could reasonably be hoped to be got in the form of return, and this tendency has led, especially in the poorest districts and with the smallest holdings, to a rent being offered and accepted often quite out of proportion to the actual value of the land, though in few instances do the very highest rents attainable seem even in these cases to have been exacted. The Act now proposed was to abolish one passed in 1860 which had reduced all tenant and landlord transactions in Ireland to simple matters of free contract, and to interpose the authority of the State between the two. It legalized what were known as the "Ulster customs;" awarded compensations for all improvements made by the tenant or his predecessors, and in case of eviction for any cause except non-payment of rent a further compensation was to be granted, which might amount to a sum equal to seven years' rent; it also endeavoured to a partial extent to establish peasant proprietorship. That it was a conscientious attempt to deal with a very intricate and perplexing problem may fairly be conceded, at the same time it has been its misfortune that it proved satisfactory to neither of the two classes chiefly concerned, being denounced by the one as the beginning of spoliation, by the other as a mere worthless, and utterly contemptible attempt at dealing with the necessities of the case.

A third measure—the Irish Education Act—was proposed the following session, but as it resulted in failure, was popular with no party, and failed to pass; it need not be entered into even briefly. 1874 saw a dissolution of Parliament and a General Election, which resulted in the defeat of the Liberals, and the return of the Conservatives to office. Before this, a new Irish constitutional party pledged to the principle of Home Government, had grown up in the House of Commons, at first under the leadership of Mr. Butt, afterwards with new aims and widely different tactics under that of Mr. Parnell. In 1879 an agrarian movement was set on foot in Ireland, chiefly

THE LAND LEAGUE. 409

through the instrumentality of Mr. Davitt, which has since become so widely known as the Land League. It was almost immediately joined by the more extreme members of the Irish Parliamentary party. Meetings were held in all directions, and an amount of popular enthusiasm aroused which the more purely political question had never succeeded in awakening. Subscriptions poured in from America. A season of great scarcity, and in some districts of partial famine, had produced an unusual amount of distress, and this and the unsettled state of the Land Question all helped to foster the rising excitement. The country grew more and more disturbed. Several murders and a number of agrarian outrages were committed, and the necessity of strengthening the hands of the executive began to be felt by both the chief political parties alike.

In 1880 the Liberal party returned to power after the General Election, and 1881 witnessed the passage through Parliament of two important Irish measures. The first of these was a Protection of Life and Property Bill brought in in January by Mr. Forster, then Chief Secretary of Ireland. As was to be expected, this was vehemently opposed by the Nationalist members, who retarded it by every means in their power, one famous sitting of the House on this occasion lasting for forty-two hours, from five o'clock on the Monday afternoon to nine o'clock on the Wednesday following, and then only being brought to an end by the authority of the Speaker. By March, however, the Bill passed, and in the following month, April 7th, a new Irish Land Act was brought forward by Mr. Gladstone, and was passed after much opposition the following autumn.

The full scope and purport of this Act it is far beyond the limits of these few remaining pages to enter upon. Although, to some extent an outcome of the Act of 1870, it cannot in strictness be called a mere development or completion of it, being in many respects based upon entirely new principles. The most salient of these are what are known as the " three Fs," namely—Fixity of Tenure, Fair Rent, to be decided by a Land Court, and Free Sale. As regards the last two, it has been pointed out with some force that the one practically does away with the other, the only person benefited being the immediate occupier, at whose departure that fierce competitive desire for the land which is the real root of the whole difficulty being allowed freer play than ever. With regard to the first, its effect may be briefly stated as that of reducing the owner to the position of a rent charger or annuitant upon what had before been his own estate, thereby depriving him—even where want of means did not effectually do so—of all desire to expend capital upon what had henceforth ceased to be his property, and over the management of which he had almost wholly lost control. That this is a change of a very large and sweeping character it is needless to say. Henceforward ownership of land in Ireland is no longer ownership in the ordinary sense of the word. It is an ownership of two persons instead of one, and a divided ownership, even where two people work together harmoniously, is as most of us are aware, a very had he to a great degree planned the murder and helped to draw the others into it, but had actually selected the very weapon by which it was accomplished, so that of all the miscreants engaged in the perpetration he was perhaps the deepest dyed and the most guilty.

Since then, and indeed all along, the struggle in Ireland itself has been almost wholly an agrarian one. The love of and desire for the land, rather than for any particular political development, is what there dominates the situation. A heavy fall of prices has led to a widespread refusal to pay rent, save at a considerable abatement upon the already reduced Government valuations. Where this has been refused a deadlock has set in, rents in many cases have not been paid at all, and eviction has in consequence been resorted to. Eviction, whether carried out in West Ireland or East London, is a very ugly necessity, and one, too, that is indelibly stamped with a taint of inhumanity. At the last extremity, it is, however, the only one open to any owner, *qua* owner, let his political sympathies or proclivities be what they may, so that it does not necessarily argue any double portion of original sin even on the part of that well-laden packhorse of politics—the Irish landlord—to say that his wits have not so far been equal to the task of dispensing with it.

Within the last two years only one question has risen to the surface of politics which gravely affects the destinies of Ireland, but that one is of so vast and all-important a character that it cannot be evaded. The question I mean, of course, of Home Rule. Complicated as its issues are, embittered as the controversy it has awakened, dark still as are its destinies, its history as a piece of projected, and so far unsuccessful, legislation has at least the merit of being short and easily stated. In the month of December, 1885, just after the close of the general election, it began to be rumoured as forming part of the coming programme of the Liberal leader. On April 8, 1886, a Bill embodying it was brought forward in the House of Commons by Mr. Gladstone; upon June 7th, it was rejected upon the second reading by a majority of thirty, and at the general election which followed was condemned by a large majority of the constituencies.

And afterwards? What follows? What is its future destined to be? Will it vanish away, will it pass into new phases, or will some form of it eventually receive the sanction of the nation? These are Sphinx questions, which one may be excused from endeavouring to answer, seeing that the strongest and most far-reaching heads are at this moment intent upon them—not, so far as can be seen, with any strikingly successful result. The Future is a deep mine, and we have not yet struck even a spade into it.

In every controversy, no matter how fierce the waves, how thick the air with contending assertions, there is almost always, however, some fact, or some few facts, which seem to rise like rocks out of the turmoil, and obstinately refuse to be washed or whittled away. The chief of these, in this case, is the geographical position, or rather juxtaposition, of the two islands. Set before a stranger to the whole Irish problem—if so favoured an individual exists upon the habitable globe—a map of the British islands, and ask him whether it seems to him inevitable that they should remain for ever united, and we can scarcely doubt that his reply would be in the affirmative. This being so, we have at least it will be said one fact, one sea-rock high above the reach of waves or spray. But Irishmen have been declared by a great and certainly not an unfavourable critic— Mr. Matthew Arnold—to be "eternal rebels against the despotism of fact." If this is so—and who upon the Irish side of the channel can wholly and absolutely deny the assertion?—then our one poor standing-point is plucked from under our feet, and we are all abroad upon the waves again. Will Home Rule or would Home Rule, it has been asked, recognize this fact as one of the immutable ones, or would it sooner or later incline to think that with a little determination, a little manipulation, the so-called fact would politely cease to be a fact at all? It is difficult to say, and until an answer is definitely received it does not perhaps argue any specially sloth-like clinging to the known in preference to the unknown to admit that there is for ordinary minds some slight craning at the fence, some not altogether unnatural alarm as to the ground that is to be found on the other side of it. "Well, how do you feel about Home Rule now that it seems to be really coming?" some one inquired last spring, of an humble but life-long Nationalist. "'Deed, sir, to tell the truth, I feel as if I'd been calling for the moon all me life and was told it was coming down this evening into me back garden!" was the answer. It is not until a great change is actually on top of us, till the gulf yawns big and black under our very eyes, that we fully realize what it means or what it may come to mean. The old state of things, we then begin to say to ourselves, was really very inconvenient, very trying to all our tempers and patience, but at least we know the worst of it. Of the untravelled future we know nothing. It fronts us, with hands folded, smiling blankly. It may be a great deal better than we expect, but, on the other hand, it may be worse, and in ways, too, which as yet we hardly foresee. Whatever else Home Rule may, would, could, or should be, one thing friends and foes alike may agree to admit, and that is that it will mark an entirely new departure—a departure so new that no illustration drawn from the last century, or from any other historical period, is of much avail in enabling us to picture it to ourselves. It will be no resumption, no mere continuation of anything that has gone before, but a perfectly fresh beginning. A beginning, it may be asked, of what?

LIX.

CONCLUSION.

"CONCLUDED not completed," is the verdict of Carlyle upon one of his earlier studies, and "concluded not completed," conscience is certainly apt to mutter at the close of so necessarily inadequate a summary as this. Much of this inadequacy, it may fairly be confessed, is individual, yet a certain amount is also inherent in the very nature of the task itself. In no respect does this inadequacy press with a more penitential weight than in the case of those heroes whose names spring up at intervals along our pages, but which are hardly named before the grim necessities of the case force us onwards, and the hero and his doings are left behind.

Irish heroes, for one reason or another, have come off, it must be owned, but poorly before the bar of history. Either their deeds having been told by those in whose eyes they found a meagre kindness, or else by others who, with the best intentions possible, have so inflated the hero's bulk, so pared away his merely human frailties, that little reality remains, and his bare name is as much as even a well-informed reader pretends to be acquainted with. Comparing them with what are certainly their nearest parallels—the heroes and semi-heroes of Scotch history—the contrast strikes one in an instant, yet there is no reason in the nature of things that this should be. Putting aside those whose names have got somewhat obscured by the mists of the past, and putting aside those nearer to us who stand upon what is still regarded as debateable ground, there are no lack of Irish names which should be as familiar to the ear as those of any Bruce or Douglas of them all. The names of Tyrone, of James Fitzmaurice, of Owen Roe O'Neill, and of Sarsfield, to take only a few and almost at random, are all those of gallant men, struggling against dire odds, in causes which, whether they happen to fit in with our particular sympathies or not, were to them objects of the purest, most genuine enthusiasm. Yet which of these, with the doubtful exception of the last, can be said to have yet received anything like a fair meed of appreciation? To live again in the memory of those who come after them may not be—let us sincerely hope that it is not—essential to the happiness of those who are gone, but it is at least a tribute which the living ought to be called upon to pay, and to pay moreover ungrudgingly as they hope to have it paid to them in their turn.

Glancing with this thought in our minds along that lengthened chronicle here so hastily over-run, many names and many strangely-chequered destinies rise up one by one before us; come as it were to judgment, to where we, sitting in state as "Prince Posterity," survey the varied field, and judge them as in our

CONCLUSION. 419

wisdom we think fit, assigning to this one praise, to that one blame, to another a judicious admixture of praise and blame combined. Not, however, it is to be hoped, forgetting that our place in the same panorama waits for another audience, and that the turn of this generation has still to come.

AUTHORITIES.

Adamnan, "Life of St. Columba" (*trans.*).
Arnold (Mâtthew), "On the Study of Celtic Literature."

Bagwell, "Ireland under the Tudors."
Barrington (Sir Jonah), "Personal Recollections," "Rise and Fall of the Irish Nation."
Brewer, "Introduction to the Carew Calendar of State Papers."
Bright (Rt. Hon. J.), "Speeches."
Burke (Edmund), "Tracts on the Popery Laws," "Speeches and Letters."

Carlyle, "Letters and Speeches of Cromwell."
Carew, "Pacata Hibernia."
Cloncurry, "Life and Times of Lord Cloncurry."
Clogy, "Life and Times of Bishop Bedell."
Cornwallis Correspondence.
Croker (Rt. Hon. W.), "Irish, Past and Present."

Davis (Thomas), "Literary and Historical Essays."
Davies (Sir John), "A Discoverie of the True Causes why Ireland was never Subdued."
Dennis, "Industrial Ireland."
Domenach (Abbé), "Larerte Erinn."
Dymock (John), "A Treatise on Ireland."
Duffy (Sir Charles Gavin), "Four Years of Irish History."

Essex, "Lives and Letters of the Devereux, Earls of."

Froude (J. A.), "History of England," "The English in Ireland."

Giraldus Cambrensis, "Conquest of Ireland," Edited by J. Dimock, Master of the Rolls Series, 1867; "Topography of Ireland," Edited by J. Dimock, Master of the Rolls Series, 1867.
Green, "History of the English People."
Grattan, "Life and Speeches of Rt. Hon. Henry Grattan."

Halliday, "Scandinavian Kingdom of Dublin."
Hennessy (Sir Pope), "Sir Walter Raleigh in Ireland."
Hardiman, "History of Galway."
Howth (Book of), from O'Flaherty's "Iar Connaught."

Joyce, "Celtic Romances."

Kildare (Marquis of), "The Earls of Kildare."

Lodge, "Desiderata Curiosa Hibernica."
Lecky, "History of England in the Eighteenth Century," and "Leaders of Public Opinion in Ireland."
Leland, "History of Ireland."

Maine (Sir H.), "Early History of Institutions," "Village Communities, East and West."
Max Müller's Lectures.
M'Gee (T. Darcy), "History of Ireland."
McGeoghegan, "History of Ireland."
Mitchell (John), "History of Ireland."
Montalembert, "Monks of the West."
Murphy (Rev. Denis), "Cromwell in Ireland."
Madden, "History of Irish Periodical Literature."
McCarthy (Justin), "History of Our Own Times."

O'Connor (T. P.), "The Parnell Movement."
O'Flaherty, "Iar Connaught."

Petty (Sir W.), "Political Anatomy of Ireland."
Petrie (Dr.), "Round Towers of Ireland."

Prendergast, "Tory War in Ulster," "The Cromwellian Settlements."

Richey (A. G.), "Lectures on the History of Ireland."

Smith (Goldwin), "Irish History and Irish Character."
Spenser (Edmund), "View of the State of Ireland."
Stokes (Miss), "Early Christian Architecture of Ireland."
Stokes (Professor George), "Ireland and the Celtic Church."

Tone (Wolfe), "Autobiography."

Vere de (Aubrey), "Queen Meave and other Legends of the Heroic Age," and "Legends of St. Patrick."

Walpole, "Kingdom of Ireland."
Webb (Alfred), "Compendium of Irish Biography."
Wilde (Sir W.), "Lough Corrib," and "The Boyne and the Blackwater."

Young (Arthur), "Tour in Ireland."

INDEX.

A

Abercromby, Sir Ralph, 359
Act of Supremacy, 152
Act of Uniformity, 278
Adamnan, 43
Adare, 188
Affane, battle of, 183
Aidan (Saint) and Irish monk, 45
Alcansar, battle of, 184
Allen, an Irish priest, 184
Allen, hill of, 14
Allen, John, Archbishop of Dublin, 146
Allen, the Fenian prisoner, 406
Andrews, Dean of Limerick, 237
Angareta, mother of Giraldus, 78
Angelsea, settlement of, 67
Anglo-Norman invasion, 76
Annals of Lough Cè, 109
Anselm (Saint), Archbishop of Canterbury, 81
Arctic hare, the, 4
Ard-Reagh, or Over-king, 91
Ardscul, battle of, 108
Arklow Head, 93
Armagh, Book of, 33
Armagh, cathedral of, burnt by Thorgist, 55
Armdu, a Viking, 68
Arran, isles of, 38
Art McMurrough, or Art Kavanagh, 119; master of Leinster, 119; has recourse to Blackrent, 123; entertained by Richard II., 120; knighted, 120; thrown into prison, 120; released, 120; he hastens to Meath, 121; defeats the royal army, 121; he again meets Richard II. in battle, 121; victorious, 123
Ascendency, the Protestant, 307
Ashton, Sir Arthur, a royalist officer, 261
Askeaton, castle of, 187; destroyed, 188
Association, Loyal National Repeal, 386
Attainder, Bill of, drawn and passed, 287
Athenry, battle of, 110; enfeebled state, 175
Athlone, fortress of, 104, 292
Athy, bridge of, 128
Aughrim, battle of, 293
Augustine (Saint), 44
D'Aguilar, Don Juan, 215
D'Avaux, Count, envoy to James II., 283

B

Baculum Cristatum, or Staff of St. Patrick, 158
Baggotrath, battle of, 260
Bagnall, Sir Henry, 198; Tyrone marries his sister, 201; becomes his enemy, 201; he marches against Tyrone, 204; he is shot, 205; his army defeated, 205; fort of Blackwater surrendered, 205

426 INDEX.

Ballinasloe, town of, 293
Baltimore, stronghold of pirates, 127
Baltinglass, Lord, 189
Bannockburn, battle of, 108; its effects on Ireland, 108
Bannow, bay of, or "FitzStephen's stride," 83
Barnabie FitzPatrick, 157
Barries descendants of Nesta, 76
Barri, Robert de, 83
Barrington's Bridge, 107
Barrymore, Lord, 141
Beare O'Sullivan, 215
Bedell, bishop of Kilmore, 245
Beltane, Celtic festival of 1st May, 14
Belgic, colony of, 6
Bellingham, Sir Edward, 162
Belrath, castle of, 141
Ben Edar, now Howth, 17
Benignus, first disciple of St. Patrick, 35
Benturb, battle of, 255
Bermingham, Sir John de, victor of Athenry, 110, 111
Beresford, Chief Commissioner of Customs, 351
Bernard, Saint, of Clairvaux, 81
Betas, Celtic houses of hospitality, 14
Black-rent, use of, 119, 123, 129
Blackwater river, 183; battle of, 203
Blaney, Mr., member for Monaghan, 243
Book of Aicill, Aryan law, 25
Book of Armagh, 33
Book of Howth, the, 140
Borough, Lord, deputy, 203
Boulter, Archbishop of Armagh, 304, 320
Boyle, primate, 280
Boyne, battle of the, 288
Bramhall, primate, 277
"Brass Band," 403
Brehons, judges or law makers, 19, 25
Brian Boru, or Boruma, 60, 61; he defeats the Danes, 61; seizes throne of Cashel, 63; over-runs Leinster, 63; subdues Ossory, 63; attacks Meath, 63; burns the stronghold of Tara, 63; becomes Ard-Reagh in Malachy's place, 63; he is called Brian of the Tribute, 64; he becomes master of Ireland, 64; his victory at Clontarf, 66; he marches against Brodar, 68, 69; is killed, 69; mourned and buried, 69, 70.
Bridget (Saint), 47; sacred fire of, 47
Brodar, a Viking, 66; killed Brian, 67
Brown, Archbishop of Meath, 159; deprived, 161
Bruce, Edward, in Ireland, 107; battle of Bannockburn, 108; its effects, 108; Bruce lands at Carrickfergus, 108; defeats Richard de Burgh, 108; defeats Sir Edmund Butler at Ardscul, 108; victorious at Kells, 108; meets his brother, 108; is crowned king, 109; devastates the country, 109; defeated and killed at Dunkalk, 110
Bruce, King Robert of Scotland, 108
Burren, district of the, in North Clare, 269
Burgh, Sir William FitzAldelm de, 103
Burgundy, Duchess of, 132, 136
Burke, Edmund, 330
Burke, Mr. Thomas, murder of, 411

C

Calvagh O'Donnell, 167
Camden, Lord (Lord-Lieutenant), 359
Campion, historian, the, 125
Carew, Sir George, 213, 215, 216, 226
Carew, Sir Peter, 178; his atrocities, 178
Carey, James, the informer, 412
Carhampton, Lord, 358

INDEX.   427

Carle Canuteson, 67
Carlow, 154
Carneg, rock of, 84
Carnot, 355
Catholic Confederacy, 249
Catholic Relief Bill carried, 381
Cashel, Synod of, 92
Castlehaven, 215
Castlereagh, Lord, Chief Secretary, 370
Caulfield, Lord, Governor of Charlemont, 243
Cavan, Lord, 365
Cavendish, Lord Frederick, murdered, 411
Cerd or Nuad of "the Silver hand," 9
Charlemont, Lord, 330
Charles I., accession, 231 ; he sends Strafford to Ireland, 231, 235, 238 ; his death, 279
Chester Castle, attack on, projected, 405
Chesterfield, Lord, Lord-Lieutenant, 344
Claims, Court of, 275
Clan Nairn, 17
Clann Dichin, a malediction, 20
Clanricarde, Earl of, 105
Clarence, Lionel, Duke of, 114
Cliach, plains of, 14
Clocthech, round towers of, 56
Clogher, Bishop of, 241
Clonard, town of, 47
Clonmacnois, high altar at, 47
Clonmel, 262
Clontarf, battle of, 71, 74 ; strand of, 66
Clyn, Franciscan historian, 109
Cole, Dean of St. Paul's, story of, 163
Cole, Sir William, Governor of Enniskillen, 243
Coleraine, 243
Colkilla, hill of, 14
Colman, Bishop, 46
Columba (Saint), born, 43 ; his character, 42, 43 ; he leaves Ireland, 43 ; visits Scotland, 43 ; and Iona, 44

Connaught, landowner's case of, 230
Connaught, treaty of, 103
Connemara, anciently Iar Connaught, 8
Conciliation Hall, 386
Confederates, Young Irelanders, 395
Con O'Neill (Earl of Tyrone) 154
Cong, plains of, 7
Conyers, Clifford, Sir, Governor of Connaught, 209
Cooke, Under-Secretary of State, 351
Coote, Sir Charles, 244, 246, 273
Cork, town of, 119
Cormac, MacArt, 23
Cormac O'Conn, King, 11
Cornwallis, Marquis, Lord-Lieutenant, 365
Corrib Lough, 104
Cowper, Lord, 411
"Coyne and livery," 183
Croagh Patrick, mountain of, 34
Crofty, hill of, 247
Crom a Boo, war cry of the Fitzgeralds, 138
Cromwell, Henry, Lord-Lieutenant, 76
Cromwell in Ireland, 261 ; he takes Drogheda, 261 ; Wexford, 262 ; Kilkenny, 262 ; Clonmel, 262 ; his army sickens, 263 ; Ireland under his rule, 264 ; the struggle continues, 264 ; Limerick and Galway yield at last, 264 ; close of civil war, 265 ; his methods, 266 ; Catholic evictions, 267 ; his treatment of Sir Phelim O'Neill, Lord Mayo, and Lord Muskerry, 267 ; his death, 272
Crint, or stringed harp, 52
Cruachan, mountain of, 35
Curragh of Kildare, 14

D

Danaans, tribe of, 8
Danes, 53
Danes, Dublin, 67

Danes of Limerick, 58–61
Dangen, ancient name of Phillipstown, 162
Dashda, or Druid chieftain, 53
Davis, John, Sir, 95–117; he is elected Speaker, 227; quarrel which followed, 227, 228
Davis, Thomas (poet), 290
Davitt, Michael, Mr., 409
Declaration of Rights by Grattan, 320
Declaratory, Act of George I., 322
"Defenders," Association of, 345
Delvin, Lord, 191
Dermot McMurrough, King of Leinster, 83
Derry, town of, 171
Desmond, Earl of, taken to London, 176; vacillates about rebelling, 185; his death, 192
Desmond-Sugane or Straw, Earl of, 200
Dillon, Mr., 391
Donald, Chief of Ossory, 90
Donegal, chapels in, 43
Donore, hill of, 280
Douchad, son of O'Brien, 74
Dowdal, Archbishop of Armagh, 159
Downpatrick, town of, 99
Drapier Papers by Swift, 317
Drogheda, Parliament of, 138
Drogheda, taken by Cromwell, 261
Dublin Castle, 240; plot to seize it, 241; frustrated, 242
Dublin, Philosophical Association of, 311
Dublin, Society of, 311
Duffy, Sir Charles Gavin, 390
Dundalk, battle of, 110
Dungannon, Matthew, Baron of, 165
Dunsany, Lord, 247

E

Edgecombe, Sir Edward, 135
Edward, I., 107
Edward II., 108; Battle of Bannockburn, 108
Edward III., 113; he summons landowners, 114; appoints Lionel, Duke of Clarence, viceroy, 114; Statute of Kilkenny is passed, 115
Elizabeth, Queen, 165; entertains Shane O'Neill at Court, 68; account of his visit, 168; Ireland during her reign, 171–172
Emmett, Robert, 376
Emmett, Thomas Addis, 354
Encumbered Estate Court, 400
Enniskillen, town of, 247
Eochaidh king, tale of, 35
Essex, Robert Devereux, Earl of, 206; take the command in Ireland, 208; proceeds against Tyrone, 208; his disasters, 208; takes Cahir Castle, 208; meets Lugane Earl, 208; meets Tyrone at Lagan, 209; returns to England, 210
Eva, daughter of Dermot, 86
Everard, Sir John, 227, 228

F

Falkland, Lord, 231
Famine, the first symptoms of, 396; great distress, 397; Mr. Forster reports, 397; Relief Act passed, 399; the ruin which followed it, 400; after effects, 403
Fedlim O'Connor, king of Connaught, 108
Fenian prisoners, rescue of, at Manchester, 405
Fenian rising, 401
Fenni or Fenians, 11
Fercal, tribes of, 161
Ferns, town of, 83
Finn, McCumal, 14
Finn or Fingal, father of Ossian, 11
Finnvarragh, king of the fairies, 21
Firbolgs, race of, 6
Fitton, Sir Edward, 176
Fitzgerald, Lord Edward, 354–359
Fitzgerald, Maurice, 83

Fitzgerald, Mr., member for Clare, 380
Fitzgerald, Raymond (le Gros), 85
Fitzgerald, Sir James, 191
Fitzgerald, Sir John, 191
FitzHenry, Robert and Meiler, sons of Nesta, 76
Fitzmaurice, Lady, 188
Fitzmaurice of Lexnaw, 111
Fitzmaurice, Sir James, 178; breaks into rebellion, 178; relations between him and Sir James Perrot, 179; burns Kilmallock 179; marches into Ulster, 179; burns Athlone, 179; joins the Mac-an-Earlas, 180; lays Galway waste, 180; crosses the Shannon, 180; surrenders and takes the required oaths at Kilmallock, 180; sails to France, 180; returns, 184; his death, 187
FitzSimons, Walter, Archbishop of Dublin, 137
FitzStephen, Robert, 83
FitzUrse of Louth, 111
Fitzwilliam, Lord, Lord-Lieutenant, 349-350
Fitzwilliam, Sir William, Lord-deputy, 199
Flood, Rt. Hon. Henry, 323
Foltbar and Feradach, Legends, 16
Formorians, race of, 5
Forster, Mr. W. E., 397
Forty-shilling Freeholders, Bill of, 349
"Four Masters," the annals of the, 9
Foyle, Lough, 165
Freeman's Journal, 322
Fuidhar, or "broken man," 28

G

Gall (Saint), 36
Galway, bay and town of, 104
Galway, Jury of, 247
George, Duke of Clarence, 129

Gerald de Barri, Gerald of Wales, or Giraldus Cambrensis, 78; grandson of Nesta, 78; priest and chronicler, 78; his character as a writer, 78
Gerald, 8th Earl of Kildare, son of Geroit Mor, 130
Gerald of Windsor, husband to Nesta, 76
Geraldines, 101; Giraldus' opinion of them, 101; ancestors of Earls Kildare and Desmond, 102; important position, 102; their keep at Maynooth, 102; power in Ireland, 102; Geroit Mor, or Gerald the Great, 7th Earl of Kildare, 130
Gilbert, Sir Humphry, 179
Gilla Dacker and his horse, legend of, 14
Ginkel, Dutch general of William III., 291
Gladstone, Mr. W. E., 406; disestablished the Irish Church, 406; introduced Irish Land Act of 1870, 407; of 1881, 409; imprisoned members of Land League, 411; proposed measure of Home Rule of 1886, 414
Glenmama near Dunlaven, 68
Godred, King of Man, 87
Gormanstown, Lord, 249
Granard, Lord Justice, 280
Grattan, Henry, 328; his loyalty and patriotism, 328; he enters Parliament, 330; his eloquence, 330; Declaration of Rights, 330; retires into private life, 332; protests against the Union, 332; member of English Parliament, 332; his death and burial, 333
"Great Darcy of Platten," 132
Gregory, Pope, 44
Grey, de Wilton, Lord-deputy, 189
Grey, Leonard, Lord, Deputy, 151, 152
Griffiths, Sir Richard, Irish geologist, 312

430 INDEX.

H

Habeas Corpus Act, 351
Hadrian IV., Pope, 81
Hamilton, Sir Richard, 282
Harcourt, Lord, 325
Hardi, French General, 365
Harvey, Bagenal, United Irishman and general of the rebels, 363
Hasculph, Danish Governor, 86-87
Hatton, Sir Christopher, "an Undertaker," 194
Heber and Heremon, sons of Milesius, 10
Hoadly, Archbishop of Armagh, 320
Hoche, General, 355
Hoche, vessel called the, 365
Home Rule, the question of, 44
Howth, Earl of, 134, 136
Humbert, French general, 364
Hy-Nial, or royal house of O'Neil, 42, 52

I

Iar Connaught, mountains of, 104
Ireland, Primeval, 1; its early vicissitudes, 3; South European plants in, 5; early history of, 5-11; its legends, 13-21; Celtic Ireland, 23; early laws of, 26-29; St. Patrick's visit to, 32; the Northern scourge of, 50; invasion by Anglo-Normans, 76; King John in, 98-100; invasion of, by Edward Bruce, 107; Richard II. visits to, 119; attempt to force Protestantism upon, 158-160; Molyneux's, "The case of," &c., 313; Union of Great Britain and Ireland, 367-376
Ireland, the future of, 413
"Ireland, Young," party, 390-395
Irish Catholic Association, 407
Irish Celts, 25
Irish Church, disestablishment of, 409
Irish Education Act, 408
Irish elk, 4
Irish export of woollen goods forbidden, 309
Irish famine, 396-403
Irish hare, 4
Irish heroes, 418
Irish Land Act, 407
Irish volunteers, 336-340
Inchiquin, Lord, 256
Iona, 44

J

James II. recalls Lord Ormond, 280; restores Catholics to office, 280; his treatment of Protestants, 281-282; his flight to France, 282; arrives in Ireland, 283; his reception, 284; besieges Londonderry, 285; goes to Dublin, 286; is defeated at the battle of the Boyne, 288; his flight, 289
John, the Mad Berserker-warrior, 87
Jones, Michael, Colonel, 259
Jones, Paul, pirate, 326
Joyce's, Mr., "Celtic Romances," 13

K

Kelts, battle of, 99
Keogh, Judge, 403
Kerry, defence of, 215
Kerry, plants and animals in, 5
Kildare, Dean of, 149
Kildare, house of, 102; earls of, 130, 134, 150; "Silken Thomas," 147; vice-deputy, 147; renounces allegiance to England, 147; takes Dublin, 148; burns Trim and Dunboyne, 149; is defeated, 150; imprisoned and hanged, 150
Kilkea, castle of, 144
Kilkenny, castle of, 105
Kilkenny, statutes of, 115
Killala, Bishop of, 365
Kilmallock burnt, 179; church of, 179
Kimbaoth, prince of Milesia, 10

King's County, 52
Kinsale, harbour of, 215
Knights of Glyn, 102 ; of Kerry, 102
Knockma, a hill of, 8
Knocktow, battle of, 144; cause of, 106

L

Lacy, Hugo de, viceroy of Henry II., 92
Lagan, ford of, 209
Lalor, James, 393
Lambay, stand of, 55
Lambert, Simnel, 331 ; received in Dublin and crowned, 134; defeated at Stoke, 135 ; taken prisoner and appointed turnspit, 135
Land League, the, 409
Land Lepers, 53, 59
Lanfranc, Archbishop of Canterbury, 81
Langan, Comte de, 288
Laoghaire, King of Meath, 34
Larkin, Fenian hanged, 406
Lecky's, Mr., "History of the Eighteenth Century," 300
Lee, Captain, 199
Leix, town of, 161
Leland the historian, 10
Liffy river, 87
Lilibullero, anti-Catholic song, 283
Limerick, articles of, 295
Limerick, first siege of, 291
Limerick, treaty of, 295
Limerick, wood and town of, 117
Lindsfarne, peninsula of, 45
Londonderry, siege of, 285
Lovell, Lord, 135
Lucas, Charles, 323
Luinagh Tyrlough, 195
Lundy, governor of Londonderry, 285

M

Mac-an-Earlas, sons of Clanricarde, 191

Macarthy, Colonel, 288
McCarthy, Dermot, 90
Maccumactheneus, St. Patrick's chronicler, 34
Magan, betrayer of Lord Edward Fitzgerald, 361
Maguire, Lord, 241
Mahon, King of Munster, 61
Malachy or Melachin, Ard-Reagh, 52
Malby, Sir Nicolas, governor of Connaught, 187
Mananan MacLir, Legend of Gilla Dacker, 17
Marshall, William, Earl of Pembroke, 103
Maryborough anciently Campa, 162
Mary, Queen of England, 163 ; her death, 164
Maynooth, castle of, 102
Mayo, Lord, 267
Mayo mountains, 8
Maxwell, Colonel, 362
McGeoghan, Abbè, historian, 1
McGillapatrick, Lord of Upper Ossoy, 168
McHugh, 191
McMahon, Hugh, chief of Monaghan, 192
McMurrough, Dermot, King of Leinster, 83, 241
McMurrough, son of Dermot, 83
McToole, Sir Owen, 197
McWilliam, Burke of Galway, 154
McWilliam Eighter, and McWilliam Oughter, the Nether and Further Burkes, 111
McWilliam of Clanricarde, 142
Meagher, 391
Meath, plains of, 8
Mila de Cogan, Norman governor of Dublin, 87
Milcho chieftain, 3
Milesians or Scoti, 9, 10
Mitchell, John, 391
Molyneux, Thomas, Dr., 311
Molyneux, William, the "Ingenious Molyneux," 311
Montalembert, M. de, 40
Montmorency, Henry de, 85

Mortimer, Roger, viceroy, 110
Mountgarrett, Lord, 249
Mountjoy, Charles Blount, 211; his character, 211; establishes military stations, 213; defeats by starvation, 213; defeats Tyrone and the Spanish fleet, 216
Moytura, prehistoric battle of the southern, 7
Muckern, or Mulkearn noi, 187
Mullingar, town of, 292
Munroe, General, 255
Murhertach, house of, 74
Murphy, Father John, 362
Murphy, Father Michael, 304

N

Nation, The, newspaper, 390
Neil Grey, 167
Newtown Butler, battle of, 288
Norris, General Sir Henry, 206
Norris, Sir Thomas, 194
Norsmen, or Northmen, or Danes, 7, 53-56
Northern Star, newspaper, 358
Nuad, King of the Tuatha-da-Danaans, 7-9

O

"Oakboys," Society of the, 345
O'Brian, Prince of Thomond, 90
O'Brien, race of, 60
O'Brien, Smith, 391
O'Brien, the Fenian, 406
O'Byrnes, 128
O'Carroll of Argial, 91
O'Connell, Daniel, makes his first speech, 379; his energy, 379; sets on foot the Irish Catholic Association, 379; carries Catholic rent, 380; contests the county of Clare, 381; his character, 382; his efforts to procure repeal, 385; his enmity to secret societies, 385; founds the Loyal National Repeal Association, 386; his prosecution, 387; found guilty and imprisoned, 387; his last appearance and death, 389
O'Connell, John, 391
O'Connor, Roderick, the Ard-Reagh, 75, 84-91
O'Connors of Connaught, 74
Octennial Bill, the, 325
O'Curry, 53
O'Dogherty, Sir John, 198
O'Donnel, Calvagh, 167
O'Donnel, of Tyrconnel, 167
O'Donnell, Hugh, or Red Hugh, 200.
O'Donnell, murder of Carey, 412
O'Donnell, Rory, 221
O'Donovans, 63
O'Driscoll's piratical clan of West Cork, 27
O'Dynor, Dermot, or Dermot of the Bright Face, 17
O'Flaherty, Edmund, 403
Oilen-an-Oir, or Gold Island, 185
Ollamhs or Sennachies, head bards, 19
O'Lochlin of House of O'Neill, 74
O'Moore, Rory or Roger, 241
O'Neill, Owen, 248
O'Neill, Shane, called the Proud, 165; his character, 166; his eloquence, habits, and morals, 166; his encounter with Sussex, 167; his visit to the English Court, 168; receives title of Captain of Tyrone, 169; returns to Ireland, 169; Sussex attempt to poison him, 169; his descent on the Scots, 170, and on Connaught, 170; his last disaster and death, 172, 173
O'Neill, Sir Phelim, 241
O'Neills, or Hy-Nials, 60-74
Orange Lodges, institution of, 345
O'Reilly of Brefny, 167
O'Rorke, chieftain of Connaught, 91
O'Rorke of Brefny, chieftain of Leinster, 91

INDEX. 433

Ormond, house of, 105-128
Ossian, poet and bard, 11-35
Ossory, clan of, 84
Oswald, King of Northumbria, 44
Oswin, King of Northumbria, 46
O'Toole, Garrot, 191
O'Toole, St. Lawrence, Archbishop of Dublin, 86
Oulart, hill of, 362
Owel, Lough, near Mullingar, 55

P

Paladius, missionary, 33
Parnell, Mr., 411
Parnell, Sir John, 371
Parsons, Sir William, 242
Patrick (Saint), his birth, 33; lands in Ireland, 33; visits to Meath and to Connaught, Antrim, and Armagh, 34; legends of, by Mr. Aubrey de Vere, 35
"Peep of Day Boys," Society of, 345
Pelham, Sir William, Lord-deputy, 188
Penal Code, the, 300
Perkin Warbeck, 136, 137
Perrot, Sir John, 176-179
Peter's Pence, collection of, 79
Petrie, George, LL.D., 7
Petty, Sir William, his survey of Ireland, 271
Philip II., King of Spain, 183
Phœnix organization, 404
Phœnix Park tragedy, 411
Picts, 53
Pierce, Captain, 173
Plunkett, Dr., Archbishop of Dublin, 279
Portland, Duke of, 350
Poynings' Act, 138
Poynings' Act repealed, 287
Poynings, Sir Edward, 148
Preston, Colonel, 249
Protection of Life and Property Bill, 409

R

Raleigh, Sir Walter, 190-191
Rents, Black, 17, 123
Rents, Fair Rent and Free Sale, 410
Rents, Rack, 28
Rents, Stipulated, 28
Ribbon Association, 385
Richard II. lands at Waterford, 119; his meeting with Art McMurrough, 119; entertains the chiefs, 120; receives their oaths of allegiance, 120; returns to Ireland, 122; encounters Art McMurrough, 122; leaves Ireland, 123
Rupert, Prince, 259; his arrival at Kinsale, 259

S

Sadleirs, John and James, 403
Sanim Celtic Festival (November 1st), 14
Sarsfield, Patrick, 280
Saunders, Pope's Legate, 184
Schomberg, Duke of, 288
Schwartz, Martin, Dutch General, 135
Scoti, tribes of the, 9
Scullobogue, barn of, 363
Sebastian, King of Portugal, killed at the battle of Alcansar, 184
Senchus Mor, ancient law-book, 25, 28
Shannon, Lord, 322
Shannon, river, 91
Shiel, Richard Lalor, 379
Sidney, Henry, Sir, 174; becomes Lord-deputy, 174; appoints presidents in the provinces, 176; his scheme for reducing expenses, 177; his visits to Munster and Connaught, 179
Sigurd, Earl of Orkney, 66
Silvermine hills of Tipperary, 291
Simon, priest and tutor to Lambert Simnel, 135

Sitric, a Viking, 67
Skeffington, Sir William, 148
Slemish mountains, 33
Sligo, town of, 254
Smerwick, town of, 185
Somerset, Edward Earl of Glamorgan, 254
South European Plants in Ireland, 5
Southern Moytura, 7
Spanish Armada, 197
Spenser, Edmund, poet, 190
Stanihurst, historian, the, 131
Steelboys, Society of, 345
St. John, Sir Oliver, deputy, 231
St. Leger, Sir Wareham, "Undertaker," 194
St. Ruth, General, 292
Stephen, Head Fenian centre, 405
Stokes, battle of, 135
Stokes, Miss Margaret, 312
Stone, Archbishop of Armagh, 320
Strafford, Wentworth, in Ireland, 232; orders subsidy of £100,000, 234; he overawes the juries, 234; his character, 235; his suppression of the woollen trade, 235; founds the linen trade, 235; clears the sea of pirates, 235; sets a Court of High Commission to work, 237; his treatment of Archbishop Ussher, 237; his account of his dealings with Convocation, 237; his return to England, 239; tried for treason, condemned, and executed, 239; effect of his death in Ireland, 239
Strangford Lough, 33
Strongbow, Earl of Pembroke, 82; his marriage with Eva, 86; takes Waterford, 86; is besieged in Dublin, 87; flees to Waterford, 88; thence to England, 88; meets Henry, 88; and returns to Ireland, 89
Stukeley, Thomas, Sir, 170, 184
Sulcost, battle of, 61
Surrey, Earl of, deputy, 145

Swift, Jonathan, Dean of St. Patrick's, 315; his character, 315; his Drapier Papers, 317; his attack on Wood's patent, 315; his popularity, 319
Swords in Meath, 247

T

Talbot, Richard, Earl of Tyrconnel, 208
Tanist laws of succession, 27
Tara in Meath, 63; battle of, 63
Tenant League Confederation, 403
Tenure, Fixity of, 410
Thomond, Lady, 303
Thomond, Lord, 247
Tower, the "Tower Earl" of Desmond, 192
Townshend, Lord, 325
Towton, battle of, 129
Tuam, Archbishop of, 254
Tuatha-da-Danaans, race of, 7
Turgesius or Thorgist, 55
Turlough, grandson of Brian, 82
Tyrconnel, Lady, 289
Tyrconnel, Richard, Earl of, 280
Tyrconnel, Rory O'Donnell, Earl of, 221
Tyrone, Hugh O'Neill, Earl of, 199; receives his title from Elizabeth, 199; contrasted with Shane, 199; his religious views, 200; arbitrary arrest of his brother-in-law, 200; marries Bagnall's sister, 201; prepares for rebellion, 202; assumes the title of the O'Neill, 202; is victorious over Bagnall, 205; meets Essex at Lagan, 209; struggle with Mountjoy, 214; he hurries south to meet the Spaniards, 215; encounters Mountjoy and is defeated, 216; reported plot against England, 220; flies the country, 221; dies in exile, 222

U

Union, Pitt's plan of, 268
Union, the, 367

INDEX.

United Irishmen newspaper, 394
United Irishmen, the Society of, 386
Ussher, Archbishop of Armagh, 163; treatment of by Strafford, 237

V

Vere, Aubrey de, Mr., Legends of St. Patrick, 35
Vinegar Hill, 363
Volunteers, Irish, the, 334-340

W

Ware Papers, 163
Waterford, town of, 262; defence of, 86; Danes of, 85; Richard II. lands at, 122
Wexford, town of, 83; castle of, 87; siege by Cromwell, 262
Whitby, Synod of, 46
Whiteboys, outrages of, 342-344
Wicklow, landing of St. Patrick in, 33
William of Orange in Ireland, 288; he lands at Carrickfergus, 288; meets James's army, is victorious at the battle of the Boyne, 289; offers free pardon, 290; besieges Limerick, 291; his evidence about the treaty of Limerick, 296
Willoughby, Sir Francis, Governor of Dublin, 246
Winter, Admiral, 187
Wolfe, Tone, 354; leader of United Irishmen, 354; meets Lord Edward Fitzgerald in Paris, 355; his scheme of descent, 355; descent fails, 357; a fresh attempt, 358; again fails, 361; is arrested on board the *Hoche*, 361; condemned and dies in prison, 366
Wood, patentee of halfpence, 317

Y

Yellow Ford, battle of the, 203
"Young Ireland," party of, 388, 390

The Story of the Nations.

MESSRS. G. P. PUTNAM'S SONS take pleasure in announcing that they have in course of publication a series of historical studies, intended to present in a graphic manner the stories of the different nations that have attained prominence in history.

In the story form the current of each national life will be distinctly indicated, and its picturesque and noteworthy periods and episodes will be presented for the reader in their philosophical relation to each other as well as to universal history.

It is the plan of the writers of the different volumes to enter into the real life of the peoples, and to bring them before the reader as they actually lived, labored, and struggled—as they studied and wrote, and as they amused themselves. In carrying out this plan, the myths, with which the history of all lands begins, will not be overlooked, though these will be carefully distinguished from the actual history, so far as the labors of the accepted historical authorities have resulted in definite conclusions.

The subjects of the different volumes will be planned to cover connecting and, as far as possible, consecutive epochs or periods, so that the set when completed will present in a comprehensive narrative the chief events in the great STORY OF THE NATIONS; but it will, of course not always prove practicable to issue the several volumes in their chronological order.

The "Stories" are printed in good readable type, and in handsome 12mo form. They are adequately illustrated and furnished with maps and indexes. They are sold separately at a price of $1.50 each.

The following is a partial list of the subjects thus far determined upon:

THE STORY OF *ANCIENT EGYPT. Prof. George Rawlinson.
" " " *CHALDEA. Z. A. Ragozin.
" " " *GREECE. Prof. James A. Harrison,
            Washington and Lee University.
" " " *ROME. Arthur Gilman.
" " " *THE JEWS. Prof. James K. Hosmer,
            Washington University of St. Louis.
" " " *CARTHAGE. Prof. Alfred J. Church,
            University College, London.
" " " BYZANTIUM.
" " " THE GOTHS. Henry Bradley.
" " " *THE NORMANS. Sarah O. Jewett.
" " " *PERSIA. S. G. W. Benjamin.
" " " *SPAIN. Rev. E. E. and Susan Hale.
" " " *GERMANY. S. Baring Gould.
" " " THE ITALIAN REPUBLICS.
" " " HOLLAND. Prof. C. E. Thorold Rogers.
" " " *NORWAY. Hjalmar H. Boyesen.
" " " *THE MOORS IN SPAIN. Stanley Lane-Poole.
" " " *HUNGARY. Prof. A. Vámbéry.
" " " THE ITALIAN KINGDOM. W. L. Alden.
" " " EARLY FRANCE. Prof. Gustave Masson.
" " " *ALEXANDER'S EMPIRE. Prof. J. P. Mahaffy.
" " " THE HANSE TOWNS. Helen Zimmern.
" " " *ASSYRIA. Z. A. Ragozin.
" " " *THE SARACENS. Arthur Gilman.
" " " TURKEY. Stanley Lane-Poole.
" " " PORTUGAL. H. Morse Stephens.
" " " MEXICO. Susan Hale.
" " " *IRELAND. Hon. Emily Lawless.
" " " PHŒNICIA.
" " " SWITZERLAND.
" " " RUSSIA.
" " " WALES.
" " " SCOTLAND.

* (The volumes starred are now ready, December, 1887.)

G. P. PUTNAM'S SONS
NEW YORK   LONDON
27 AND 29 WEST TWENTY-THIRD STREET   27 KING WILLIAM STREET, STRAND

www.ingramcontent.com/pod-product-compliance
Lightning Source LLC
Chambersburg PA
CBHW031955300426
44117CB00008B/777